Volume II

Involvement:
Social and Sexual Relationships
in the Modern World

By John Stott

Basic Christianity
Basic Introduction to the New Testament
What Christ Thinks of the Church
The Preacher's Portrait
Confess Your Sins
The Epistles of John
Men Made New
Our Guilty Silence
Only One Way
Christ the Controversialist
Understanding the Bible
Guard the Gospel
Balanced Christianity
Christian Mission in the Modern World
Baptism and Fullness
Christian Counter-Culture
Understanding Christ
God's New Society
Between Two Worlds
God's Book for God's People
One People (Expanded and Updated)
Involvement, Volumes I & II

Volume II

Involvement:
Social and Sexual Relationships
in the Modern World

John Stott

A Crucial Questions Book

Fleming H. Revell Company
Old Tappan, New Jersey

Unless otherwise indicated, Scripture quotations are from the Holy Bible, *New International Version*, Copyright © 1973, 1978 by the International Bible Society, used by permission of Zondervan Bible Publishers.

Involvement: Being a Responsible Christian in A Non-Christian Society, and this volume are published in Great Britain as one book, *Issues Facing Christians Today*, by Marshall Pickering, Ltd.

Library of Congress Cataloging in Publication Data
(Revised for volume 2)

Stott, John R. W.
    Involvement.
    Vol. 2 has title: Social and sexual relationships
in the modern world.
    First published in 1984 under title: Issues
facing Christians today.
    Bibliography: p.
    Includes index.
    1. Christian life—Anglican authors.   2. Church and
social problems.   3. Evangelicalism.   4. Sex—Religious
aspects—Christianity.   I. Title.
BV4501.2.S789   1985   261.8   84-24826
ISBN 0-8007-1418-0 (v. 1)
ISBN 0-8007-1438-5 (v. 2)

Publisher's Foreword

IN A WORLD THAT HAS BECOME AN INTERRELATED GLOBAL VILLAGE of 4.5 billion men, women, and children, the problems of human existence have reached crisis proportions. Modern man stretches to achieve new heights, but his very advances in technological and scientific realms sometimes threaten him with the loss of life's most precious gifts—and even life itself. In the midst of the crises, Christians believe there exists the possibility for unprecedented good, for the flourishing of freedom, and for peace. This hopeful outlook is itself possible in a violent, threatened world because the Christian views the world from the center point of history, the Cross, where God dealt redemptively with the crux of the human problem.

While the Christian does not doubt God's ability nor His final victory, he struggles to know and to implement God's plan. Thankfully, there is an ongoing discussion of contemporary problems as Christians wrestle with agendas for action. As the publisher of the Crucial Questions series, we earnestly hope that these volumes will contribute positively to that discussion. Although the viewpoints expressed by the authors in this series may not always be those of the publisher, we are grateful for the opportunity to present them to the public, and we trust that these volumes will serve to stimulate Christians to fulfill their role as salt and light in today's world.

Contents

Conclusion

Abbreviations

The biblical text quoted is normally that of the New International Version. If another text is used, this is stated.

Arndt-Gingrich *A Greek-English Lexicon of the New Testament and Other Early Christian Literature* by William F. Arndt and F. Wilbur Gingrich (University of Chicago Press and Cambridge University Press, 1957).

AV The Authorised (King James) Version of the Bible, 1611.

JB The Jerusalem Bible (Darton, Longman and Todd, 1966).

NASB The New American Standard Bible (Moody Press, Chicago, 1960).

NEB The New English Bible (NT 1961, 2nd edition 1970; OT 1970).

NIV The New International Version of the Bible (Hodder & Stoughton, NT 1974; OT 1979).

RSV The Revised Standard Version of the Bible (NT 1946, 2nd edition 1971; OT 1952).

Introduction

ONE OF THE MOST NOTABLE FEATURES OF THE WORLDWIDE EVAN-
gelical movement during the last ten to fifteen years has been
the recovery of our temporarily mislaid social conscience. For
approximately fifty years (c.1920–70) evangelicals were preoccupied with the task of defending the historic biblical faith
against the attacks of liberalism, and reacting against its 'social
gospel.' But now we are convinced that God has given us social
as well as evangelistic responsibilities in his world. Yet the
half-century of neglect has put us far behind in this area. We
have a long way to catch up.

The two volumes entitled *Involvement* are my own modest
contribution to the catching-up process. In Volume I, subtitled
'Being a Responsible Christian in a Non-Christian Society,' I
addressed myself both to some important introductory questions (e.g. whether Christians have a social responsibility,
whether we can think straight on ethical questions, and whether
we have any influence anyway), and to four global issues (the
nuclear threat, human rights, the environmental debate, and
North-South economic inequality). In this book, which is Volume II and is subtitled 'Social and Sexual Relationships in the
Modern World,' I take up four contemporary social issues
(work and unemployment, labor relations, race, and poverty)
and four more questions which may broadly be labelled 'sexual' (feminism, marriage and divorce, abortion, and the homosexual challenge). The source of both volumes may be traced to
1978/9, when Michael Baughen, now Bishop of Chester, but

then Rector of All Souls, invited me to preach a series of occasional sermons under the title 'Issues Facing Britain Today.' Several of these chapters began their life in the pulpit, and subsequently grew into lectures at the London Institute for Contemporary Christianity, whose *raison d'être* is to help people develop a Christian perspective on the complexities of the modern world.

I confess that several times in the course of writing I have been tempted to give up. I have felt now foolish and now presumptuous to attempt such an undertaking. For I am in no sense a specialist in moral theology or social ethics, and I have no particular expertise or experience in some of the fields into which I trespass. Moreover, each topic is complex, has attracted an extensive literature, only some of which I have been able to read, and is potentially divisive, even in a few cases explosive. Yet I have persevered, mainly because what I am venturing to offer the public is not a polished professional piece but the rough-hewn amateur work of an ordinary Christian who is struggling to think Christianly, that is, to apply the biblical revelation to the pressing issues of the day.

For this is my concern. I begin with a commitment to the Bible as 'God's Word written,' which is how it is described in the Anglican Articles and has been received by nearly all churches until comparatively recent times. Such is the basic presupposition of this book; it is not part of my present purpose to argue it. But Christians have a second commitment, namely to the world in which God has placed us. And our two commitments often seem to be in conflict. Being a collection of documents which relate to particular and distant events, the Bible has an archaic feel. It seems incompatible with our western culture, its space probes and microprocessors. Like every other Christian I feel myself caught in the painful tension between these two worlds. They are centuries apart. Yet I have sought to resist the temptation to withdraw from either world by capitulation to the other.

Some Christians, anxious above all to be faithful to the revelation of God without compromise, ignore the challenges of the modern world and live in the past. Others, anxious to respond to the world around them, trim and twist God's revelation in their search for relevance. I have tried to avoid both traps. For the Christian is at liberty to surrender neither to antiquity nor to modernity. Instead, I have attempted with integrity to submit to the revelation of yesterday within the realities of today. It is not easy to combine loyalty to the past with sensitivity to the present. Yet this is our Christian calling: to live under the Word in the world.

Many people have helped me develop my thinking. I thank the 'apostolic succession' of my Study Assistants—Roy McCloughry, Tom Cooper, Mark Labberton, Steve Ingraham, and Bob Wismer—who have compiled bibliographies, assembled groups for the discussion of sermon topics, gathered information and checked references. Bob Wismer has been specially helpful in the final stages, having read the manuscript twice and made valuable suggestions. So has Frances Whitehead, my secretary for twenty-eight years, in addition to typing the manuscript, which has been shared by Vivienne Curry. Steve Andrews, my present study assistant, has been meticulous in proof correcting. I also thank friends who have read different chapters and given me the benefit of their comments—Oliver Barclay, Raymond Johnston, John Gladwin, Mark Stephens, and Roy McCloughry, Myra Chave-Jones and my colleagues at the London Institute—Andrew Kirk (Associate Director) and Martyn Eden (Dean). I am particularly grateful to Jim Houston, founding Principal and now Chancellor of Regent College, Vancouver, whose vision of the need for Christians to have an integrated world view has stimulated both my own thinking and the founding of the London Institute.

JOHN STOTT
June 1984

Part I

Social Issues

Chapter One

Work and Unemployment

WORK OCCUPIES SUCH A SIGNIFICANT PLACE IN MOST PEOPLE'S lives that, if we are Christians, we must know how to think Christianly about it and about the trauma of unemployment. After all, the average worker still divides his (or her) day into three more or less equal periods—eight hours' sleep, eight hours' work, and eight hours' leisure. So our work occupies a third of our day, indeed a half of our waking hours. We also acknowledge the importance of work by our habit of defining people in relation to it. Although convention teaches us to ask 'how do you do?' the real question which interests us is 'what do you do?'

Now please let me say it before you think it: a clergyman is the last person in the world to write about work. For, as everybody knows, he has not done an honest day's work in his life. As the old saying goes, he is 'six days invisible and one day incomprehensible'! Some years ago I was travelling by train in South Wales when a rather drunk Communist miner entered my compartment. When he discovered that I was a pastor, he treated me to a lecture (in his sing-song Welsh accent) on work: 'It's time you became productive, man; you're a parasite on the body politic.'

19

So, then, with the possible exception of the clergy (and, of course, the unemployed), we are all workers. In consequence, we need a philosophy of work which will determine our attitude to it.

Attitude to Work

Some people are very negative towards their job and give the impression that, if possible, work is something to be avoided. This view has been well expressed in this doggerel:

> *I don't mind work*
> *If I've nothing else to do;*
> *I quite admit it's true*
> *That now and then I shirk*
> *Particularly boring kinds of work;*
> *Don't you?*
> *But, on the whole,*
> *I think it's fair to say*
> *Provided I can do it my own way*
> *And that I need not start on it today—*
> *I quite like work!*

The same rather casual attitude to work was illustrated by the following message, which the head of a New York firm put on its notice board: 'Some time between starting and quitting time, without infringing on lunch periods, coffee breaks, rest periods, story-telling, ticket-selling, holiday planning, and the rehashing of yesterday's television programs, we ask that each employee try to find some time for a work break. This may seem radical, but it might aid steady employment and assure regular paychecks.'

Other people tolerate their job as a necessary nuisance, a way of earning a living, and a tedious consequence of the Fall. I was astonished to read this latter concept recently in a serious book: 'The orthodox view of work, which has been accepted by most managers and industrial psychologists is a simple one, and fifty years of industrial psychology and more than a century of managerial practice have been founded upon it.' What is it? It 'accepts the Old Testament belief that physical labour is a curse imposed on man as a punishment for his sins, and that the sensible man labours solely in order to keep himself and his family alive or . . . to enable him to do the things he really likes. . . .[1] The author evidently knows more about industry than Scripture. For according to Scripture work is a blessing, not a curse, and it is the Creation not the Fall which has made us workers.

This second attitude to work, which regards it as either meaningless in itself or at best a necessary means to some quite different end (e.g. facilitating leisure pursuits), is the same in principle as the Christian view that work is a useful sphere of witness. To be sure, the Christian is a witness to Christ in every situation, but it is very inadequate to see the work place as having no Christian significance in itself, but only as a well-stocked lake to fish in.

Yet another group of people have no particular understanding of their work. They have never stopped to think about it. They simply accept it. They are rather like H. L. Mencken, often referred to as 'the sage of Baltimore,' who once said: 'I go on working for the same reason that a hen goes on laying eggs.'[2] In other words, work is part of our human nature. Man is a compulsive worker, as a hen is a compulsive layer of eggs.

Those who are trying to develop a Christian mind on work, however, turn first to creation. The Fall turned some labour into drudgery (the ground was cursed, and cultivation became possible only by toil and sweat), but work itself is a consequence of our creation in God's image. God himself is represented in Genesis 1 as a worker. Day by day, or stage by stage, his creative plan unfolded. Moreover, when he saw what he had made, he pronounced it 'good.' He enjoyed perfect job-satisfaction. His final act of creation, before resting on the seventh day, was to create human beings, and in doing so to make them workers too. He gave them some of his own dominion over the earth and told them to exercise their creative gifts in subduing it. So from the beginning men and women have been privileged stewards of God, commissioned to guard and develop the environment on his behalf.

Then in the second account of creation, which concentrates on man, we read: 'Now the Lord God had planted a garden. . . . The Lord God took the man and put him in the Garden of Eden to work it and take care of it' (Genesis 2.8, 15). Thus God planted the garden and God created the man. Then he put the man he had made into the garden he had planted, and told him to cultivate and protect it. As he had put the earth in general into man's charge, now in particular he committed the garden to him. Later (Genesis 4.17ff.) Adam's descendants are pictured as building cities, raising livestock, making and playing musical instruments, and forging tools of bronze and iron. It seems, in fact, to be the Middle Stone Age which is being described.

Here then are God the worker, together with man the worker sharing God's image and dominion. And (Christians will want to add) there is Jesus the worker, demonstrating at the carpenter's bench the dignity of manual labour. In the light of these revealed truths about God, Christ, and man, what is the Christian understanding of work?

Self-fulfilment

First, work is intended for the fulfilment of the worker. That is, an important part of our self-fulfilment as human beings is to be found, according to God's purpose, in our work. We can affirm this with confidence in view of the very first instruction which God addressed to man and woman: 'Be fruitful and increase in number; fill the earth and subdue it' (Genesis 1.28). Here are three successive commands, each leading logically to the next. They could not subdue the earth without first filling it, and they could not fill it without first reproducing themselves.

This original and composite commandment expresses, then, a basic aspect of our vocation as human beings.

We have already seen, when thinking about our responsibility for the environment, that our dominion over nature is due to our likeness to God. Or, to express the same truth in different terms, our potential for creative work is an essential part of our God-likeness. Our Creator has made us creative creatures. Dorothy Sayers was right then in her epigram: 'Work is not primarily a thing one does to live, but the thing one lives to do.'[3] Since the Creator has given us gifts, he intends them to be used. He wants us to be fulfilled, not frustrated.

Pope John Paul II is clear and outspoken about the fundamental place of work in human life. In his encyclical on 'Human Work' entitled *Laborem Exercens* he writes: '*Work is one of the characteristics that distinguish* man from the rest of creatures, whose activity for sustaining their lives cannot be called work.'[4] From the early chapters of Genesis 'the church is convinced that work is a fundamental dimension of man's existence on earth.'[5] For this reason, he continues, 'human work is a *key*, probably *the essential key*, to the whole social question.' If the latter is 'making life more human,' as the Second Vatican Council said it was, 'then the key, namely human work, acquires fundamental and decisive importance.'[6] So then, 'work is a good thing for man,' not only because through work he transforms nature to serve his needs, but because through it 'he also *achieves fulfilment* as a human being, and indeed, in a sense, becomes "more a human being." '[7]

It would probably be an exaggeration to affirm that work is actually 'indispensable' to our humanness. But at least we can say that if we are idle (instead of active) or destructive (instead of creative), we are denying a basic aspect of our humanity, contradicting God's purpose for our lives, and so forfeiting a part of our own fulfilment. This does not mean, of course, that a child, a hospital patient or a retired person is not a human being because they cannot work. Nevertheless, a child wants to grow up, and a sick person to get well, in order to be able to serve. Similarly, retired people are wise to seek an active retirement in which they have opportunities for constructive service, even if it is unpaid. Pessimistic as the Preacher was in Ecclesiastes, regarding the meaninglessness of life lived without God, and about 'toilsome labour under the sun,' he was able to be positive about man's daily work: 'A man can do nothing better than to eat and drink and find satisfaction in his work.' Again, 'there is nothing better for a man than to enjoy his work . . .' (Ecclesiastes 2.24; 3.22)

The concept of self-fulfilment through work is certainly much more difficult in some countries and regions (where the choice of job is extremely limited), and in particular kinds of work. The mining of coal (or for that matter of copper, tin, gold, and diamonds) involves dirt, discomfort, and danger, and everything should be done by mine owners to reduce risks and unpleasantness. Then there is the tedium of the factory assembly line. E. F. Schumacher did not exaggerate when he wrote about monotonous work: 'Mechanical, artificial, divorced from nature, utilizing only the smallest part of man's potential capacities, it sentences the great majority of workers to spending their working lives in a way which contains no worthy challenge, no stimulus to self-perfection, no chance of development, no element of Beauty, Truth or Goodness.'[8]

He drives home the anomaly of this by pointing out that 'the modern world takes a lot of care that the worker's body should not accidentally or otherwise be damaged' and, if it *is* damaged, provides for his compensation. But what about 'his soul and his spirit'? 'If his work damages *him*, by reducing him to a robot— that is just too bad.'[9] He then quotes Ananda Coomaraswamy that 'industry without art is brutality.' Why? Because it damages the worker's soul and spirit.[10] Schumacher's solution is in the 'small is beautiful' concept with which his name will always be associated. But even in large factories (e.g. in the manufacture of Volvo cars in Sweden), attempts are being made to relieve monotony and increase responsibility by job-swapping or job rotation within a team. Indeed, we should support every attempt to 'enrich' or 'humanize' working conditions.

Other manual jobs, although not tedious like the assembly line, are thought by some to be 'menial' or 'demeaning.' Take refuse collection as an example. It can involve the handling of rubbish that is filthy or smelly or both. Yet it is, of course, a vital service to public health and hygiene, and as such should provide a measure of job satisfaction. I read in 1970 of Dennis Sibson, a dustman (or in the American tongue, 'garbage collector') from Middleton in Lancashire, who was awarded a Churchill travelling fellowship, which he used to study refuse collection and disposal on the European continent. He had previously been a clerk, a coalman, a window cleaner, a tool-setter and a decorator. But he said he found refuse work (he had had fourteen years of it) 'most satisfying to himself and most useful to the public.'[11]

The Service of Man and God

Work is intended not only for the fulfilment of the worker, but also for the benefit of the community. One can imagine that Adam did not cultivate the Garden of Eden merely for his own enjoyment, but to feed and clothe his family. Throughout the Bible the productivity of the soil is related to the needs of society. Thus, God gave Israel a 'land flowing with milk and honey,' and at the same time issued instructions that the harvest was to be shared with the poor, the alien, the widow, and the orphan. Similarly in the New Testament, the converted thief is told not only to stop stealing, not only to start working with his own hands, but to do so in order that he 'may have something to share with those in need' (Ephesians 4.28).

The knowledge that our work is beneficial and appreciated

adds considerably to our sense of job satisfaction. I understand that Henri De Man's studies in Germany between the wars, and the Hawthorne experiments which were conducted at the same time at the Chicago plant of the Western Electric Company, were the first pieces of scientific research into this now well-accepted fact. The Hawthorne studies in particular showed 'that workers would increase their output even when the lights were dimmed to the strength of moonlight, if they thought that their labours were considered by other people to be important and significant.'[12]

Certainly the Bible regards work as a community project, undertaken by the community for the community. All work needs to be seen as being, at least to some degree, public service. This principle throws light on the discussion about the purpose(s) of business. It is acknowledged by all that a successful business must make a profit; provide adequate wages, good prospects, and pleasant working conditions for the work force; invest in research and development; declare a dividend for shareholders; pay taxes to the government; and serve the public. The point of controversy concerns the order in which these six purposes should be placed. Many business people insist that profit must head the list, since otherwise the firm will sink. And everybody agrees that profit is indispensable as an index of efficiency and a condition of survival. But Christians feel uncomfortable about giving priority to profit, lest it seems that the chief end of the company is self-service (although, of course, there is a distinction between retained profits and distributed profits).

It appears more consistent with the Christian emphasis on 'ministry' to give priority to the provision of whatever goods or services the company offers the public. We then, of course, have to add immediately that in order to serve the public, and so stay in business and/or expand in order to do so, the firm must not only pay its workforce and its taxes, but also make a profit out of which to plough something back for research and renewal of equipment, and to declare a dividend. In other words, all six obligations of a business dovetail with one another. Some prefer to visualise them as the spokes of a wheel, in which priority is not given to any one purpose, rather than as the layers of a pyramid. Yet the Christian mind still wants to insist that service to the community should come first. After all, it is not only true that a firm cannot serve the public without making a profit; it is also (and perhaps more) true that it cannot make a profit if it does not serve the public acceptably.

More important even than the service of the community is the service of God, though they cannot be separated. Christians believe that the third and highest function of work is that through it God should be glorified, that is, that his purpose should be revealed and fulfilled. E. F. Schumacher also gives three purposes of human work, as follows:

> First, to provide necessary and useful goods and services.
> Second, to enable every one of us to use and thereby perfect our
> gifts like good stewards.
> Third, to do so in service to, and in cooperation with others, so
> as to liberate ourselves from our inborn egocentricity.[13]

Now it seems to me that his first purpose is my second, and his second my first. It is when we come to the third that we differ. Schumacher sees life as a school, God as the Schoolmaster, and work as one of the chief means by which our chronic human self-centredness is reduced, if not eradicated. 'In the process of doing good work,' he writes, 'the ego of the worker disappears.'[14] I do not wish to deny the wholesome ego-diminishing influences of work. But it seems to me that an even higher vision of work is to see it as being for the glory of God. How is this?

God has deliberately arranged life in such a way as to need the cooperation of human beings for the fulfilment of his purposes. He did not create the planet earth to be productive on its own; human beings had to subdue and develop it. He did not plant a garden whose flowers would blossom and fruit ripen on their own; he appointed a gardener to cultivate the soil. We call this the 'cultural mandate' which God gave to man. I like the story of the cockney gardener who was showing a parson the beauty of his garden, with its herbaceous borders in full summer bloom. Duly impressed, the parson broke out into spontaneous praise of God. The gardener was not very pleased, however, that God should get all the credit. 'You should 'ave seen this 'ere garden,' he said, 'when Gawd 'ad it all to 'isself!'[15] He was right. His theology was entirely correct. Without a human cultivator, every garden quickly degenerates into a wilderness.

Usually we emphasise the indispensability of *God's* part. We sing at the Harvest Festival

We plough the fields and scatter
The good seed on the land,
But it is fed and watered
By God's almighty hand.

The opposite, however, would be equally true. We might sing instead

God plants the lovely garden
And gives the fertile soil,
But it is kept and nurtured
By man's resourceful toil.

We should not be shy to declare this. It is not being proud; it is true. God does indeed provide soil, seed, sunshine, and rain, but we have to do the ploughing, sowing, and reaping. God provides the fruit trees, but we have to tend and prune the trees, and pick the fruit. As Luther once commented, 'God even milks the cow through you.' Of what use to us would be God's provision of an udder full of milk, if we were not there to extract it?

So there is cooperation, in which indeed we depend on God but also (we say it reverently) he depends on us. God is the Creator; man is the cultivator. Each needs the other. In God's good purpose creation and cultivation, nature and nurture, raw materials and human craftsmanship go together.

This concept of divine-human collaboration is applicable to all honourable work. God has humbled himself and honoured us by making himself dependent on our cooperation. Take the human baby, perhaps the most helpless of all God's creatures. Children are indeed a 'gift of the Lord,' though here too the parents cooperate. After the birth it is as if God drops the newborn child into the mother's arms and says 'now you take over.' He commits to human beings the nurturing of each child. In the early days the baby remains almost a part of the mother, so close are they to one another. And for years children depend on their parents and teachers.

Even in adult life, although we depend on God for life itself, we depend on each other for the necessities of life. These include not only the basic needs of physical life (food, clothing, shelter, warmth, safety, and health care) but also everything which makes up the richness of human life (education and recreation, sport, travel and culture, music, literature, and the arts), not to mention spiritual nurturing. So whatever our job—in one of the professions (education, medicine, the law, the social services, architecture or construction), in national or local politics or the civil service, in industry, commerce, farming or the media, in research, management, the services or the arts, or in the home, we need to see it as being cooperation with God, in serving the needs of human beings and so helping them fulfil his purpose and grow into human maturity. In some jobs the cooperation is direct, and therefore easy to perceive. The farmer plants and sows; God gives the increase. Or in medicine. The words of Ambroise Paré, the sixteenth-century French surgeon, sometimes described as 'the founder of modern surgery,' are inscribed on a wall of the École de Médicine in Paris: 'I dressed the wound, but God healed him.'

In other kinds of work the cooperation is indirect, in which case we need insight to grasp it. When asked whether his doctoral research in solid state physics was 'useful,' Robert Newport replied, 'Well, it's not directly related to anything.' But then he went on: 'I hope that later my findings will link up with those of others and the results will be applied in industry.' That is an example of what I mean.[16] And, although I have developed in a specifically Christian way this principle of looking beyond the immediate to the ultimate, it is surely applicable to very many jobs undertaken by non-Christians.

The story is told of a man who was taking a walk down a country lane, when he came across a stone quarry in which a number of men were working. He questioned several of them about what they were doing. The first replied irritably, 'Can't you see? I'm hewing stone.' The second answered without looking up, 'I'm earning £100 a week.' But when the same question was put to the third man, he stopped, put his pick down, stood up, stuck out his chest and said, 'If you want to know what I'm doing, I'm building a cathedral.' So it is a matter of how far we can see. The first man could not see beyond his pick, and the second beyond his Friday paycheck. But the third man looked beyond his tools and his wages to the ultimate end he was serving. He was cooperating with the architect. However small his particular contribution, he was helping to construct a building for the worship of God.

So *laborare orare*, 'work is worship,' provided that we can see how our job contributes, in however small and indirect a way, to the forwarding of God's purpose for mankind. Then whatever we do can be done for the glory of God (1 Corinthians 10.31).

Some years ago I was given the opportunity by the Medical Officer of Health for the Port and City of London to see something of his responsibilities. We were shown round by T. L. Mackie, who at that time was the Port of London's Chief Health Inspector. His enthusiasm for his work was infectious, and in a letter he sent me the following week he divulged its origin. He wrote: 'the work covers a rather comprehensive field of preventive medicine and environmental health control. . . . To work for one's own ends, the pay packet, the "perks," security of tenure and eventual pension, is not enough for me. I like to think that I am responsible for a part of the greater human field pattern whereby we all subscribe of our best to the whole effort for human welfare according to our talents, and obey the will of our wonderful Creator. . . . With this trend of thought and outlook, I go into action each day happily. . . .'

In the light of the three purposes for work which we have been considering, we should be ready to attempt a definition.

Work is the expenditure of energy (manual or mental or both) in the service of others, which brings fulfilment to the worker, benefit to the community, and glory to God.

Fulfilment, service, and worship (or cooperation with God's purpose) all intertwine, as indeed our duties to God, others, and self nearly always do. Certainly self-fulfilment cannot be isolated from service, for job satisfaction is not primarily attained by a fair wage, decent conditions, security, and a measure of participation, important as these are. It arises from the job itself, and especially from that elusive thing 'significance.' And the main component of significance in relation to our job is not even the skill and effort we put into it, but the sense that through it we are contributing to the service of the community and of God himself. It is service which brings satisfaction, discovering ourselves in ministering to others. We need not only to develop this perspective on our own work, but, if we are employers or managers, to do our utmost to develop it in our workforce.

In 1981, I was shown round the Handicrafts Centre in Dacca,

Bangladesh, which is operated by HEED (the Health, Education, and Economic Development project). Here young people from refugee camps were being taught a skilled trade, either carpet making or tapestry, weaving or straw art. What impressed me most was the degree of their concentration on what they were doing. They hardly noticed us, and did not even look up as we walked by. They were absorbed in their craft. Their work had given them dignity, significance, a sense of self-worth through service.

The Trauma of Unemployment

When we have grasped how central a place work occupies in God's purpose for men and women, we see at once how serious an assault on our humanness unemployment is. Referring to the unemployed in the north of England during the Depression years, William Temple wrote: 'the gravest and bitterest injury of their state is not the animal (physical) grievance of hunger or discomfort, nor even the mental grievance of vacuity and boredom; it is the spiritual grievance of being allowed no opportunity of contributing to the general life and welfare of the community.'[17] It is a shocking experience to be declared 're-dundant,' and still worse to have to think of oneself thus. Many people live in fear of it happening to them.

In 1963 the total number of unemployed in the United Kingdom (excluding school-leavers) was 500,000. By 1977 this had trebled to one and a half million. Then from 1980 the figures climbed steeply, so that between 1980 and 1982 the 1977 figure doubled to three million, where (the experts gloomily tell us) it is likely to stay for the rest of this century. Three million people represent about 13 percent of the workforce: so one person in eight is out of work. The true figure may be higher still, partly because of the number of unregistered unemployed people and partly because some industries and businesses are still over-manned. Certain groups are particularly hard hit. More than a million (37.5 percent) are young people under the age of twenty-five. The percentages are also higher than the average among ethnic (especially coloured) groups, disabled people, and unskilled workers in regions like Northern Ireland, South Wales, and the big cities of Scotland and the north of England.

On the European continent the figures vary considerably from country to country. According to the statistics published by the Department of Employment in September 1983, the percentage of the workforce unemployed was highest in Belgium (18.6 percent) and lowest in Switzerland (0.9 percent). In Japan it was 2.5 percent, in the United States 9.2 percent, in Australia 9.8 percent, and in Canada 11.2 percent.

When we turn from the West to the South, however, the statistics of unemployment are appalling. It is reckoned that at least three hundred million people (some say as many as five hundred million) are unemployed in the developing countries of the Third World, and that this represents approximately 35 percent of the workforce, whereas the average in the West (bad as it is) is about ten percent.

Moreover, it seems certain that, at least in the immediate future, the problem is going to get worse. Developing nations will become increasingly industrialised and compete in world markets, over steel, ships, and manufactured goods. Microelectronics will complete the Industrial Revolution. Computers will take over the running of factories, the ploughing of fields (by driverless tractors), and even the diagnosing of diseases. There will be no sense in trying to resist this development, like the nineteenth-century Luddites who went round smashing factory machines, beginning in 1811 with the newly-installed knitting machines in the hosiery factories of Nottingham. We have to come to terms with it.

Unemployment is not a problem of statistics, however, but of people. In the Third World, where no wage-related unemployment benefit is available, it is often a question of actual survival, but in the West the suffering is more psychological than physical. It is a poignant personal and social tragedy. Industrial psychologists have likened unemployment to bereavement, the loss of one's job being in some respects similar to the loss of a relative or friend. They describe three stages of trauma. The first is shock. A young unemployed man in our congregation spoke of his 'humiliation,' and an unemployed woman of her 'disbelief,' since she had been given assurances that her job was safe. A restaurateur felt 'immediately degraded' and said to himself, 'I've become a statistic, I'm unemployed.' On hearing that they have been sacked or made redundant, some people are angry, others feel rejected and demeaned. Their self-image has suffered a bitter blow, particularly if they have dependents they cannot now provide for. Unemployment brings tension and conflict to their family life. At this stage, however, they are still optimistic about the future.

The second stage is depression and pessimism. Their savings are exhausted and their prospects look increasingly bleak. So they lapse into inertia. As one man summed it up, 'I stagnate.' Then the third stage is fatalism. After remaining unemployed for several months and being repeatedly disappointed in their applications for jobs, their struggle and hope decline, their spirit becomes bitter and broken, and they are thoroughly demoralised and dehumanised. There are now more than a million people in Britain who have been unemployed for over a year, and about a quarter of them are under the age of twenty-five.

Solutions and Palliatives

How should Christians react to the problem of unemployment? The ultimate solution belongs to the realm of macroeconomics. Everybody seems to be agreed that unemployment is due to the current world recession, and that it can be overcome only by more trade bringing more demand, bringing more jobs. But experts do not agree on how this growth can be secured. In Britain 'making industry more competitive' is the cry from government, employers, and unions.

To this end some advocate a massive reflation of the economy by government investment and job creation. Others hope to stimulate a more dynamic economy by private (though government-encouraged) investment. Others accept Schumacher's 'small is beautiful' dictum and believe we should turn from huge capital-intensive enterprises to modest labour-intensive projects. Yet others believe that the new microprocessor technology will force this decentralisation upon us anyway. In the short term the silicon chip will undoubtedly decrease jobs (and in any case, they add, jobs which robots can do are not fit for rational human beings); but in the long term, they add, the Microprocessor Revolution—like the Industrial Revolution two hundred years ago—will create more jobs.

The 1979 report commissioned by the Department of Employment, entitled *The Manpower Implications of Micro-Electronic Technology*, was tentatively optimistic. Its authors pointed out that 'the evidence from the economic history of the entire industrial age is that technological change has been beneficial to aggregate employment' and that 'western industrialised countries have experienced an almost continuous period, since 1945, of both rapid technological change and increasing employment.[18] Sir Fred Catherwood in his contribution to the 1981 London Lectures was equally optimistic and gave a number of examples.[19]

Turning from long-term to short-term remedies, or from solutions to palliatives, there seems to be more agreement. Successive governments have done much in their regional policies, Vocational Youth Training (for school leavers), retraining schemes, and job creation programmes. The Manpower Services Commission operates both a Youth Opportunities Programme and a Community Enterprise Programme. There is room also for more voluntary initiatives. BURN (the British Unemployment Resource Network) is an umbrella organisation for such. It includes centres for the unemployed sponsored by the Trades Union Congress and by Local Trades Councils; autonomous groups of unemployed people seeking to help themselves and one another; and cooperative schemes to launch small new businesses. The church can initiate programmes too; I shall come to this later.

Various proposals are also being made not so much to increase demand for labour as to decrease supply. The principle behind them is to redistribute the same amount of work by spreading it over more people. One arrangement being canvassed is 'job-splitting' or 'job-pairing,' by which the same job is shared between two people, who work either a 'week in-week out' or a 'morning-afternoon' rhythm, giving them more freedom, although also of course less pay. Other people are urging the reduction of the weekly total of hours worked, the strict curtailment of overtime, the banning of 'black economy' jobs, the extension of annual leave, the provision of more sabbaticals, and earlier voluntary retirement.

Has the Christian church any specific contribution to make?

I have been encouraged by reading David Bleakley's two books, *In Place of Work . . . The Sufficient Society*, 'a study of technology from the point of view of people,' and *Work: The Shadow and the Substance*, 'a reappraisal of life and labour.' They contain much food for thought and much stimulus to action. He does not underestimate the impact of the new microtechnology, or the magnitude of the social change it is already beginning to introduce.

On the contrary, 'By the year AD 2000 our world will have been transformed beyond recognition,' he writes.[20] 'We are in the midst of a revolution that will count as one of the most momentous in the history of human society.'[21] In the light of this,

his first concern is that we shall learn lessons from the Industrial Revolution and not repeat them. The introduction of the new technology cannot be resisted; but it should be carefully controlled and 'kept compatible with the human needs of the society in which it takes root.'[22] Also, we have somehow to ensure that this time the benefits of the microelectronic revolution, and the burdens of adjustment to it, are evenly shared. Otherwise, another disastrous 'two-nation' situation will emerge, separating the beneficiaries from the casualties.[23]

The Role of the Church

In the present transition period David Bleakley believes that the church should have a key role. In the Industrial Revolution it missed its opportunity, and ever since the working masses of Britain have been alienated from it. This must not happen again. The church could keep Britain united during the dangerous period of industrial transformation. And, since the unemployed (the chief casualties) have no union to represent them or plead their cause, the church could be the voice of the voiceless. It is well placed to do so. 'Straddling as it does the whole spectrum of the community, it can be a unique lobby, articulating the Christian social demand and encouraging its people to discover and apply . . . such demands through national and local church initiatives.'[24]

Let me spell out at least three ways in which the church can and should be helping.

First, many of us need to change our attitudes towards the unemployed, and persuade the public to do the same. Those who have been schooled in the values of the so-called 'Protestant work ethic' (industry, honesty, resourcefulness, thrift, etc.) tend to despise those who are losers in the struggle to survive, as if it were their fault. No doubt there are a few work-shy people who do not want a job and prefer to sponge on the community. But they must constitute a tiny minority. The great majority of unemployed people want to work, but cannot find a job. They are victims of the recession and of the new technology. There is need therefore for more Christian sympathy towards them and more pastoral care. We have to repent of looking down on the unemployed, or of even imagining that the words 'workless' and 'worthless' might be synonyms. I was chagrined to hear of a man in our church who, after being unemployed for two years, stayed away from public worship because he was scared of being asked what he was doing and, on the discovery that he was out of work, of being made to feel a failure. But at least within the Christian community no stigma should be attached to unemployment. Paul's dictum 'if a man will not work, he shall not eat' (2 Thessalonians 3.10) was addressed to voluntary not involuntary unemployment, to the lazy, not the 'redundant.' So we need to welcome and support the unemployed in the local church; otherwise our pious talk about 'the Body of Christ' becomes a sick joke.

Secondly, the church can take its own initiatives. For some twenty-five years now an increasing number of local congregations have come to realise that the buildings they inherited from the past are both too large for their needs and unsuitable for their responsibilities. Many have therefore developed imaginative plans to preserve (and usually remodel) an area for worship, and convert the rest for other purposes, especially for appropriate service to the local community. Then, in order to indicate its new multi-purpose character, some have dropped the traditional word 'church' and renamed their building (or complex) a 'Christian Centre.' Some such centres accommodate a children's play group or nursery school, a club for 'Mums and Toddlers,' a luncheon club and chiropody service for old people, an open youth group, a coffee bar, etc. They are also beginning to be used to serve the unemployed.

CAWTU (Church Action With The Unemployed),[25] founded in 1982 and sponsored by a number of denominations, emphasises three areas in which local churches can take the initiative. The first is 'Pastoral Care (coping with being out of work).' Why not open a 'drop-in centre' or 'resource centre' on church premises, where unemployed people can find companionship, information, a library, refreshments, and recreation? Secondly, 'Work Experience (a better chance to get jobs).' Why not sponsor one of the schemes suggested by the Manpower Services Commission—either under their 'Youth Opportunities Programme' to provide young people with work experience, or under their 'Community Enterprise Programme' to provide long-term adult unemployed people with temporary work of benefit to the community? Thirdly, 'Job Creation (new jobs and permanent work).' This might involve creating a new job at the church (in administration or maintenance), or starting a neighbourhood cooperative (for odd jobs), or launching a new business (joining with others to set it up). CAWTU produced a leaflet entitled 'Creating New Jobs—a guide to help get you started.'

The following are some examples of local Christian initiatives. The Portrack Workshop on Teeside in the north of England, which is supported by a dozen or more congregations, employs forty-five disabled people in a factory which both makes toys and repairs school desks. Its success is partly due to skilled management, including young managers temporarily seconded by local firms.[26]

In Northampton some Christians have formed a workers' cooperative which, after purchasing food in bulk, stores and packages it and then distributes it to retailers.

'Traidcraft' was set up in 1979 by eight Christian businessmen to provide a European market for Third World products. It has created forty jobs in its own office and warehouse in Newcastle-upon-Tyne, and some 2,500 in developing countries.

Westcliff Baptist Church in Essex operates an enterprising 'Temporary Employment Scheme,' whose object is to provide local unemployed people with a worthwhile life-style while they are looking for permanent work. In 1983 seventy unemployed people were meeting three times a week for social and educational activities, and for voluntary service (e.g. with the elderly and the handicapped). Also twenty long-term unemployed people were being funded by the Manpower Services Commission for different kinds of community work. Unemployed people run the scheme themselves.

The Mayflower Family Centre in the East End of London pays unemployed people to undertake community service.

A church in Leeds has reduced its worship area to accommodate three hundred instead of three thousand, while 'the rest of the church serves as an industrial training and community centre where local young people receive commercial, industrial, and catering training.'[27]

Several Church of England dioceses have appointed an Unemployment Officer, with special responsibility to inform young people of organisations available to help them.

Moulsham Mill, near Chelmsford, Essex, ceased operating as a mill in 1979 (after many centuries), and has been taken over by 'Interface,' part of the Social Care division of the Chelmsford Diocese's Department of Mission. It is being converted to provide training workshop facilities; forty-one people on the long-term unemployment register will be recruited to restore it.

The Bridge Project, based at Bow in East London, was launched in 1982 by a group of Christian organisations (e.g. British Youth for Christ and Frontier Youth Trust) to create new jobs. By the end of the year it was helping thirty-six new businesses get off the ground. It offers both advice and administrative help to entrepreneurs.

Thirdly, in seeking to involve unemployed people in constructive activity, the church should also make, publicise and act on the distinction between 'work' and 'employment.' Although all employment is work (we are not paid for doing nothing), not all work is employment (we can work without being paid for it). What demoralises people is not so much lack of employment (not being in a paid job) as lack of work (not using their energies in creative service). Conversely, what gives people a sense of self-respect is significant work. Adam was not paid for cultivating the Garden of Eden. The housewife who works at home and students who work at their books are not usually paid (though some of them are agitating to be paid).

I know that the salary check is important, and that those receiving unemployment benefit tend to feel parasites (quite falsely, since they have themselves contributed to Social Security). Nevertheless, work significance is more important than wage or salary in giving us a sense of self-worth. To employ people to dig holes and fill them up again brings pay without significance; to work creatively but voluntarily brings significance without pay. Of the unemployed people I have known personally, several have spent time in study; one who had a camera used the opportunity to improve his photographic techniques in the hope that later he would be able to make Christian audiovisuals, while a young woman spent many hours visiting and supporting some alcoholic friends who lived in the flat below her.

The current social revolution will not leave any of us untouched. If the average working week is reduced first to thirty-five hours, and then to thirty, how shall we spend our extra free time? Should the church not be both suggesting and offering some constructive alternatives to television and video? Creative leisure, though unpaid, is a form of work. The possibilities are numerous: 'Do-it-yourself' repairs, redecorations, and improvements at home; servicing the car, motorbike or bicycle; self-education through evening classes, correspondence courses or Open University; cultivating the garden or allotment, growing your own vegetables, keeping pigs or chickens; working with wood or metal; dressmaking, knitting, and embroidery;

making music; painting, pottery, sculpting; reading and writing; and where possible doing these things together, spending more time with family and friends.

Then there is the whole sphere of community service through the local church or a voluntary organisation, or taking one's own initiative: visiting the sick, the elderly, or prison inmates; redecorating an old person's home; working with mentally- or physically-handicapped people; baby-sitting; collecting other people's children from school; teaching backward children, or ethnic families for whom English is a second language, to read and write; helping in the local hospital, school, club or church.

Some readers will doubtless dismiss all this as a typical middle-class reaction, quite unpractical for working class unemployed people in towns. And to some extent this is true. I am not so stupid as to recommend people who live in a flat in an inner city area to keep pigs! But in principle I still appeal to the great biblical truths on which we have been reflecting: Mankind by creation is creative; we cannot discover ourselves without serving God and our neighbour; we must have an outlet for our creative energies. So, if the unemployed have no facilities for the range of activities I have mentioned, and they are not available elsewhere in the community, should not the church provide them? Is it impossible for the church to make available a workshop (and tools), a garage or studio, in which people can both learn and practise new skills? And could not most local churches develop a much broader programme of service to the local community? Increasing numbers of unemployed, semi-employed and retired people will need to be encouraged to use their leisure time creatively. As a result of automation, as Marshall McLuhan wrote twenty years ago, 'we are suddenly threatened with a liberation that taxes our inner resources of self-employment and imaginative participation in society.'[28]

The Christian understanding of work as self-fulfilment through the service of God and neighbour should have several wholesome consequences. We shall value our own work more highly; see to it that those we may employ are able to do the same; feel deeply for the unemployed, and try to ensure that though out of employment they are not out of work. In summary, all of us should expect to remain workers all our lives, so that even after we have retired, we may spend whatever energy we have left in some form of service.

Chapter Two

Industrial Relations

RIGHT ATTITUDES TO WORK ARE ESSENTIAL TO OUR ENJOYMENT OF it; right relationships at work are equally important. Men and management may be highly motivated, and yet at the same time deeply dissatisfied because they are at loggerheads with one another.

Britain has a bad record of industrial relations. The trough was the winter of 1978–79, which was described at the time as a situation of 'industrial civil war.' There were strikes of bakers, refuse collectors, road haulage and railway workers, hospital workers and ambulance drivers, journalists, teachers, and social workers. The number of working days lost through industrial action in 1978 is said to have been 9,306,000. It was probably higher, since records are not always accurately kept. Sir Francis Boyd, the former political editor of *The Guardian* commented: 'The social turmoil of this dreadful winter has shown the British to be more full of hatred and bitterness towards each other than at any time since the General Strike of 1926.' The community turned sour.

This situation was of concern to all thoughtful people, but especially to Christians, for we are in the business of right relationships. John V. Taylor, Bishop of Winchester, has justly

45

called God's Kingdom 'the Kingdom of right relationships.'[1] Reconciliation is at the top of the Christian agenda, because it lies at the heart of the gospel. Sin disrupts relationships; salvation rebuilds them. Jesus came on a mission of reconciliation. He is the supreme Peacemaker, and tells his followers to be peacemakers too.

Moreover, relationships at work are particularly important. God means work, as we have seen, to be a cooperative enterprise in which we collaborate with him and others for the common good. Britain and her allies experienced this solidarity during World War II, when united against a common evil, but that unity soon fell apart afterwards and no common cause has yet been found which could restore it.

The Biblical Principle of Mutuality

As in the other topics of this book, my task is not to presume to recommend policies (which is the task of those involved in government, employment, and unions, and for which I have no expertise), but rather to try to clarify biblical principles so that we can think straight and take whatever action is appropriate to our position and responsibility.

I invite you therefore to reflect on the situation in Israel after King Solomon died. I recognise that an industry or business is not a kingdom, and that any analogy between them is bound to be only partial. Yet there are some parallels. The early united monarchy (under Saul, David, and Solomon) had not been uniformly absolutist. At times there had been a reasonable degree of consultation, as when David 'conferred with' his officers, and then with the whole assembly, about bringing the ark to Jerusalem. He did not wish to make a unilateral decision, but to take action only 'if it seems good to you and if it is the will of the Lord our God.' Then after consultation, we are told, 'The whole assembly agreed to do this, because it seemed right to all the people' (1 Chronicles 13.1–4).

David's son and successor Solomon, however, despite all his

wisdom and greatness, was a despot. His ambitious building programme had been completed only by the use of forced labour. Industrial relations (if I may use this term) were at an all-time low. So when he died, the people described his oppressive regime as a 'heavy yoke' and appealed to his son Rehoboam to lighten it. When Rehoboam consulted his father's elder statesmen, they advised him, 'If . . . you will be a servant to these people and serve them . . . they will always be your servants' (1 Kings 12.7). This splendid principle was rejected by Rehoboam, and in consequence the kingdom split into two. But this principle remains the essential basis of every constitutional monarchy (the motto of the Prince of Wales has since the fourteenth century been *Ich dien*, 'I serve') and indeed of every democratic institution.

First, it embodies the principle of *mutual service:* 'if you will serve them, they will serve you.' Jesus himself went beyond a prudential arrangement (we serve in order to be served) and affirmed that true leadership must be interpreted in terms of service ('whoever wants to become great among you must be your servant'). Later, Paul stated it ('Each of you should look not only to your own interests, but also to the interests of others'), and went on to illustrate it from the incarnation and death of Jesus.[2]

Secondly, it is mutual service based on *mutual respect.* One might say it is service based on justice, and not on expediency alone. To be sure, expediency enters into it ('you serve them and they will serve you'), but the principle's real foundation is justice, namely that the other party is a group of human beings with human rights, created in God's image as we have been, and therefore deserving our respect, as we deserve theirs. To oppress the poor is to insult their Maker; to serve them honours him.[3] It is this truth which lay behind the many detailed social instructions of the Old Testament, for example, to pay servants their wages the same day, to care for the deaf and the blind, to have compassion on the widow and orphan, to leave the gleanings of the harvest to the poor and the alien, and to administer justice impartially in the courts. And the same principle also lay behind the New Testament instructions to masters and servants to respect each other, for they served the same Lord and were responsible to the same Judge.

Turning from biblical principle to contemporary reality, the contrast is stark. What prevails is industrial strife, in which each side suspects the other of self-seeking, and so indulges in it too. Each seeks his own interests rather than the other's. It is an adversary situation born of suspicion and rivalry, instead of a situation of mutual service born of respect and trust.

In addition, one cannot escape the fact that strife is deeply embedded in our stratified British society. Confrontation between management and unions is often a reflection of the class divisions which continue to undermine our national unity. As David Steel, the Liberal Party leader, put it before the 1979 General Election: 'The major single defect in British society has been, and remains, its class-ridden nature. We see class division bedevilling so many aspects of our national life, particularly industrial relations. . . . Compared with the United States and our successful European competitors, Britain still has very deep and damaging class divisions. Our two major parties are mirror images of the two sides of industry, so that our industrial and class conflicts are perpetuated in our political system.' Many people feel underprivileged and alienated. It is not greed that motivates them, so much as grievance.

Let me cite a rather extreme example. A. J. M. Sykes has described the work attitudes of navvies on a hydroelectric construction site in North Scotland in 1953.[4] The labour force of 208 men lived in a camp; 108 were Irish, 87 Scots, 12 Poles, and one a Spaniard. 'All the employers in the industry were regarded as being entirely ruthless, holding their workers in contempt and having not the slightest interest in their welfare. . . . The management and staff interviewed, both in this camp and elsewhere, made no attempt to hide their contempt; in more than one interview they referred to the men as "animals," and the kindest estimates of them placed them as people outside society. Neither side expected any consideration from the other, or gave it. The navvies in discussing the industry, constantly used such phrases as "it's every man for himself," "you've got to be able to look after yourself" and "you get no quarter in this game.". . . .'[5] The men's attitude to the trade unions was similar: 'The idea that union officials might be genuinely concerned with their members' interests rather than their own, was regarded as naive. . . .' 'In short, the navvies regarded trade unions not as *their own* organisations but as external bodies, membership of which was incompatible with their independence as individuals.'[6]

Such a situation, one need hardly say, is wholly incompatible with the mind and spirit of Jesus Christ, and in his name we should set ourselves resolutely against it. But how? How can mutual suspicion be replaced by mutual service, and competition by cooperation?

The transforming influence of mutual respect has been well illustrated in the experience of the American industrialist Wayne Alderson. For four generations the Aldersons had been coal miners. During his boyhood Wayne's father would come home from the pit saying 'if only they'd value me as much as they value the mule' (it was easier to replace a miner than a well-trained mule), while his three brothers who had jobs in the local steel works would say 'if only they would value us as much as they value the machines.' Thus the importance of human *value* was instilled into him in his formative years and was later to flower in his 'Value of the Person' concept.

In the early 1970s Wayne Alderson became Vice-President of Operations in the Pittron Corporation, which had a steel foundry in Glassport, Pennsylvania, near Pittsburgh. The firm was struggling to survive after a disastrous eighty-four day strike, which left an aftermath of implacable bitterness and re-crimination between management and men. Mr. Alderson con-ceived a plan for better production, quality, relationships, and morale which he called 'Operation Turnaround.'

Determined to end the old management style of confronta-tion, he called for cooperation instead, walked daily through the foundry, greeted the men by name, asked them about their work and home, visited them when they were sick, in fact treated them like human beings. At the request of a few of them he then started a small Bible study, which grew into a brief 'chapel' service in a storage room underneath a furnace. As a result of the mutual confidence which he developed with the men, absenteeism and labour grievances virtually disappeared, while productivity and profits rose substantially. The old sterile days of confrontation were over. People called it 'the Miracle of Pittron.' After nearly two years Pittron was sold and Wayne Alderson lost his job. He started an itinerant ministry as speaker, consultant, and peacemaker, to spread his 'Value of the Person' vision. Its three key ingredients, he says, are love (a positive 'I'm for you' attitude), dignity (people count) and re-spect (appreciation instead of criticism). He goes on: 'Christ is at the centre of the Value of the Person approach. But even an atheist can accept the worth of the person.'[7]

Similarly, 'I am committed,' writes Kenneth N. Hansen, Chairman of the Board of ServiceMaster Industries Inc., 'to using work to help people develop, rather than to using people to accomplish the work as the end.'

Once there is a desire for mutual respect and mutual service, there will be at least three consequences.

Abolish Discrimination

The first is that discrimination will be abolished—both the realities and the symbols, which together perpetuate an un-wholesome 'them-us' confrontation.

For example, has there ever been a justification for paying workers by the hour and the week, and higher grades an annual salary? Or for insisting that wage earners clock in, while salaried staff do not have to? Or for restricting workers to the company canteen, while providing the rest with a posh 'staff restaurant'? In recent years many companies have put an end to such offensive distinctions, but many have not. 'We know there are "untouchables" on other continents,' commented Jock Gilmour, a shop steward in the British car industry; 'what we haven't recognised is that our own industrialised society can have its untouchables too.' I know, of course, that my three examples are trivial in themselves, but they are status symbols which appear deliberately to give self-respect to some and deny it to others. And behind these symbols of discrimination lies the reality of social injustice, namely the excessive disparity between the high-paid and the low-paid.

As I suggested in chapter 7 of Volume One, in which we were thinking about 'North-South Economic Inequality,' I do not think total egalitarianism should be the Christian goal, for God himself has not made us identical in either our natural or our spiritual endowments. What the Christian should oppose is the inequality of privilege, and what we should seek to ensure is that all differentials are due to merit, not privilege. In fact, it is a healthy and confidence-building arrangement when discrimination is limited to pay and does not extend to hidden perquisites for senior management (e.g. private health care, 'top hat' pension schemes, and free theatre tickets).

Wage differentials have been a major source of unrest and conflict. Barbara Wootton wrote back in 1962 of 'the apparent irrationality, as judged by *any* standard, of our present wage and salary structure. One may search in vain for the rational compound of skill, responsibility, effort, and working conditions of a system which would explain why the ward sister in a general hospital should be paid (at the top of her scale) about one-sixth of the salary of the Dean of Westminster (sc. of Westminster Abbey); why the male probation officer should start at about one-quarter of the top transatlantic pilot's rate, or at his maximum just pass the starting rate of the university lecturer in Greek; or why the sub-officer in the Fire Brigade should end a little above where the graduate school teacher began; and why the police constable after six years' experience should get for his full-time employment about five-sixths of the salary of a part-time governor of the BBC.'[8]

Yet human beings have a built-in sense of fair play, so that in all industrial relations arguments there are appeals to 'fairness,' and complaints of 'unfair practices.' This concept is the central focus of the book *Social Values and Industrial Relations*, subtitled 'a study of fairness and inequality.'[9] Already in 1881 Engels had described the expression 'a fair day's wage for a fair day's work' as 'the old time-honoured watchword of British industrial relations.'[10]

Surely then, it should be possible to evaluate, compare and classify jobs with a view to a graduated pay scale (the Netherlands introduced such a scale nationally in the postwar years). Is it really beyond the wit and wisdom of human beings to devise a commonly agreed scale on some kind of point system according to qualifications and length of training, skill and craftsmanship, mental and manual effort, risk and responsibility, achievement, experience and length of service, working conditions (including dirt, discomfort, danger, and tedium), supply and demand?

It is notoriously difficult, but surely not impossible, to compare clerical, manual, and skilled jobs. Such a wage/salary structure would have to be worked out by management and labour together; should ideally include the whole range from directors through managers to workers; would have to be seen to be just (every differential having a rational justification); and would overcome jealous conflicts, and the present uneven leapfrogging of claims and settlements.

I confess that I have admired the Scott Bader Commonwealth ever since I first read about it in E. F. Schumacher's *Small Is Beautiful* (1973) and subsequently corresponded with Ernest Bader. Mr. Bader is a Quaker, who came to England from Switzerland before World War I. The company he founded is a leading producer of plastics, and in 1951 he converted it into a 'Commonwealth' in which 'there are no owners or employees' because they are 'all co-owners and co-employees.' In 1979, Schumacher (who was a director) wrote: 'we have settled the maximum spread between the highest paid and the lowest paid; that is, before tax. It may shock many people [egalitarians, he must mean] that, in spite of a lot of goodwill from all concerned, that spread is still one to seven. There is no pressure from the community that it should be narrowed, because it is understood that this spread is necessary. But of course this includes everybody, the lowest paid juvenile compared with the highest paid senior employee.' The scale is reviewed and fixed by 'a sort of parliament of workers.'[11]

There must be differentials. But unwarranted discrimination in pay, conditions or promotion—'unwarranted' because based on privilege not merit—must be abjured. It is incompatible with social justice, and with the Christian ideal of mutual respect.

Increase Participation

It seems to be increasingly recognised that the workers in any enterprise, on whose skill and labour its success largely depends, should have a share in both decision-making and profits. Although some directors and managers resist this, and naturally feel threatened by it, the principle accords with natural justice. I want to concentrate on the concept of decision-making, since the Christian mind discerns in it a basic component of humanness.

However we define the 'Godlikeness' of mankind, it will surely include the capacity to make choices and decisions. Adam in the Genesis story is certainly regarded, and therefore treated, by God as a morally responsible person. True, the first command addressed to him was identical with that addressed to the living creatures of the sea, namely 'be fruitful and increase in number' (Genesis 1.22,28), and the injunction to them did not denote that they had freedom of choice. Yet, what animals do by instinct, humans do by free decision. The divine mandate to subdue the earth clearly implies responsibility, and a higher degree still is implicit in the words, ' "You are free to eat from any tree in the garden; but you must not eat from the tree of the knowledge of good and evil ..." ' (2.16,17). Here side by side are a liberal permission and a single prohibition. It is assumed that Adam was able both to distinguish between 'you may' and 'you must not,' and to choose between them. Moreover God held him responsible for his choice.

Christian tradition has always taught this biblical truth, that moral freedom is an essential ingredient in the dignity of human personhood. 'For the supreme mark of a person,' wrote William Temple, 'is that he orders his life by his own deliberate choice.'[12] In consequence, he adds, 'society must be so arranged as to give to every citizen the maximum opportunity for making deliberate choices and the best possible training for the use of that opportunity. In other words, one of our first considerations will be the widest possible extension of personal responsibility; it is the responsible exercise of deliberate choice which most fully expresses personality and best deserves the great name of freedom.'[13] Intuitively people know this. They want to be treated as adults with freedom to decide things for themselves; they know that if decision-making is taken away from them, their humanness will be demeaned. They will be reduced either to a child instead of an adult, or to a robot instead of a person.

The essential difference between a 'community' and an 'institution' is that in the former, members retain their freedom to choose, while in the latter it is to some degree taken away from them. Erving Goffman's interesting book *Asylums* is, strictly speaking, an investigation into 'the social situation of mental patients and other inmates.'[14] But he begins with some general observations. What he calls a 'total institution' is a place of residence or work where people 'lead an enclosed, formally administered round of life.'[15] This includes hospitals, orphanages, old people's homes, prisons, army barracks, boarding schools, monasteries and (I would have thought, although they are non-residential) many factories. In such places, the day's activities are 'tightly scheduled' and 'imposed from above by a system of explicit formal rulings and a body of officials.'[16] The key factor is the bureaucratic control, and the existence of a 'basic split between a large managed group, conveniently called "inmates," and a small supervisory staff.'[17] 'Characteristically, the inmate is excluded from knowledge of the decisions taken regarding his fate.'[18] Therefore in 'total institutions' an inmate ceases to be 'a person with adult self-determination, autonomy and freedom of action.'[19]

So important do I believe this to be, if Christians are to help create genuine community life, and protest against the dehumanising effects of institutional life, that I will give several examples and then come back to our topic of industrial relations. Before looking at the factory from this perspective, we will look at the school or college, the hospital, and the prison.

Christians distinguish sharply between education and indoctrination. Indoctrination is the process by which the teacher imposes his or her viewpoint on the malleable mind of the child; in true education, however, the teacher acts as a catalyst to develop the child's ability to learn by observation and reasoning. The former is oppressive, the latter genuinely liberating. To be sure, the teacher cannot and should not adopt a position of complete neutrality, for children need guidance as they grow in discernment. Yet the crucial question is which mind is given pride of place—the teacher's mind as it instructs the children's, or the children's as they learn how to use their mind, in order to make their own value judgments and moral decisions. This process of self-education in interaction with teachers should be even more evident in universities and colleges, and also in churches where the preacher should never treat his congregation as nothing more than an absorbent sponge.[20]

The students' demands of the 1960s also seemed right, namely that, since it is their education which is at stake, they should have a say in academic questions of curriculum and examinations, and an opportunity to evaluate their teachers' performance. School children and college students, as their age and maturity increase, should be given growing opportunities to make their own decisions.

Prison is very different, of course, because inmates have had their freedom taken from them following a fair trial, by the judicial authority of a court. It cannot be right to treat prisoners as if they were free citizens. Nevertheless, they should not be treated as if they were slaves or robots either. They are still adult human beings, still persons who bear God's image, even while being punished for their offences. I was struck by Chuck Colson's comment on this in one of the contributions he made to the 1979 London Lectures in Contemporary Christianity. Reflecting on his experience of incarceration, following his involvement in the Watergate cover-up, he said: 'You make absolutely no decisions for yourself. The time of your meals, your work assignments—everything is decided for you. You have an overwhelming sensation of helplessness. Your individual identity is destroyed.'[21]

Turning now to the medical field, there is a constant danger that the doctor-patient relationship, already unnatural because of the awe in which doctors are held, will degenerate further beyond paternalism to control. The patient remains a person, and when decisions have to be made affecting his health and even his life, he should be left free to make them. Although it is obviously difficult for doctors to explain to their patients complex medical conditions and procedures in nontechnical language, yet they are under obligation to do their best to do so; otherwise the notion of 'informed consent' to treatment, surgery or research would be meaningless. According to the Nuremberg Code of 1946–49, 'the voluntary consent of the human subject is absolutely essential.' This means not only that there shall be no duress, but that he 'should have sufficient knowledge and comprehension of the elements of the subject matter involved as to enable him to make an understanding and enlightened decision. . . .'[22] Similarly, the 1964 Helsinki Declaration on human experimentation (drawn up by the World Medical Association) included the clause that 'clinical research on a human being cannot be undertaken without his free consent after he has been fully informed.'[23]

Yet patients often feel that they are being bypassed, and even manipulated, because they are kept in the dark about their condition and treatment, and are consequently powerless. Solzhenitsyn gives us a moving example of this in Oleg Kostoglotov, the chief character he created in his book *Cancer Ward*.[24] Like Solzhenitsyn himself, Oleg had been in a concentration camp before he entered the cancer ward. Indeed throughout the book Solzhenitsyn seems to be drawing a subtle parallel between prison and hospital, especially in the fact that neither prisoners nor patients are allowed to make any decisions for themselves. Oleg has a sturdy independence of mind and spirit, however. 'Everything that's gone wrong in my life,' he says, 'has been because I was too devoted to democracy. I tried to spread democracy in the army, that is, I answered my superiors back.'[25]

Ludmila Afanasyevna Dontsova, who is in charge of the radiotherapy department, reacts strongly against what she regards as his uncooperative attitude. 'You will go home when I consider it necessary to interrupt your treatment,' she says with great emphasis. 'Ludmila Afanasyevna!' responds Oleg in exasperation. 'Can't we get away from this tone of voice? You sound like a grown-up talking to a child. Why not talk as an adult to an adult? . . . You see, you start from a completely false position. No sooner does a patient come to you than you begin to do all his thinking for him. . . . And once again I become like a grain of sand, just like I was in the camp. Once again nothing *depends* on me.'[26] Then later, writing to his friends, and describing the ward's barred windows, bunk beds, terrified inmates, one-by-one processing, as if he were in prison, Oleg goes on: 'By some right . . . they [the doctors] have decided, without my consent and on my behalf, on a most terrible form of therapy—hormone therapy.'[27]

I return at last to industry and to industrial relations. I realise that western hospitals are not like those in the Soviet Union during Stalin's oppressive regime, and that in any case there are differences between factories on the one hand and schools, colleges, prisons, and hospitals on the other. Nevertheless, I have been anxious to show that decision-making is a basic right of human beings, an essential component of our human dignity.

The cry for industrial democracy, in order to facilitate a greater participation of workers in their own enterprise, does not make factories a special case, but is the expression within industry of the universal cry for the humanisation of society. We now take political democracy for granted, and are grateful to those who struggled long to secure universal suffrage so that ordinary citizens might share in governing their country and in making the laws they are then required to obey. Is not the propriety of industrial democracy equally self-evident? Already forty years ago William Temple wrote: 'The cause of freedom will not be established till political freedom is fulfilled in economic freedom.'[28] He looked back with feelings of horror to the oppressive beginnings of the Industrial Revolution: 'the pioneers showed little respect for the personality of those who earned their living by working in factories and mills. They were often called "hands"; and a hand is by nature a "living tool," which is the classical definition of a slave.'[29]

Indeed, in a historic letter to the *Leeds Mercury* in 1830, Richard Oastler, a Christian landowner in Yorkshire, had the courage to draw this very analogy three years before Wilberforce and his friends had secured the abolition of slavery in the British colonies. 'Thousands of our fellow creatures and fellow subjects both male and female are at this moment existing in a state of slavery more horrid than the victims of that hellish system of colonial slavery.' He went on to refer particularly to little children from seven to fourteen years of age, who were working thirteen hours a day in the factories, with only a half-hour break.[30]

We have come a long way in a hundred and fifty years, thank God. And yet we still have some way to go. William Temple continued: 'The worst horrors of the early factories have been abolished, but the wage earners are not yet fully recognised as persons, for . . . the "workers" usually have no voice in the control of the industry whose requirements determine so large a part of their lives.'[31] He states the principle in these clear terms: 'Every citizen should have a voice in the conduct of the business or industry which is carried on by means of his labour.'[32]

At the heart of many industrial disputes (so I understand from my reading) is the question of rules and rule-making—not just *what* the rules require or forbid, but *who* makes the rules and *why*. Management is often dictatorial in making or changing rules, regarding this as 'managerial prerogative.' Workers, on the other hand, usually go by what they call 'C and P' (Custom and Practice), the unwritten but established conventions of the place. The *Donovan Report*[33] emphasised the tension between these two systems, the 'formal' (official agreements) and the 'informal' (unwritten procedures), and expressed its dislike of this situation. It is the difference between rules from above and from below, and so between two different kinds of authority, power wielded from above and commonsense or custom from below.

Moreover, each side sees the need to legitimise its rules. This necessity is the particular emphasis of the book *Ideology and Shop-Floor Industrial Relations* (1981).[34] It discusses the process of legitimisation in industrial relations, the arguments which each side uses to justify or challenge rules, and the ideology, worldview or value-system which lies behind this process. Industrial relations are broader than rules and rule-making, however. The whole policy and programme of the company are concerned. It has to be admitted that in many companies the workers lack self-respect because they lack responsibility. They feel oppressed and powerless. The 'them and us' mentality is enforced because other people make all the decisions (remote, faceless people), while their role is exclusively to react, and indeed to obey. The analogy with slavery, though very inexact, is yet instructive at this point. Christians opposed slavery because human beings are dehumanised by being *owned* by someone else. Christians now should oppose all forms of labour in which human beings are *used* by someone else. True, the evil is much smaller, because the work is undertaken voluntarily and is regulated by a contract. Yet it is a contract which diminishes humanness if it involves the relinquishing of personal responsibility and the undertaking to obey without consultation.

Christians will agree that at the very least there should be a procedure of consultation, and, more important, that this should not be a piece of window dressing but a genuine discussion early in the planning process which is reflected in the final decision. After all, *production* is a team process, in which the workers' contribution is indispensable; should not *decision-making* be a team process too, in which the workers' contribution is equally indispensable? Self-interest undoubtedly lies at the root of each side's viewpoint. Managers tend to begin their thinking with profit, on which the company's survival depends; whereas workers tend to begin with rising costs and therefore wages, on which their personal survival depends. Their different starting points are understandable. But in discussion each side comes to understand the other's legitimate concerns, and then to see that the two, far from being incompatible, are in fact interdependent.

Once the principle of worker-participation has been conceded, there can be a legitimate difference of opinion about the best ways and means to ensure it. Indeed a variety of structures have been advocated and tried from thorough consultation at all levels to the election of worker-directors. More experiments would be valuable.[35]

The majority report of the *Bullock Committee on Industrial Democracy* (1977) recommended a positive partnership between management and labour in developing a corporate strategy for the company, and in making and implementing decisions. They expressed themselves in favour of the company having employee directors.

In May 1978 the Labour Government issued a white paper on *Industrial Democracy*, which accepted the principle of participation. If this Government had had the opportunity to produce legislation on this basis, they would have (1) *obliged* employers in companies of more than five hundred employees to discuss with representatives of the work force all major proposals affecting them, including plans for investment, merger, expansion, and contraction; (2) *encouraged* companies to develop a two-tier board structure (a policy board and a management board) and to arrange for employees to be represented on the policy board; and (3) *given a statutory right* to employees in firms of more than two thousand to be represented on the policy board alongside the shareholders' representatives. A minority report disagreed, on the grounds of lack of evidence and size of risk.

Reactions to these proposals were mixed, though on the whole they were more hostile than friendly. The Confederation of British Industry (CBI), representing the employers, said they thought that the Bullock committee had been given biased terms of reference, and that they were more concerned to give workers control of the company than participation in it. The Unions were negative because they believed board representation and collective bargaining to be fundamentally incompatible. Historically, it has been by collective bargaining that the Trade Unions have undermined the undisputed power of the employers and indeed secured some power of their own over wages and conditions of work. In other words, both sides understandably wanted to preserve their present power, even if this meant a continuing degree of confrontation.

I doubt if any Christian would disagree with the way Robin Woods, at that time Bishop of Worcester and Chairman of the Church of England's Board for Social Responsibility, summed the situation up in a letter to *The Times:* 'it is consistent with Christian vision that society should develop in such a way that each person can exercise his God-given ability to make choices, to take responsibility, and to share in shaping his own environment. We believe that employees have a stake in their company which is at least as significant as that of the shareholders.'[35]

The second kind of participation is profit-sharing. Another clear biblical principle seems to be involved, namely that ' "the worker deserves his wages" ' (1 Timothy 5.18). Presumably then there should be some correlation between work and wage. If a company prospers, shared power (responsibility) should bring shared profit. If shareholders benefit from profit, so should workers, whether in bonuses or company stock or deferred benefits (e.g. pension). The 'pact' between the British Liberal and Labour parties at the end of the 1970s introduced the idea of tax incentives for firms which developed profit-sharing schemes.

The credit for being first in the profit-sharing field seems to belong to the John Lewis Partnership in Oxford Street, London. John Lewis was twenty-eight years old when he opened a small drapery shop there in 1864. By the turn of the century his son Spedan had become troubled in conscience that he, his father, and his brother as shareholders were jointly drawing from the business substantially more than all their employees put together. So he determined to devise a more equitable division of the rewards of industry, and in 1920 the first distribution of 'Partnership Benefit' was made, representing an extra seven weeks of pay. Spedan Lewis later made two irrevocable settlements in trust for the benefit of the workers.

From 1928 to 1970 the 'Partnership Bonus' (as it is now called) was made in the form of stock, but since 1970 it has been wholly in cash. The company's policy is stated thus: 'After paying preference dividends and interest, and providing for amenities, pensions, and proper reserves, the remainder of the profits in any year is distributed to the members of the Partnership in proportion to their pay. In this way the profits are shared among all who work in the business.' The percentage of the total profits applied to the Bonus rose from 12 percent in 1967 to 20 percent in 1980, and has been even higher since.

Such an arrangement was innovative in the '20s. Today similar profit-sharing schemes or profit-linked share plans are multiplying in Britain, Continental Europe, and North America. The 'Wider Share Ownership Council' was established in 1958 to promote such schemes.[36]

Both aspects of participation (decision-making and profit-sharing) appeal to the Christian mind on the ground not only of expediency (increased industrial peace and productivity) but also of justice (workers have a right to share in power and profits).

Emphasise Cooperation

The fundamental concept of mutual respect and mutual service, whose implications for industry we are exploring, should lead not only to the abolition of discrimination, but also to the increase of participation and so of cooperation.

Trade unions developed in the nineteenth century to protect workers against exploitative bosses. Since workers had no rights under British Company Law at that time, they were forced to organise themselves from outside. Over the years they have secured great gains for labour, both in wages and in conditions. They were therefore absolutely necessary; without their sense of collective responsibility and their persistent struggles labour would still be exploited today. It is true that now a union will sometimes forfeit public sympathy by a stance that is more political than industrial, by unreasonable demands and unjustified strike action, or by violence in the picket lines. But it is also true that many trade unionists work hard and long to find solutions to conflict in the face of incompetent or intransigent managers, and that their patient work often goes unacknowledged. The tragedy is, however, that the first loyalty of the workers tends to be given to their union rather than their firm, and that confrontation is now built into the very structures of industry. Why should we assume that this structural confrontation is inevitable and therefore everlasting? Why must the language of 'winning' and 'losing,' whenever there is an industrial dispute, be perpetuated? Why should we not dream of, and work towards, the day when better structures will be developed which express cooperation? The Labour Government's white paper *Industrial Democracy*, to which I have already referred, defined the goal as 'a positive partnership between management and workers, rather than defensive coexistence.' When management and labour are locked in confrontation, the public also suffers; when they cooperate in the service of the public, their relations to each other improve.

An example, of how the atmosphere and attitudes of a whole company can change, will serve to illustrate some of the principles we have been considering.

Towards the end of the 1960s, Gerald Snider, an American businessman, worked for a multinational company whose identity it is not necessary to divulge. He found himself Vice-President and General Manager of a group of European companies. He was in fact Acting President, since the ultimate responsibility for them was his.

He told me the story of one particular company which, when he assumed responsibility for it, was in extremely bad shape. The factory's product was inferior in design and quality. The plant was dirty, the machinery out-of-date, and the environment bad. Although wages were competitive, the workers took little interest in their work and were suspicious of management, even hostile. Absenteeism was rampant. As many as 20 percent of the work force did not show up on Mondays. In consequence, to make up for absenteeism, the plant was seriously overstaffed. Indeed, one of Gerald Snider's first acts was to declare four hundred of the eighteen hundred workers redundant. It was an extremely unpleasant task, but the only alternative would have been to close the plant down.

As he thought about the whole situation, it became clear to him that the fundamental cause of the factory's malaise was the bad relationships between the workers and their supervisors. To be sure, each employee maintained the required contact with those above and below him. But it was more a ritual than a relationship. The factory was organised by directives which descended from on high through five levels—from managing director through plant manager, personnel manager, supervisor and foreman to the production workers. There was no consultation and no intelligent, willing cooperation. Indeed, there were no genuine relationships at all.

Gerald Snider saw that, if the factory was to survive, it was necessary not only for the quality of its product to be acceptable to the marketplace, but for the employees at every level both to understand the company's objectives and to cooperate in order to achieve them. So he decided to take an unheard-of step. He would call the entire work force together, in order to take them into his confidence and explain the situation to them. Immediately the most strenuous objections were raised. 'It isn't done,' he was told; 'you fellows in the United States may get away with it, but in our country we don't do things that way.' A whole week of discussion followed, in which managers and supervisors (who felt threatened by what they thought would be the undermining of their authority) advanced every contrary argument they could think of. But the General Manager was adamant.

So one day at 11:45 A.M., for a quarter-of-an-hour of the company's time, everybody assembled in the factory's auditorium. Mr. Snider outlined the serious situation which had arisen on account of the poor quality of the product and the poor performance of the work force. Indeed, of all the companies for which he was responsible in Europe, theirs showed the lowest production and the highest absenteeism. He then propounded his programme for survival. On the one hand, the company was prepared to invest millions of pounds in modernising equipment and tools, and in improving the work environment. On the other, he asked for their whole-hearted cooperation. Absenteeism would have to stop. There could be no more Saturday work at double or treble time; what had to be done must be done during the working week.

Above all, he added, he was anxious to improve relationships and simplify communication between all levels. He was even now giving them a direct account of the factory's problems, goals, and needs. He wanted them to have equally direct access to management and to him personally, for he was convinced that if mutual understanding could grow, mutual responsibility would grow with it. So, when the plant opened at seven o'clock the following morning, he would be there and available to them.

To his surprise, and to the personnel department's astonishment (since they had prophesied that the men would not accept a direct approach from the General Manager), his speech was greeted with loud applause. And when he walked through the factory floor early the following morning, already the old sullenness had gone. Men smiled as he passed. Some also made suggestions, especially the foremen, who occupy a key position between management and labour. A daily meeting between them began, which resulted in a number of useful suggestions. Another important decision was to close the two dining rooms previously reserved for executives and supervisors, so that everybody would eat in the same restaurant, sharing the same conditions and the same food, and having the same opportunity to meet, know and trust one another.

Gradually too the General Manager's other promises were fulfilled. Modern equipment was installed. The factory was redecorated. The washrooms were cleaned. The new procedures for open communication continued to be fostered. So as the management's good faith became evident, the workers' good faith increased. Production went up significantly. Absenteeism was reduced from over 20 percent to under 5 percent. The quality of the product improved. The crisis was over.

Gerald Snider was brought up in a Christian home, and has remained a practising Christian. Although he modestly disclaims any self-conscious application of Christian principles to his business life, and although he did not put forward his proposals for the survival of his factory as a specifically 'Christian' solution to the problem, nevertheless his actions reflected the teaching of the Bible. On the one hand, he was convinced of the dignity of work in God's intention ('if you can't enjoy your work, you shouldn't be there,' he said to me). On the other, he recognised the value of human beings as God's supreme creation in his own likeness. In the production process, therefore, workers must not be treated as 'objects,' who receive directives from the top without explanation or consultation, but rather as 'subjects,' who are given the chance to understand their contribution to the whole enterprise, and who participate in it with a good will.

Cooperation cannot be engineered by itself; it is a by-product of a common vision and goal. This fact is increasingly recognised by those who pursue that elusive thing called 'good management.' The main emphasis of Thomas J. Peters and Robert H. Waterman, Jr. in their best-selling book *In Search of Excellence* is the necessity, if a company is to succeed, of 'shared values,' which unite and motivate the entire workforce. After investigating the management techniques of America's sixty-two best-run companies, they developed the '7-S McKinsey Framework,' which they present as an alliterative 'managerial molecule.' The six outer satellites are Strategy, Structure, Systems, Style, Staff, and Skills, but the nucleus at the centre, round which all these revolve, is 'Shared Values,' alternatively described as 'superordinated goals.'[37] One of the most vital of these is respect for people, both employees and customers. 'Treating people—not money, machines or minds—as the natural resource' is of paramount importance (p. 39).

Japanese management has largely been built on this kind of American foundation. Why, then, is Japanese industry often more productive than American? What is the secret of the economic prowess of the Japanese? Richard Tanner Pascale and Anthony G. Athos set out to answer these questions in their book *The Art of Japanese Management*. In particular, they investigated the Matsushita Electric Company.

They found that this large corporation was using all the American principles of management (Japanese people joke that 'BA' stands for 'Been to America'!). But they also found something else. Matsushita not only composed an 'employees' creed' (which includes a reference to 'the combined efforts and cooperation of each member of our Company') and seven 'spiritual values' (one of which is 'harmony and cooperation'), but has actually set these to music.

'Matsushita was the first company in Japan to have a song and a code of values. "It seems silly to Westerners," says an executive, "but every morning at 8:00 A.M., all across Japan, there are 87,000 people reciting the code of values and singing together. It's like we are all a community." '[38]

Messrs. Pascale and Athos recognise that this emphasis on cooperation has a strongly cultural origin. The Americans prize 'independence,' but the Japanese 'interdependence.' Of a person who has difficulties in relating to others Americans say 'he hasn't found himself,' the Japanese 'he doesn't belong' (p. 122). So all members of the workforce belong to a 'work group' of about ten people, in which harmony is developed, and to which loyalty is expected. It is not suggested that this kind of cultural arrangement can be transferred *tout simple* from Japan to Europe or America. Nevertheless, the contrast between the competitive individualism of the West and the productive cooperation of the East which they describe is surely significant. Company morale arising from shared values is easier to develop in small businesses; if huge corporations are to experience it, they may need to break into smaller autonomous units.

The shared values of a company will inevitably include a recognition of its multiple responsibilities. In his trailblazing books *The Future of Private Enterprise* (1951) and *The Responsible Company* (1961), George Goyder considered the alternatives of 'a form of private enterprise based on the profit motive' and 'a form of public enterprise called nationalisation' and proposed 'a third and better way through the creation of responsible industrial companies, neither wholly private nor wholly public.'[39] His concern was to make companies accountable not only to their shareholders (which was at that time their only obligation according to Company Law in Britain), but also to their workers, their consumers, and the community at large. George Goyder went on to propose how this could be done legally, in particular by adding to the company's 'Memorandum of Association,' a clause which would define its general purposes. In order to bring private industry under social control without depriving it of freedom, he further suggested that every firm, in addition to an annual financial audit, should establish a triennial 'social audit' relating to pricing policies (affecting consumers), labour relations (affecting employees), and local interests (affecting the community). 'The social audit,' he wrote, 'is the natural result of business accepting its full responsibility.'[40] Such a firm, being half way between a private and a public company, might well be called 'a Participating Company.'[41]

It seems clear then, that every company should define its goals and assign a priority order to them. In 1975 the CBI approved a report of its Company Affairs Committee entitled 'The Responsibility of the British Public Company.' Its paragraph 22 reads: 'While law establishes the *minimum* standard of conduct with which a company must comply . . . , a company like a person must be recognised as having functions, duties and moral obligations that go beyond the pursuit of profit and the specific requirements of legislation.' So several organisations, and some individual companies, have issued a 'Code of Practice' which summarises their ideals and goals. For example, a thorough 'Code of Business Ethics' has been produced by CABE, the Christian Association of Business Executives.[42]

Of course, every firm must make a profit, but its priority concern should be the public whom the company (management, shareholders, and workers together) exists to serve. Just as the first responsibility of hospital workers is their patients, of teachers their pupils, and of lawyers and social workers their clients, so the first responsibility of every business and industry is their customers—not just because the survival of the enterprise depends on pleasing the public, but because service to the public is its *raison d'être*. In addition, the company itself is best served when management, labour, and shareholders are united in serving the public. 'If you serve them, they will serve you.'

The Church should be the first community in which class stratification and a 'them-us' mentality are overcome. If the followers of Jesus Christ cannot develop relationships of respect and trust, across social barriers, we can hardly blame the world for failing. But improved relationships need not be limited to the Church. We should work expectantly for greater respect and cooperation in every segment of human society. We should not acquiesce in industrial conflict or be pessimistic about resolving it. For all human beings, though fallen and self-centred, have an inborn sense of dignity and justice. So better relations are possible.

Chapter Three

The Multiracial Dream

ON AUGUST 28, 1963 MARTIN LUTHER KING, JR., WHO WAS equally committed to nondiscrimination and to nonviolence, in other words to justice and peace, led a march of 250,000 people, three quarters of whom were black and one quarter white, to Washington, D.C. And there he shared his dream of a multiracial America:

> I have a dream that one day on the red hills of Georgia the sons of former slaves and the sons of former slave-owners will be able to sit down together at the table of brotherhood.
>
> I have a dream that one day even the state of Mississippi, a state sweltering with the heat of injustice. . . . and oppression, will be transformed into an oasis of freedom and justice.
>
> I have a dream that my four little children will one day live in a nation where they will not be judged by the color of their skin but by the content of their character. . . .
>
> I have a dream that one day in Alabama, with its vicious racists . . . little black boys and black girls will be able to join hands with little white boys and white girls as sisters and brothers. . . .
>
> With this faith we will be able to transform the jangling discords of our nation into a beautiful symphony of brotherhood.
>
> With this faith we will be able to work together, to stand up for freedom together, knowing that we will be free one day. . . .[1]

It is right for Christians to dream this dream, for God has given us in Scripture a vision of the redeemed as 'a great multitude that no one could count, from every nation, tribe, people and language, standing before the throne . . .' (Revelation 7.9). That dream, we know, will come true. Meanwhile, inspired by it, we should seek at least an approximation to it on earth, namely a society characterized by racial justice (no discrimination) and racial harmony (no conflict). Perhaps even the word 'multiracial' is not specific enough, and 'interracial' would be better, since the South African Nationalist government describes its vision of separate 'homelands' as 'multiracial development,' and that is not at all how the word should be used. I do not know a more careful definition of racial integration than that given by Roy Jenkins when he was Home Secretary: 'I define integration,' he said, 'not as a flattening process of assimilation, but as equal opportunity, accompanied by cultural diversity, in an atmosphere of mutual tolerance.'[2]

Before considering the biblical basis for racial integration, I think we need to look at some examples of 'racism,' both historical and contemporary, and be aware of the false foundations on which it is built.

Slavery and the American Racial Problem

It is not possible to jump straight to the contemporary problem of race in Europe and America, and ignore the evils of slavery and of the slave trade out of which it has largely sprung. Although slavery was abolished in the British colonies 150 years ago, no sensitive Briton can meet a West African or West Indian, without seeing them as probable descendants of slaves, or visit their countries without remembering the appalling traffic in human beings in which Britain engaged for at least two hundred years. Similarly, no sensitive American can confront the race issue in the United States today without looking back beyond the Civil War to the cruelty and degradation of life on the plantations.

It is generally accepted that 'the slave has three defining characteristics: his person is the property of another man, his will is subject to his owner's authority, and his labor or services are obtained through coercion.'[3] Being regarded as nothing but movable and disposable property, slaves were normally deprived of elementary human rights, e.g. the right to marry, or to own or bequeath possessions, or to witness in a court of law. Although slavery of different kinds and degrees was universal in the ancient world, it is inexcusable that the professedly Christian nations of Europe (Spain and Portugal, Holland, France, and Britain) should have used this inhuman practice to meet the labour needs of their New World colonies. Worse still, practising Christians developed an elaborate defence of slavery on the grounds of social and economic necessity (there was no other source of labour in the colonies to provide raw materials for the Industrial Revolution in Europe), racial superiority (Negroes deserved no better treatment), biblical permission (Scripture regulates but nowhere condemns slavery), humanitarian benefit (the trade transferred slaves from African savagery to American civilisation), and even missionary opportunity (African infidels would be introduced to Christianity in the New World). The blatant rationalisations of slave-owners make one blush with embarrassment today.

The inherent evil of slavery (which in principle is the evil of racism also) is that it affronts, indeed denies, the people's God-like dignity as human beings. Being the property of their owners, slaves were advertised for sale alongside horses and cattle, mules and pigs, corn and plantation tools. Having first been captured, chained, shipped and branded, they were then auctioned, forced to work, often separated from wife and children, if recalcitrant flogged, if escaped pursued by bloodhounds, and if caught killed.

Some writers argued that the reason why they were property is that they were animals. In his *The History of Jamaica* (1774), Edward Long developed the outrageous argument that in the

Creator's 'series or progression from a lump of dirt to a perfect man' African Negroes are inferior to human beings. 'When we reflect on . . . their dissimilarity to the rest of mankind, must we not conclude that they are a different species of the same genus?'[4] The French author J. H. Guenebault went even further in his *The Natural History of the Negro Race* (1837). Having given his opinion of the physical form and mental inferiority of Negroes, he wrote: 'It is then impossible to deny that they form not only a race, but truly a species, distinct from all other races of men known on the globe.' They belong to 'the ape genus,' he declared, and placed them somewhere between orangutans and white human beings.[5]

A third inferiority theory, popularized by Ulrich B. Phillips in his *American Negro Slavery* (1918), is that Negroes were children. He was evidently fond of Negroes in a paternalistic way, but could not take them seriously as adults. Stanley M. Elkins in his book *Slavery* (1959) examines the familiar image of the plantation slave as 'Sambo.' He was 'docile but irresponsible, loyal but lazy, humble but chronically given to lying and stealing. . . . His relationship with his master was one of utter dependence and childlike attachment: it was indeed the childlike quality that was the very key to his being.'[6] The Sambo stereotype was of 'the perpetual child incapable of maturity.'[7] Professor Elkins goes on to develop the thesis that Negro 'infantilism' was due neither to race, nor to culture, nor even to slavery in general, but to the absolutist structure of the North American plantation system. He draws a striking analogy between the victims of North American slavery and those of Nazi concentration camps, for the latter (if they survived) were 'reduced to complete and childish dependence upon their masters,' namely the SS guards.[8] Thus, the same mechanism operated in Negro plantation and Nazi concentration camp, since both were hideous forms of slavery, and the victims of both were subjugated into infantilism.[9]

The horror of eighteenth-century slavery, then, was that it regarded men and women as tools, animals or children. In consequence, they were thought to have an inborn inferiority. Christian opponents of slavery found it necessary, therefore, to demonstrate that Negro slaves were human beings who were in no way inferior to others. So Wilson Armistead, a Quaker businessman from Leeds, subtitled his book *A Tribute for the Negro* (1848) 'a vindication of the moral, intellectual and religious capabilities of the coloured portion of mankind, with particular reference to the African race.' He dedicated it to three Negroes and 'many other noble examples of elevated humanity in the Negro ... beautifully designated "the image of God cut in Ebony." ' His intention, he wrote, was to demonstrate 'from facts and testimonies that the white and the dark coloured races of man are alike the children of one Heavenly Father and in all respects equally endowed by him,' and to prove 'that the Negro is indubitably and fully entitled to equal claims with the rest of mankind.'[10]

This brief excursus into slavery is far from being irrelevant, for the racist, although of course he concedes the humanness of black people, nevertheless also holds that they have an inborn inferiority. He may defend his position as a so-called 'scientific theory of race,' or merely cherish 'vague notions about a unilinear evolution "from monkey to man" ' which 'encourage him to believe that such "races" are "lower" in the "scale" of evolution than is the group to which he belongs; that there is a hierarchy of "races." '[11]

It was to demolish this illusion that Dr. Ashley Montagu wrote his definitive book *Man's Most Dangerous Myth: The Fallacy of Race.* Of course he agrees, as a physical anthropologist, that mankind may be divided into four 'major groups' (Caucasoid, Mongoloid, Negroid, and Australoid) and into many smaller 'ethnic groups' (by nationality, language, culture etc.). But he insists that these groupings are arbitrary, overlapping, and fluid; that they merely describe populations whose distinctions are due partly to cultural development (as a result of geographical separation) and partly to 'temporary mixtures of genetic materials common to all mankind';[12] and that the differences are definitely *not* due to 'inborn physical and mental traits' which are ineradicable.[13] Indeed, that concept of 'race' is a superstition, 'the witchcraft of our time,'[14] and a stratagem invented to justify discrimination.

Columbus Salley and Ronald Behm begin their book *What Color is your God?*[15] with three historical chapters tracing the development of the racial problem in America. The first ('Christianity and Slavery') takes us up to the Civil War (1863). The second ('Christianity and Segregation') runs from 1863 to 1914, and is the period following the Civil War, in which 'Black Codes' were formulated to give blacks some permissions, but to keep them weak and inferior. The Ku Klux Klan was formed. White churches were segregated and silent, while black churches were conformist and otherworldly. The third period runs from 1914 to today ('Christianity and Ghettoization'). It began with the mass migration of blacks to the cities of the North and West, and the consequent 'Great White Exodus' from the same cities. 'Institutional racism' restricted blacks to certain areas and certain roles, and gave them inferior education, housing, and employment. There were riots and lynchings. Again in this period, as in the previous ones, the church was largely mute and ineffective.

In the 1960s, however, the search for black identity and power led to the more organised Civil Rights movement, and so to the legislation which ended segregation and discrimination. Even this was only a beginning, however. In 1968 the National Advisory Commission on Civil Disorders, which had been appointed by President Lyndon B. Johnson, reported (the 'Kerner Report'). This was its conclusion: 'Our nation is moving toward two societies, one black, one white—separate and unequal.'

Further, 'segregation and poverty have created in the racial ghetto a destructive environment totally unknown to most white Americans. . . . White institutions created it, white institutions maintain it, and white society condones it.' Thoughtful Americans are deeply disturbed by the continuing situation. 'Racism is American society's most exposed weakness,' wrote Ashley Montagu. 'It is America's greatest domestic failure, and the worst of its international handicaps.'[16]

German Anti-Semitism and South African Apartheid

Anti-Semitism in Germany and apartheid in South Africa seem at first sight so different from one another as to be entirely unsuitable for comparison. There is an obvious difference between Jews and blacks, for example, and in the laws relating to them. In particular, the unspeakable outrage of the 'Holocaust' has no parallel in South Africa. Nevertheless, although it will shock some readers to learn this, the theory of 'race' on which both systems rest is almost identical. So is the sense which many Germans and South Africans have expressed that they are 'destined to rule,' and must at all costs preserve their racial 'purity.'

In *Mein Kampf*, published eight years before he came to power, Hitler had already extolled the splendour of the Aryan race. 'Every manifestation of human culture, every product of art, science and technical skill, which we see before our eyes today is almost exclusively the product of the Aryan creative power. . . . it was the Aryan alone who founded a superior type of humanity; . . . he is the Prometheus of mankind, from whose shining brow the divine spark of genius has at all times flashed forth. . . .'[17] Borrowing his ideas from Wagner's dream of Germanic greatness, Nietzsche's notion of a 'daring ruler race,' and Darwin's concept of the ruthless struggle needed for survival, he developed both his illusions of Aryan destiny and his insane phobia of the Jews, who, he declared, were economically, politically, culturally, religiously and morally destroying civilisation.[18] The insulting and irrational language he used of them is unrepeatable. He dared even to claim that in dealing with them he would be acting on behalf of the Almighty Creator.[19] In this he was able to quote Christian scholars who had developed a 'Creation Theology' to justify racism. Paul Althaus, for example, recognising marriage, family, race, and *Volk* as God's order of creation, wrote: 'We champion the cause of the preservation of the purity of the Volk and of our Race.'[20] Hitler himself knew, it seems, that this racial theory of an Aryan *Herrenvolk* ('master race') had no scientific basis. In private he conceded this. Yet he continued to use it because he needed it as a politician: 'With the conception of race, National Socialism will carry its revolution abroad and recast the world.'[21]

The origins of the Afrikaners' sense of divine destiny are bound up with their history. When the Dutch first arrived at the Cape of Good Hope (1652), they saw themselves as the heirs and bearers of European Christian civilisation. And when their Great Trek began in 1835, and they travelled in ox wagons North and East to escape from British rule, their conviction of a special destiny increased. They saw a parallel between themselves and the Old Testament people of God. Their trek was a new exodus, a divine deliverance from alien oppression, and on their arduous journey they were tested like Israel in the wilderness. The hostile black nations they had to overcome were their equivalent to the Amalekites and the Philistines. After the Battle of Blood River, in which they defeated the Zulus, they entered into a solemn covenant with God, and the Transvaal and the Orange Free State were their promised land to which God brought them. This sacralisation of their early history has imprinted itself on the Afrikaner consciousness. They think of themselves as a chosen people, an elect nation. 'Afrikanerdom is not the work of men,' said Dr. D. F. Malan, the Nationalist leader who became Prime Minister in 1948, 'but the creation of

God.'[22] Thus most Afrikaners believe that they have a Messianic vocation, that they are born to rule, and that God has called them to preserve Christian civilisation in Africa.

Added to their history (which has given them this sense of destiny) is their theology (which has given them their theory of race). This combination of history and theology undergirds their determination to ensure their distinct survival by means of apartheid. For, says the Dutch Reformed Church, 'the Scriptures ... teach and uphold the ethnic diversity of the human race' and regard it as a 'positive proposition' to be preserved. Consequently, 'a political system based on the autogenous or separate development of various population groups can be justified from the Bible.'[23] The way this view of separate development is presented is often evenhanded, for an equal concern is expressed that *all* racial groups will be preserved intact. Nevertheless, the impression is clearly given that the Nationalist Government's primary concern is the preservation of white Afrikanerdom, and at that in a position of superiority. Certainly Dr. Verwoerd was frank enough to say to Parliament in 1963: 'Keeping South Africa white can mean only one thing, namely white domination; not leadership, not guidance, but "control" supremacy.'

The parallel between German National Socialists and South African Nationalists, then, which some will doubtless find offensive but which really cannot be refuted, lies in the resolve at all costs to maintain 'racial purity,' and to legislate for it by prohibiting mixed marriages. In *Mein Kampf* Hitler wrote that miscegenation was to be opposed with the utmost vigour in order to preserve the purity of Aryan stock. Intermarriage, he declared, invariably causes physical and mental degeneration. It 'is a sin against the will of the Eternal Creator.'[24]

In South Africa the Prohibition of Mixed Marriages Act became law in 1949. It made marriage between 'Europeans and non-Europeans' (i.e. between 'whites' and 'nonwhites') illegal, while an act of 1968 extended this law to include South African male citizens domiciled outside the country. Professor Dupreez tries to give this legislation a theological basis. 'Is it God's will,' he asks, implying that it is not, 'that all the nations he has created in such rich diversity should now be equalised and assimilated, through intermarriage, to a uniform and mixed race?'[25]

In response to this Nazi and South African fear of 'bastardisation,' two points need to be made. First, there is no such thing as pure racial stock. We are all of us mongrels. 'Not one of the major groups of man is unmixed, nor is any one of its ethnic groups pure; all are, indeed, much mixed and of exceedingly complex descent.'[26] 'Pure British blood,' for example, is a figment of the imagination. At the very least we are a mixture of Jute, Celt, Goth, Saxon, Roman, and Norman. And there is certainly a small percentage (? 6 percent) of black blood in Afrikaners. Secondly, as Ashley Montagu puts it, 'one of the most strongly entrenched popular superstitions is the belief that interbreeding or crossing between "races" . . . results in inferior offspring. . . . The commonly employed stereotype has it that the half-caste inherits all the bad and none of the good qualities of the parental stocks. . . . There is not a particle of truth in any of these statements. . . . The truth seems to be that, far from being deleterious to the resulting offspring and the generations following them, interbreeding between different ethnic groups is from the biological and every other standpoint highly advantageous to mankind. . . . It is through the agency of interbreeding that nature in the form of man's genetic system, shows its creative power.'[27]

Christians will dislike both Dr. Montagu's personification of 'nature' and his references to 'interbreeding' (a word more appropriate to animals than humans), but these expressions in no way affect the point he is making. He goes on to quote Lord Bryce in 1902 that 'all the great peoples of the world are the result of a mixing of races,'[28] and then gives numerous examples,

like crosses between Tahitian women and the English muti-
neers from the *Bounty*, between Australian aboriginals and
whites, between American Indians and Europeans, between
black and white Americans, the ethnic mixture in Hawaii, etc.'[29]

The British Record

There is no need to deny that British colonial rule brought some
positive good to the countries colonised, not so much in material terms (e.g. roads and railways), as in education, health care,
and standards of public justice. Yet these benefits have tended
to be eclipsed by attitudes of superiority or 'the British Raj
mentality.' Sometimes, I regret to say, this was presented in racial terms ominously reminiscent of the German and South
African outlook we have just considered.

Cecil Rhodes, for example, spoke of 'the predominance of
the Anglo-Saxon race' and of the need to preserve it. And successive British Secretaries of State for the Colonies talked similarly, even using the language of 'destiny,' although fortunately
such an illusion was never embodied in official policy. Racial
pride remained, however. Consequently, as Margery Perham
demonstrated in her 1961 Reith Lectures *The Colonial Reckoning,*
Africans felt themselves to be 'humiliated rather than oppressed,' and the East African cry for *uhuru* (freedom) was not
primarily for political independence but for personal dignity.[30]
Similarly, to Jomo Kenyatta the quest for the independence of
his country was 'not just a question of Africans ruling themselves, though that was the first thing; it must also mean an end
to the colour bar, to the racist slang of the settler clubs, to the
white man's patronising attitudes of half a century and more.'[31]
At a political rally at Wundanyi in January 1962, Kenyatta said
about his attitude to Europeans: 'I am not against anyone. I am
only against *ubwana*, the boss mentality.'[32]

This British boss mentality was perhaps even more obvious
in India. Paul Scott has brought it to life in his 'Raj Quartet'

novels on the decline and fall of British India, perhaps specially in the first, *The Jewel in the Crown*. Its hero is Hari Kumar, Anglicised as 'Harry Coomer,' who was sent for a while to a Public School in Britain and on his return home experienced a painful tension between his English and Indian identities. The British elite looked through him. He felt he had become invisible to white people, for 'in India an Indian and an Englishman could never meet on equal terms.'[33] It would be hard to resist Arnold Toynbee's verdict that 'the English Protestant rulers of India . . . distinguished themselves from all other contemporary Western rulers over non-Western peoples by the rigidity with which they held aloof from their subjects.'[34]

The British colonial record is a necessary background to the understanding of the last twenty-five years of racial tension in Britain. It began in 1958 when racial violence erupted in Notting Hill, London, and in Nottingham. Then the 1960s was the decade of Commonwealth Immigration Acts (1962, 1965, 1968, and 1971). Of course every country has the right and the duty to limit the number of its immigrants. What made many Christians ashamed, however, was the way this legislation both reduced Commonwealth citizens with British passports (e.g. Kenyan Asians) to the status of aliens and was weighted against *coloured* immigrants (e.g. no restriction was placed on immigrants from the Republic of Ireland). To balance this, we were very thankful that in 1972 Ugandan Asians evicted by Idi Amin were granted a free entry into Britain. But now the British Nationality Act of 1981 has created three distinct kinds of British citizenship, is weighted against coloured people, and for the first time limits the right of British citizenship. What was formerly granted to all children born on British soil is now the right only to those whose parents are British or 'settled' (with unrestricted stay). Despite lobbying by the churches, the Act fails to express the true, multiracial character of British society.[35]

The sixties was also the decade in which racial tension was fomented by the inflammatory speeches of Enoch Powell, then MP for Wolverhampton South West, near Birmingham. He spoke of the 'madness' of allowing such a large inflow of coloured immigrants, of 'watching the nation heaping up its own funeral pyre,' of 'seeing the River Tiber foaming with much blood' and of Britons 'becoming strangers in their own country.' So, since to control immigration is one thing and to achieve racial integration is another, the *Race Relations Acts* of 1968 and 1976 were passed, the first creating the Race Relations Board to hear complaints and attempt reconciliation, the second creating the Commission for Racial Equality, which was given some teeth to enforce the law.

But in 1967 the National Front was formed out of a coalition of extreme right wing movements. Its declared policy was to halt immigration, promote the repatriation of coloured immigrants, support White Rhodesia and fight Communism. Its leaders (Colin Jordan, John Tyndall, and Martin Webster) had all been involved in Nazi activities and been ardent admirers of Hitler. Here are some representative statements which these three leaders have made.

Colin Jordan said in 1959, 'I loathe the Blacks—we're fighting a war to clear them out of Britain.'[36] John Tyndall (chairman of the National Front until 1974) wrote a pamphlet in 1966 entitled 'Six Principles of British Nationalism,' whose fourth was concerned with the preservation of the British 'race': 'We therefore oppose racial integration and stand for racial separateness.'[37] And Martin Webster wrote in 1975 that 'racialism is the only scientific and logical basis for nationalism. . . . we seek to preserve the identity of the British nation. . . . If the British people are destroyed by racial interbreeding, then the British nation will cease to exist.'[38] It is not difficult to detect in these intemperate utterances the same myth of racial purity and racial superiority which found expression in Nazi policy and is now enshrined in the doctrine of apartheid. I am ashamed to have to record that the myth is held by anyone in Britain. Fortunately, it is not embodied in any British laws, and the National Front is only a tiny minority.

This is not to say that there is no racial discrimination in Britain, however. The conclusion of David J. Smith, based on research projects carried out by 'Political and Economic Planning,' was that even since the 1968 Race Relations Act (he was writing before the 1976 Act) 'discrimination is still widespread.'[39] In employment, for example, 'there is still very substantial racial discrimination against Asians and West Indians' and this is 'mostly based on colour prejudice.'[40] As for accommodation, the percentage of people belonging to ethnic minorities who are owner-occupiers is much higher than with the general population, partly because 'discrimination against applicants for rented accommodation is still substantial,' and partly because 'buying their own home is . . . a way of getting poor housing cheaply,' especially in decaying inner city areas.[41]

The decay and deprivation of the inner city (especially in housing, education, and employment) were the background causes of the street riots in Brixton (South London) in April 1981, and in Toxteth (Liverpool), Manchester, Nottingham, Leeds, and other cities soon afterwards. Lord Scarman, who was commissioned by the Home Secretary to investigate and report, concluded that these communal disturbances were not premeditated, but spontaneous, and that 'there was a strong racial element in the disorders.' In short, 'the riots were essentially an outburst of anger and resentment by young black people against the police.'[42] This summary identifies that there were two main problems, the first social and racial, and the second concerning the behaviour of the police. As to the former, Lord Scarman concluded: ' "Institutional racism" does not exist in Britain; but racial disadvantage and its nasty associate, racial discrimination, have not yet been eliminated. They poison minds and attitudes: they are, and so long as they remain will continue to be, a potent factor of unrest.'[43] He recommended temporary discrimination in favour of ethnic minorities in order to right this balance. As for policing, Lord Scarman added that 'a major cause of the hostility of young blacks towards the police was loss of confidence by significant sections, though not all, of the . . . public in the police.'[44] Whether justified or not, criticisms of racial prejudice and harassment were frequently levelled at the police. Lord Scarman recommended greater police accountability and the introduction of an independent element into the police complaints procedure.

We have seen, then, that there are two kinds of 'racism,' one based on a pseudoscientific myth and the other on personal prejudice. The myth, which is foundational to Hitler's anti-Semitism, South Africa's apartheid, and Britain's National Front, was defined by UNESCO in 1967 as a 'false claim that there is a scientific basis for arranging groups hierarchically in terms of psychological and cultural characteristics that are immutable and innate.' The popular prejudice is not based on any particular theory, but is a psychological reaction to people of other ethnic groups arising usually from resentment, fear or pride.

I cannot, however, leave this question of the basis of 'racism' without alluding to the contemporary scientific dispute about the possible genetic origin of intelligence. Professor H. J. Eysenck of London University created a stir in 1971 by the publication of his book, *Race, Intelligence and Education*. The controversy was not over the assertion that on average American blacks have a slightly lower IQ than American whites, because this (I am told) has been an accepted fact since World War I during which the American army used IQ tests. Rather, it was over the interpretation of the fact. Professor Eysenck claimed that the difference was genetically determined, and he was on that account widely (and unjustly) accused of racial prejudice.

Ten years later a debate was published between him and Professor Leon Kamin of Princeton University, entitled *Intelligence: The Battle for the Mind*. Once again the fact that 'certain national, racial and cultural groups are more intelligent than others' was common ground. For example, 'Jews, Chinese and Japanese are often thought of as being particularly clever, Negroes and Mexican-Americans as being less able than average.' But 'the second and much more difficult question is whether these differences are artifacts of testing, the result of cultural factors and the outcome of deprivation, or hereditarily determined and produced by genetic factors.'[45] Professor Eysenck summarises the evidence from numerous studies and argues that 80 percent is hereditable: 'a concrete, measurable biological basis has been found for IQ' (p.72). He prefers to speak of 'probabilities' than of 'conclusions.' 'Yet to deny that these probabilities point to a genetic basis for racial differences would be to disregard well-established facts' (p.83).

Professor Kamin, on the other hand, is sharply critical of Professor Eysenck's position. 'The data on heredity and IQ,' he writes, 'are, at best, ambiguous' (p.154). In his view there is no compelling evidence for any percentage of hereditability. On the contrary, 'to most psychologists and social scientists, the obvious educational, social and economic discriminations to which blacks have been subjected seem entirely adequate to explain the difference in measured IQ' (p.140).

Clearly we have not yet heard the end of this debate. Even if it were proved beyond question, however, that certain racial groups had a lower average IQ, this would provide no possible basis for social discrimination. For we do not assess the value of human persons by the degree of their intelligence.

Nothing I have read has helped me to understand better the damage which racism does to people than *The Autobiography of Malcolm X*. His red-hot anger was due in part to 'the world's most monstrous crime' of slavery, in part to the Black American's economic dependence on White America, but above all to the humiliation caused by the white man's 'malignant superiority complex.'[46] The problem, he writes, is not 'civil rights' but 'human rights': 'Human rights! Respect as *human beings!* That's what American black masses want. That's the true problem. The black masses want not to be shrunk from as though they are plague ridden. They want not to be walled up in slums, in the ghettoes, like animals. They want to live in an open, free society where they can walk with their heads up, like men and women.'[47]

Biblical Foundations for Multiracialism

We turn from the realities of racial mythology, prejudice, and tension in the contemporary world to the biblical vision of a multiracial society. It was thoroughly developed by the apostle Paul in his famous sermon to the Athenian philosophers (Acts 17.22–31). Ancient Athens was a centre of ethnic, cultural, and religious pluralism. From the fifth century B.C. it had been the foremost Greek city-state, and when it was incorporated into the Roman Empire, it became one of the leading cosmopolitan cities in the world. As for religions, it is easy to understand Paul's comment that the Athenians were 'very religious,' for according to a Roman satirist, it was 'easier to find a god there than a man.' The city was crammed with innumerable temples, shrines, altars, images, and statues.

What then was Paul's attitude to this multiracial, multicultural, and multireligious situation? He made four affirmations.

First, he proclaimed *the unity of the human race*, or *the God of Creation*. God is the Creator and Lord of the world and everything in it, he said. He gives to all human beings their life and breath and everything else. From one man he made every nation of men, that they should inhabit the whole earth, so that human beings would seek and find him, though he is not far from any of us. For 'in him we live and move and have our being' and 'we are his offspring.' From this portrayal of the living God as Creator, Sustainer, and Father of all mankind, the apostle deduces the folly and evil of idolatry. But he could equally well have deduced from it the folly and evil of racism. For if he is the God of all human beings, this will affect our attitude to them as well as to him.

Although in terms of an intimate personal relationship God is the Father of those he adopts into his family by his sheer grace, and our brothers and sisters are fellow members of his family, nevertheless in more general terms God is the Father of all mankind, since all are his 'offspring' by creation, and every human being is our brother or sister. Being equally created by him and like him, we are equal in his sight in worth and dignity, and therefore have an equal right to respect and justice. Paul also traces our human origin to Adam, the 'one man' from whom God made us all. This is confirmed by the known homogeneity of the human race, which is asserted even by scholars who have no belief in Adam.

Here is the statement of Ashley Montagu, the physical anthropologist: 'Concerning the origin of the living varieties of man we can say little more than that there are many reasons for believing that a single stock gave rise to all of them. All varieties of man belong to the same species and have the same remote ancestry. This is a conclusion to which all the relevant evidence of comparative anatomy, palaeontology, serology and genetics points.'[48] As for human blood, apart from the four blood groups and the Rh factor (which are present in all ethnic groups), 'the blood of all human beings is in every respect the same.'[49]

This human unity is not destroyed by interbreeding. We should totally reject the fears of miscegenation entertained by Afrikaners, and Hitler's biological myth which is being revived by the National Front. In 1964 John Tyndall launched the 'Greater Britain Movement,' whose official programme said: 'For the protection of British blood, racial laws will be enacted forbidding marriage between Britons and non-Aryans. . . . A pure, strong, healthy British race will be regarded as the principal guarantee of Britain's future.'[50] There is no such substance as 'British blood.'

Secondly, Paul proclaimed *the diversity of ethnic cultures*, or *the God of history*. The living God not only made every nation from one man, that they should inhabit the earth, but also 'determined the times set for them and the exact places where they should live.' (v.26 Cf. Deuteronomy 32.8). Thus the times and the places of the nations are in the hand of God. We cannot use this fact to justify the conquest and annexation of foreign territory, although even these historical developments are not beyond God's sovereign control. Probably Paul is alluding to the primeval command to multiply and fill the earth, for such dispersal under God's blessing inevitably resulted in the development of distinctive cultures, quite apart from the later confusing of languages and the scattering under his judgment at Babel.

Now culture is the complement of nature. What is 'natural' is God-given and inherited; what is 'cultural' is manmade and learned. Culture is an amalgam of beliefs, values, customs, and institutions developed by each society and transmitted to the next generation. Human cultures are ambiguous because human beings are ambiguous. 'Because man is God's creature, some of his culture is rich in beauty and goodness. Because he is fallen, all of it is tainted with sin and some of it is demonic.'[51]

Scripture celebrates the colourful mosaic of human cultures. It even declares that the New Jerusalem will be enriched by them, since 'the kings of the earth will bring their splendour into it,' and 'the glory and honor of the nations will be brought into it' (Revelation 21.24,26). If they will enrich human life and community in the end, they can begin to do so now. Paul was a product of three cultures. By descent and upbringing a 'Hebrew of the Hebrews,' he also possessed Roman citizenship and had absorbed Greek language and concepts. We too can enhance our human life by learning other languages and experiencing other cultures. We need to ensure, therefore, that a multiracial society is not a monocultural society. We must assert both the unity of the human race and the diversity of ethnic cultures simultaneously.

The South African Nationalist Party make much of this diversity. South Africa, they argue, has never been a single nation, but a kaleidoscope of distinct racial groups, each with its own national and cultural identity. What is needed, therefore, they deduce, is not a single integrated state (the 'melting pot' model), but 'multi-national development' or 'separate freedoms,' i.e. apartheid, each racial group preserving and advancing its own uniqueness. 'We do not want intermingling of racial groups in South Africa,' Professor Dr. J. C. G. Klotze has written; 'it is in accordance with Scripture that the ideal situation would be for each people to inhabit its own country (Acts 17.26).'[52] Apart from the question whether 'nations' and 'racial groups' are the same thing, and whether Acts 17.26 includes the latter, the South African apartheid policy seems to depend on two other errors. First, the assumption is that distinct cultures can be preserved only if racial groups are segregated from each other. But this is patently untrue, as we know in Britain where the Irish, Welsh, Scottish, and English intermingle, while their cultural distinctives also survive. Not only is it unnecessary to keep apart in order to preserve our own cultures, but it is impossible to do so if we are to enjoy each other's, as God surely means us to do.

Secondly, the assumption underlying the policy to segregate racial groups in order to preserve them is that to integrate them would inevitably mean to destroy them. But integration is not the same as assimilation, and does not necessarily lead to it. On the contrary, although intermarriage should be fully permissible, natural affinities and cultural tensions are likely to keep the number of mixed marriages comparatively small.

Thirdly, Paul proclaimed *the finality of Jesus Christ*, or *the God of Revelation*. He concluded his sermon with God's call to universal repentance because of the coming universal judgment, for which God has both fixed the day and appointed the judge (vv. 30,31). Paul refuses to acquiesce in the religious pluralism of Athens or applaud it as a living museum of religious faiths. Instead, the city's idolatry provoked him (v.16)—probably to jealousy for the honour of the living and true God. So he called on the city's people to turn in repentance from their idols to God.

We learn, then, that a respectful acceptance of the diversity of *cultures* does not imply an equal acceptance of the diversity of *religions*. The richness of each particular culture should be appreciated, but not the idolatry which may lie at its heart. We cannot tolerate any rivals to Jesus Christ, believing as we do that God has spoken fully and finally through him, and that he is the only Saviour, who died, and rose again, and will one day come to be the world's Judge.

Fourthly, Paul proclaimed *the glory of the Christian Church*, or *the God of Redemption*. It is clearer in some of the apostle's letters than it is in Luke's record of this sermon that Jesus died and rose to create a new and reconciled community, his church. Thus the flow of history is being reversed. The Old Testament is the story of human scattering, of nations spreading abroad, falling apart, fighting. But the New Testament is the story of the divine ingathering of nations into a single international society. It is hinted at here in v.34 in which we are told that a few men believed, one of whom was named Dionysius, and a woman named Damaris, and a number of others. So here was the nucleus of the new community, in which men and women of all ages, and of all racial, cultural and social origins, find their oneness in Christ.

Since God has made every nation and determines their times and places, it is clearly right for each of us to be conscious of our nationality and grateful for it. But since God has also brought us into his new society, he is thereby calling us into a new internationalism. Every Christian knows this tension, and nobody more keenly than Paul who was at the same time a patriotic Jew and the apostle to the Gentiles. Christian 'internationalism' does not mean that our being members of Christ and his church obliterates our nationality, any more than it does our masculinity or femininity. It means rather that, while our racial, national, social, and sexual distinctions remain, they no longer divide us. They have been transcended in the unity of the family of God (Galatians 3.28). Raymond Johnston is right that 'a proper understanding of nationhood calls attention to the human need for *roots*, a security and an identity mediated by the community, on the basis of which each individual knows that he "belongs.". . . .'[53] Yet it needs to be added that in Christ we have found even deeper roots, and an even stronger security and identity, for through him God has called us into a new and wider unity.

The church must therefore exhibit its multiracial, multinational, and multicultural nature. There has been considerable debate in recent years whether a local church could or should ever be culturally homogeneous. A consultation on this issue concluded that no church should ever acquiesce in such a condition: 'All of us are agreed that in many situations a homogeneous unit church can be a legitimate and authentic church. Yet we are also agreed that it can never be complete in itself. Indeed, if it remains in isolation, it cannot reflect the universality and diversity of the Body of Christ. Nor can it grow to maturity. Therefore every homogeneous unit church must take active steps to broaden its fellowship in order to demonstrate visibly the unity and the variety of Christ's Church.'[54] The Report goes on to suggest how this might be done.

Only a true theology, the biblical revelation of God, can deliver us from racial pride and prejudice. Because he is God of creation, we affirm the unity of the human race. Because he is the God of history, we affirm the diversity of ethnic cultures. Because he is the God of revelation, we affirm the finality of Jesus Christ. And because he is the God of redemption, we affirm the glory of the Christian church. Whatever policies for racial integration may be developed, we should try to ensure that they will reflect these doctrines. Because of the unity of mankind we demand equal rights and equal respect for racial minorities. Because of the diversity of ethnic groups we renounce cultural imperialism and seek to preserve all those riches of interracial culture which are compatible with Christ's lordship. Because of the finality of Christ, we affirm that religious freedom includes the right to propagate the gospel. Because of the glory of the church, we must seek to rid ourselves of any lingering racism and strive to make it a model of harmony between races, in which the multiracial dream comes true.

Chapter Four

Poverty, Wealth, and Simplicity

'WEALTH INCREASING FOR EVERMORE, AND ITS BENEFICIARIES, RICH in hire-purchase, stupefied with the telly and with sex, comprehensively educated, told by Professor Hoyle how the world began and by Bertrand Russell where it will end; venturing forth on the broad highways, three lanes a side, . . . blood spattering the tarmac as an extra thrill; heaven lying about them in the supermarket, the rainbow ending in the nearest bingo hall, leisure burgeoning out in multitudinous shining aerials rising like dreaming spires into the sky; . . . many mansions, mansions of light and chromium, climbing ever upwards. This kingdom, surely, can only be for posterity an unending source of wry derision—always assuming there is to be any posterity. The backdrop, after all, is the mushroom cloud; as the Gadarene herd frisk and frolic, they draw ever nearer to the cliff's precipitous edge.'[1]

Thus Malcolm Muggeridge satirizes the affluence of the West, its materialism, superficiality, and selfishness. It is bad enough in itself; when contrasted with the *barriadas* and *favelas* of Latin America, and the ghettoes, slums, and shantytowns of other parts of the world, it becomes inexcusable. Not that the contrast between wealth and poverty corresponds neatly with the North-South divide, for the OPEC countries are rich, and poverty has not been eliminated from North America or Europe.

In Britain, for example, 'there are still over six million people, adults and children, living on incomes at or below the level of supplementary benefit, which is the state's definition of the boundary between poverty and subsistence.'[2] And more than twice that number live in relative poverty. Hence the launching in Britain in July 1982 of 'Church Action on Poverty.' The truth is that a grave disparity between wealth and poverty is to be found not only *between* nations, but *within* most nations as well. As the Latin American Roman Catholic bishops put it at Puebla in 1979: 'the cruel contrast between luxurious wealth and extreme poverty, which is so visible throughout our continent and which is further aggravated by the corruption that often invades public and professional life, shows the great extent to which our nations are dominated by the idol of wealth.'[3]

Three Approaches to Poverty

How should Christians approach the harsh fact of poverty in the contemporary world?

First, we could approach the problem *rationally*, with cool, statistical detachment. Indeed, this is where we must begin. There are approximately 4.3 billion inhabitants of planet earth, one fifth of whom are destitute. The World Bank's 1978 report, while conceding that there had been for twenty-five years 'unprecedented change and progress in the developing world,' went on: 'Yet, despite this impressive record, some 800 million individuals continue to be trapped in . . . absolute poverty: a condition of life so characterized by malnutrition, illiteracy, disease, squalid surroundings, high infant mortality and low life expectancy as to be beneath any reasonable definition of human decency.'[4] One way to bring this home to us is to consider the provision of clean, safe water. In the West it is piped into our homes and instantly available to us at the turn of a tap. None of us would dream of regarding it as a luxury. We take it for granted. Yet 50 percent of the Third World population lack it, and 75 percent of them have no sanitary facilities, so that water-borne diseases kill an estimated 30,000 people a day and fill half the hospital beds of the world. That is why the United Nations has declared the 1980s 'the Water Decade' and hopes to bring both water and sanitation to two billion people by 1990.

Meanwhile, whereas one-fifth of the world's population lack the basic necessities for survival, more than another one-fifth live in affluence and consume about four-fifths of the world's income. These wealthy nations contribute to Third World development the derisory sum of $28.6 billion, while spending twenty-one times that amount (about $600 billion) on armaments. The gross disparity between wealth and poverty constitutes a social injustice with which the Christian conscience cannot come to terms.

Secondly, we could approach the phenomenon of poverty *emotionally*, with the hotblooded indignation aroused by the sights, sounds, and smells of human need. When I last visited Calcutta airport, the sun had already set. Over the whole city hung a pall of malodorous smoke from the burning of cowdung on a myriad fires. Outside the airport an emaciated woman clutching an emaciated baby stretched out an emaciated hand for *baksheesh*. A man, whose legs had both been amputated above the knee, dragged himself along the pavement with his hands. I later learned that over a quarter of a million homeless people sleep in the streets at night, and during the day hang their blanket—often their only possession—on some convenient railing. My most poignant experience was to see men and women scavenging in the city garbage dumps like dogs. Extreme poverty is demeaning; it reduces human beings to the level of animals. To be sure, Christians should be provoked by the *idolatry* of a Hindu city, as Paul was by the idols of Athens, and moved to evangelism. But, like Jesus when he saw the hungry crowds, we should also be moved with compassion to feed them.[5]

It is not only the absolute poverty of Third World slums which should arouse our emotions, however, but also the relative (though real) poverty of the decayed and deprived inner-city areas of the West, which the affluent seldom if ever see. This was the emphasis which David Sheppard, Bishop of Liverpool, made in his 1984 broadcast Richard Dimbleby Lecture. He urged 'Comfortable Britain' to stand in the shoes of the 'Other Britain.' He spoke with deep feeling of youth and long-term unemployment, neglected housing, poor opportunities in schooling, and the sense of alienation, even desertion. He felt indignant, indeed angry, because poverty 'imprisons the spirit,' spawns 'sick human relationships' and wastes God-given talent. He described four 'keys' which could begin to unlock the prison.[6]

The third way, which should stimulate both our reason and our emotion simultaneously, is to approach the problem of poverty *biblically*. As we turn again to that book in which God has revealed himself and his will, we ask: How according to Scripture should we think about wealth and poverty? Is God on the side of the poor? Should we be? What does the Scripture say? Moreover, as we ask these questions, we have to resolve to listen attentively to God's Word, and not manipulate it. We have no liberty either to avoid its uncomfortable challenge, in order to retain our prejudices, or to acquiesce uncritically in the latest popular interpretations.

Psalm 113 seems a good place to begin. It is an invitation to Yahweh's servants, indeed to all people 'from the rising of the sun to the place where it sets,' to praise his name, since he 'is exalted over all the nations, his glory above the heavens.' It continues:

Who is like the Lord our God,
the One who sits enthroned on high,
who stoops down to look
on the heavens and the earth?
He raises the poor from the dust
and lifts the needy from the ash heap;
he seats them with princes,
with the princes of their people.
He settles the barren woman in her home
as a happy mother of children.

Psalms 113:5–9

The psalmist is affirming something distinctive—indeed unique—about Yahweh, which enables him to ask the rhetorical question 'Who is like the Lord our God?' It is not just that he reigns on high, exalted above both the nations and the sky; nor only that from these lofty heights he condescends to look far below to the heavens and the earth; nor even that on the distant earth he regards with compassion the depths of human misery, the poor discarded on the scrapheaps of life and trampled in the dust by their oppressors. It is more than all these things. It is that he actually exalts the wretched of the earth; he lifts them from the depths to the heights; 'he raises the poor from the dust and . . . seats them with princes.' For example, he takes pity on the barren woman (whose childlessness was regarded as a disgrace) and makes her a joyful mother. That is the kind of God he is. No other god is like him, for it is not primarily the wealthy and the famous with whom he delights to fraternise. What is characteristic of him is to champion the poor, to rescue them from their misery, and to transform paupers into princes.

This affirmation is many times repeated and exemplified in Scripture, usually with its corollary that the God who lifts up the humble also puts down the proud. This was the essence of Hannah's song when after years of childlessness her son Samuel was born:

> *He raises the poor from the dust*
> *and lifts the needy from the ash heap;*
> *he seats them with princes*
> *and has them inherit a throne of honor.*
>
> *1 Samuel 2.8*

This too was the theme of the Magnificat, which the Virgin Mary sang after learning that she (and not some famous, noble or wealthy woman) had been chosen to be the mother of God's Messiah. God had looked upon her lowly state, she said; the Mighty One had done great things for her, for which she gave him thanks and praise:

> *He has performed mighty deeds with his arm;*
> *he has scattered those who are proud in their inmost thoughts.*
> *He has brought down rulers from their thrones*
> *but has lifted up the humble.*
> *He has filled the hungry with good things*
> *but has sent the rich away empty.*
>
> *Luke 1.51,52*

In Psalm 113, and in the experiences of Hannah and Mary, the same stark contrast is painted, although the vocabulary varies. The proud are abased and the humble exalted; the rich are impoverished and the poor enriched; the well-fed are sent away empty, and the hungry filled with good things; powerful rulers are toppled from their thrones, while the powerless and the oppressed are caused to reign like princes. 'Who is like the Lord our God?' His thoughts and ways are not ours. He is a topsy-turvy God. He turns the standards and values of the world upside down.

Jesus himself is the greatest example of this. One of his favourite epigrams seems to have been that 'everyone who exalts himself will be humbled, and he who humbles himself will be exalted' (*see* Luke 18.14). He did not only enunciate this principle, however; he personally exhibited it. Having emptied himself of glory, he humbled himself to serve, and his obedience took him even to the depths of the cross. 'Therefore God exalted him to the highest place. . . .' (Philippians 2.5–11).

It is this principle, which pledges the reversal of human fortunes, which alone can bring hope to the poor. But who are the 'poor' whom God is said to 'raise'? And what does he do when he 'raises' them? These words demand definition.

Who are the Poor? The Paradox of Poverty

A number of studies of the biblical material have been made and published.[7] They focus on the Old Testament in which a cluster of words for poverty, deriving from six main Hebrew roots, occur more than two hundred times. These may be classified in a variety of ways, but the principal division seems to me to be threefold. First, and economically speaking, there are *the indigent poor*, who are deprived of the basic necessities of life. Secondly, and sociologically speaking, there are *the oppressed poor*, who are powerless victims of human injustice. Thirdly, and spiritually speaking, there are *the humble poor*, who acknowledge their helplessness and look to God alone for salvation. In each case God is represented as coming to them and making their cause his own, in keeping with his characteristic that 'he raises the poor from the dust.'

The first group, *the indigent poor*, are economically deprived. They may lack food or clothing or shelter, or all three. Sometimes, the biblical authors recognise, their poverty may be due to their own sin, whether laziness, extravagance or gluttony. The Book of Proverbs has much to say about this. The sluggard is exhorted to study the ways of the ant, in order to learn wisdom, for ants gather and store food during the summer, while sluggards stay in bed: 'A little sleep, a little slumber, a little folding of the hands to rest—and poverty will come on you like a bandit and scarcity like an armed man.'[8] Closely linked to laziness, as causing poverty, are greed and drunkenness: 'drunkards and gluttons become poor, and drowsiness clothes them in rags.'[9] Not only did these particular sins bring individual poverty, however. National poverty also was due to sin. For during the theocracy, when God ruled over his people Israel, he promised to bless their obedience with fruitfulness of field and orchard, and to curse their disobedience with barrenness.[10]

Generally speaking, however, the Old Testament writers saw poverty as an involuntary social evil to be abolished, not tolerated, and represented the poor (who included widows, orphans, and aliens) as people to be succoured, not blamed. They are regarded not as sinners but as 'the sinned against'—an expression popularized at the 1980 Melbourne Conference by Raymond Fung, a Baptist minister who had spent eleven years serving factory workers in Hong Kong.[11]

In the Law, God's people were commanded not to harden their hearts or close their hands against their poor brother or sister, but to be generous in maintaining those who could not maintain themselves, by taking them into their home and feeding them without charge. Their regular tithes were also to be used to support the Levites, the aliens, the orphans, and the widows.[12] If an Israelite lent money to somebody in need, he was not to charge interest on it. If he took a pledge to secure his loan, he was not to go into the house to fetch it, but to stand respectfully outside and wait for it to be brought out to him. If he took as pledge his neighbour's cloak, he was to return it before sunset because the poor person would need it as a blanket to sleep in.[13] In particular, the support and the relief of the poor were the obligations of the extended family towards its own members.

Employers were to pay their workers' wages promptly, the same day that they were earned. Farmers were not to reap their fields 'to the very edges,' nor to go back to pick up a dropped or forgotten sheaf, nor to gather the gleanings after harvesting, nor to strip their vineyard bare, nor to gather fallen grapes, nor to go over the branches of their olive trees a second time. The borders, the gleanings, and the fallen fruit were all to be left for the poor, the alien, the widow, and the orphan. They too must be allowed to share in the harvest celebrations. Every third year, a tenth of the agricultural produce was to be given to the poor. Every seventh year fields were to lie fallow, and vineyards and olive groves to be unharvested, for the benefit of the poor who could help themselves to the fruit.[14]

The Old Testament Wisdom Literature confirmed this teaching. One of the characteristics of a righteous man is that he 'is generous and lends freely,' and 'has scattered abroad his gifts to the poor'; whereas 'if a man shuts his ears to the cry of the poor, he too will cry out and not be answered.'[15] The wise teachers of Israel also grounded these duties on doctrine, namely that behind the poor Yahweh himself was standing, their Creator and Lord, so that people's attitude to him would be reflected in their attitude to them. On the one hand, 'he who mocks the poor shows contempt for their maker'; on the other, 'he who is kind to the poor lends to the Lord.'[16]

Jesus himself inherited this rich Old Testament legacy of care for the poor, and put it into practice. He made friends with the needy and fed the hungry. He told his disciples to sell their possessions and give alms to the poor, and when they gave a party to remember to invite the poor, the crippled, the lame, and the blind, who would probably be in no position to invite them back. He also promised that in feeding the hungry, clothing the naked, welcoming the homeless and visiting the sick, they would thereby be ministering to him.[17]

The second group, *the powerless poor*, are socially or politically oppressed. It was clearly recognised in the Old Testament that poverty does not normally just happen. Although sometimes it was due to personal sin or national disobedience, and to God's judgment on them, it was usually due to the sins of others, that is, to a situation of social injustice, which easily deteriorated because the poor were not in a position to change it. We do not understand the Old Testament teaching on this subject unless we see how frequently poverty and powerlessness were bracketed. At the same time, although the poor often had no human helper, they knew that God was their champion. For 'he stands at the right hand of the needy one.' Again, 'I know that the Lord secures justice for the poor and upholds the cause of the needy.'[18]

Moses' law laid emphasis on the need for impartial justice in the courts, in particular for the poor and powerless. 'Do not deny justice to your poor people in their lawsuits. . . . Do not accept a bribe, for a bribe blinds those who see and twists the words of the righteous.' 'Do not pervert justice; do not show partiality to the poor or favoritism to the great, but judge your neighbor fairly.' 'Do not deprive the alien or the fatherless of justice.' Moreover, the reason repeatedly given was that they themselves had been oppressed in Egypt, and the Lord had liberated them.[19]

The Wisdom books were as explicit as the Law books in demanding justice for the helpless. In Psalm 82 the judges were instructed to 'defend the cause of the weak and fatherless' and 'maintain the rights of the poor and oppressed.' In Proverbs 31 King Lemuel was exhorted by his mother to 'speak up for those who cannot speak for themselves, for the rights of all who are destitute,' to 'speak up and judge fairly' and 'defend the rights of the poor and needy.'[20]

It is well known that the prophets were even more outspoken. They not only urged the people and their leaders to 'seek justice, encourage the oppressed, defend the cause of the fatherless, plead the case of the widow,' and conversely forbade them to 'oppress the widow or the fatherless, the alien or the poor,' but were fierce in their condemnations of all injustice.

Elijah rebuked King Ahab for murdering Naboth and stealing his vineyard. Amos fulminated against the rulers of Israel because in return for bribes they trampled on the heads of the poor, crushed the needy, and denied justice to the oppressed, instead of letting 'justice roll on like a river, and righteousness like a never-failing stream.' Jeremiah denounced King Jehoiakim for using forced labour to build his luxurious palace. Other examples could be given. The national life of Israel and Judah was constantly tarnished by the exploitation of the poor. And James in the New Testament, sounding just like an Old Testament prophet, also inveighs against the rich. It is not their wealth in itself which he condemns, nor even primarily their self-indulgent luxury, but in particular their fraudulent withholding of wages from their work force and their violent oppression of the innocent.[21]

Over against this dark tradition of the prophets' diatribe against injustice, their predictions of the Messiah's righteous reign shine the more brightly: 'with righteousness he will judge the needy, with justice he will give decisions for the poor of the earth.'[22]

It is abundantly clear from this evidence that the biblical writers saw the poor not only as destitute people, whose condition must be relieved, but as the victims of social injustice, whose cause must be championed.

The third group, *the humble poor*, are spiritually meek and dependent on God. Since God succours the destitute and defends the powerless, these truths inevitably affect their attitude to him. They look to him for mercy. Oppressed by men, and helpless to liberate themselves, they put their trust in God. In this way 'the poor' came to be synonymous with 'the pious,' and their social condition became a symbol of their spiritual dependence. Zephaniah describes them as 'the meek and the humble, who trust in the name of the Lord,' and Isaiah as the 'humble and contrite in spirit' who tremble at God's Word.[23]

It is particularly in the Psalms, however, that the otherwise rather blurred portrait of the humble poor comes into sharp focus, for the psalter is the hymnbook of the helpless.[24] Here we listen to their expressions of dependence upon God, and to God's promises to come to their aid. They are 'the lonely and afflicted' who cry to him to be gracious to them; they commit their way to the Lord, are quiet before him, and wait patiently for him to act. They are given the assurance that 'the poor will eat and be satisfied,' that 'the meek will inherit the land,' and that 'he crowns the humble with salvation.'[25]

More striking even than these references to the poor and meek as a group, however, are the individual testimonies to Yahweh's salvation. There is Psalm 34, for example: 'This poor man called, and the Lord heard him; he saved him out of all his troubles.' As a result, he determines to 'boast in the Lord' and is confident that others who are 'afflicted' like him will hear and rejoice with him, and will in their turn call upon Yahweh. For, he goes on to affirm, 'the Lord is close to the brokenhearted and saves those who are crushed in spirit.'[26] Another example occurs in Psalm 86. The psalmist describes himself as savagely assaulted by arrogant, godless, and ruthless men. His only hope is in God. 'Hear, O Lord, and answer me,' he cries, 'for I am poor and needy. Guard my life, for I am devoted to you. You are my God; save your servant who trusts in you.' And he goes on to express his confidence that God will rescue him, because he is 'a compassionate and gracious God, slow to anger, abounding in love and faithfulness.'[27]

All this biblical teaching enables us to affirm that God succours the indigent poor, champions the powerless poor and exalts the humble poor. In each case 'he raises the poor from the dust,' whether it be the dust of penury or oppression or helplessness.

Good News for the Poor

At the risk of oversimplification, however, it will be helpful (especially if we are to judge what the Christian attitude to poverty should be) if we reduce these three categories to two, namely the material poverty of the destitute and powerless, and the spiritual poverty of the humble and meek. God concerns himself with both. In both cases 'he raises the poor from the dust,' but the way he does it is different. For the first kind of poverty is a social evil which God opposes, while the second is a spiritual virtue which he approves. Moreover, there is only one human community in which the two are combined, namely the kingdom community, the new and redeemed society in which God rules through Christ by his Spirit.

This is clear from the Old Testament expectation of the kingdom of God. God promised the coming of his ideal king, who would both judge the poor with justice and give the blessing of his rule to the humble and lowly. We meet such people in the first two chapters of Luke's Gospel, Zechariah and Elizabeth, Joseph and Mary, Simeon, and Anna. They were humble, poor believers. They were looking and waiting for the kingdom of God, in which God would throw down the mighty from their thrones and exalt the humble and meek.

Clearer still was the fulfilment through Jesus Christ. Who are the 'poor' he spoke about? Those to whom he said he had been anointed to preach the good news of the kingdom? And to whom the kingdom would be given?[28] They surely cannot be either just the materially poor (for Christ's salvation is not limited to the proletariat) or just the spiritually poor (for this overlooks his ministry to the needy). He must have been referring to both in combination. The 'poor' are those to whom the kingdom comes as great good news, partly because it is a free and unmerited gift of salvation to sinners, and partly because it promises a new society characterised by freedom and justice.

The church should exemplify both these truths. On the one hand it consists of the spiritually poor, the 'poor in spirit,' who acknowledge their bankruptcy before God. They have no righteousness to offer, no merit to plead, no power to save themselves. They know that the only way to enter God's kingdom is to humble themselves like little children and receive it as a gift. So they come as beggars, with nothing in their hands, and on their lips the publican's prayer 'God be merciful to me, a sinner.' To such Jesus says: 'Blessed are the poor in spirit, for theirs is the kingdom of heaven.' By contrast, the rich or self-satisfied, who imagine they have something to offer, are sent away empty.

On the other hand, the church must proclaim the good news of the kingdom to the materially poor, welcome them into the fellowship, and share in their struggles. Indeed, the special concern for the poor shown by the biblical authors, and more particularly by Jesus himself, has led some contemporary thinkers to speak of God's 'bias' in their favour, as in Bishop David Sheppard's recent book *Bias to the Poor*. 'I believe that there is a divine bias to the disadvantaged,' he writes, 'and that the church needs to be much more faithful in reflecting it.'[29] He concludes his analysis of deprivation in Liverpool with these words: 'If we can put ourselves in the shoes of the poor and disadvantaged, we may see how matters appear to their consciousness. . . . They are to do with the righteousness of God which has a persistent tendency to favour those at a disadvantage. They are to do with God taking flesh in the person of Jesus, living out his life in a special relation to the poor.'[30]

I confess that I am uncomfortable with the word 'bias,' since its commonest meaning is 'prejudice,' and I do not think God is 'biassed' in that sense. Less misleading is the language of the Latin American bishops. At their Second General Conference at Medellin in 1970 they spoke of a 'preference for, and solidarity with, the poor.' At their Third General Conference ten years later at Puebla in Mexico, they affirmed 'the need for conversion on the part of the whole church to a preferential option for the poor.'[31] It is because of Jesus' ministry to the poor that 'the poor merit preferential attention.'[32] 'Preferential' does not mean 'exclusive,' however, for the next chapter is entitled 'A Preferential Option for Young People.' Nevertheless, the option for the poor is 'demanded by the scandalous reality of economic imbalances in Latin America.'[33]

The 1980 Melbourne Conference quoted the Puebla Conclusions, and then echoed them in asserting that 'God has a preference for the poor.'[34] It seems to me, however, that better than the vocabulary of personal 'bias' or 'preference' is the language of mission priority. Because of God's own care for the poor, and because of their exploitation by the unscrupulous and their neglect by the church, they should now receive a 'positive' or 'reverse' discrimination. The church should concentrate its ministry where the need is greatest, to move from the centre out 'towards the periphery,'[35] to the 'sinned against,' in other words, to the poor and the oppressed.

Moreover, the church should not tolerate material poverty in its own fellowship. When Jesus said 'the poor you will always have with you' (Mark 14.7), he was not acquiescing in the permanence of poverty. He was echoing the Old Testament statement 'there will always be poor people in the land' (Deuteronomy 15.11). Yet this was intended not as an excuse for complacency but as an incentive to generosity, as a result of which 'there should be no poor among you' (Deuteronomy 15.4). If there is one community in the world in which justice is secured for the oppressed, the poor are freed from the indignities of poverty, and physical need is abolished by the voluntary sharing of resources, that community is the new society of Jesus the Messiah. It happened in Jerusalem after Pentecost, when 'there were no needy persons among them,' as Luke is at pains to show, and it can (and should) happen again today. How can we allow our own brothers and sisters in God's family to suffer want?

The church, then, as the community which is called to exemplify the ideals of the kingdom of God, should bear witness to the biblical paradox of poverty, by opposing one kind and encouraging the other. We should set ourselves both to eradicate the evil of material poverty and to cultivate the good of spiritual poverty. We should hate injustice and love humility. In these two complementary ways the gospel may be said to be 'good news for the poor,' and God may be described as on their side.

Not that our Christian concern should be confined to those poor who are church members. Although we have a special responsibility to 'the family of believers' (or, in older versions of the Bible, 'the household of faith'), we are also required to 'do good to all people' (Galatians 6.10). How will this express itself to the poor? Certainly in terms of personal philanthropy, as we seek to help needy individuals and families in our neighbourhood and further afield. But we cannot allow our duty to stop there. For the Bible itself indicates, as we have seen, that most poverty is the fault rather of society than of the poor themselves. We therefore have a social as well as a personal responsibility towards them, and this will begin with a painful appraisal of the causes of poverty. I call it 'painful' because the tendency of the affluent is to blame the poor, or to find some other scapegoat, whereas the problem may lie in the very structure of society in which we ourselves (willy-nilly) are implicated.

This is the thesis of Robert Holman's carefully researched, well written, and overtly Christian book *Poverty: Explanations of Social Deprivation.*[36] He rejects as incomplete three common scapegoat explanations—'individual' (genetic, economic or psychological inadequacies in the poor themselves), 'cultural' ('the transmission of poverty from one generation to the next,' (p. 134) and 'the deficient agent' (the inefficiency of teachers, social workers, and bureaucrats). Instead, he traces the cause of most poverty (at least in Britain) to the stratified structure of society itself, in which resources (especially income, wealth, and power) are unequally divided. 'Poverty exists,' he writes, 'in order to support or uphold these social divisions' (p.188). It is tolerated, even justified, by making it (and therefore its affluent opposite) appear merited and because it provides a useful pool of workers who have no choice but to undertake the most unattractive occupations.

Bob Holman's approach is sociological. In consequence, he avoids the polarised economic debate between those who blame poverty on capitalism, on the ground that it is inherently covetous and therefore exploits the poor, and those who blame socialism on the ground that it perpetuates the dependency of the poor and undermines the enterprise of wealth creators. Neither position has a monopoly of truth. Christians should oppose in both systems what they perceive to be incompatible with biblical faith which equally emphasises creativity and compassion, and refuses to foster either at the expense of the other.

Three Options for Rich Christians

Conscientious Christians have further questions to ask. It is one thing to discern what our attitude to the poor should be; it is another to define our attitude to poverty itself. Involuntary material poverty is a scandal, as we have seen; but what about voluntary poverty? And what is an authentically Christian attitude to money and property? What should rich Christians do?

In the context of western affluence there are three options before us. The first is to become poor, the second to stay rich, and the third to cultivate generosity, simplicity, and contentment.

First, should we *become poor?* Paul wrote: 'For you know the grace of our Lord Jesus Christ, that though he was rich, yet for your sakes he became poor, so that you through his poverty might become rich' (2 Corinthians 8.9). This voluntary self-impoverishment of Jesus was the theological ground on which the apostle based his appeal to the Christians of Greece to contribute to the relief of the Christians of Judea. Did he intend them to divest themselves of all their possessions for the sake of their Jewish brothers and sisters? Does he mean us to do the same? At first sight it seems so, and arguments have been advanced for this from the example, teaching, and early church of Jesus.

1. *The example of Jesus.*   Renouncing the wealth of heaven, Jesus was certainly born into a poor home. When Joseph and Mary came to the Temple to present their child to the Lord, they availed themselves of the law's provision for poor people and brought as their sacrifice a pair of doves instead of a lamb and a dove. During his public ministry as an itinerant preacher Jesus had no home and few possessions. To an applicant for discipleship he once said: 'Foxes have holes and birds of the air have nests, but the Son of Man has no place to lay his head.' He taught from a borrowed boat, rode into Jerusalem on a borrowed donkey, spent his last evening in a borrowed room, and was buried in a borrowed tomb. He and his apostles shared a common purse, and depended for their support on a group of women who sometimes accompanied them.[37] The poverty of Jesus seems to be beyond question.

Yet he was a carpenter by trade, which means that he belonged to the craftsman class. Professor Martin Hengel writes: 'Jesus himself did not come from the proletariat of day-labourers and landless tenants, but from the middle class of Galilee, the skilled workers. Like his father, he was an artisan, a *tektōn*, a Greek word which means mason, carpenter, cartwright and joiner all rolled into one. . . . As far as we can tell, the disciples whom he called to follow him came from a similar social milieu. . . .'[38] Moreover, the women who supported him evidently 'cared for his needs' adequately (Mark 15.41). So he was not destitute.

2. *The teaching of Jesus.*   To would-be followers Jesus said: 'Any of you who does not give up everything he has cannot be

my disciple.' The twelve apostles did this literally. Simon and Andrew 'left their nets and followed him'; James and John 'left their father Zebedee in the boat with the hired men and followed him'; and Levi-Matthew 'got up and followed him,' abandoning his tax-collector's booth and work. Similarly, Jesus told the Rich Young Ruler to sell all his possessions, give the proceeds to the poor and then follow him. It was this which prompted Peter to blurt out: 'we have left everything to follow you!'[39]

Does Jesus then expect *all* his followers to give up everything in order to follow him? The apostles did it. And the rich young man was challenged to do it. But is it a universal rule? In reply, we must be careful not to whittle down the radical summons of Jesus by a little prudential exegesis. He did say that we should store our treasure in heaven not on earth; that we must put devotion to God's rule and righteousness above material things; that we must beware of covetousness; and that it is impossible to serve God and money simultaneously.[40] But he did not tell all his followers to get rid of all their possessions. Joseph of Arimathea is described both as 'a rich man' and as 'a disciple of Jesus.' So these two were evidently not incompatible. Zacchaeus the wealthy tax-collector promised both to pay back to people he had cheated four times what he had taken, and to give half of his possessions to the poor, which presumably means that he kept the other half, apart from what he paid back to his victims. Yet Jesus said that salvation had been given him.[41] So then, when he said that no one could be his disciple unless he both 'renounced' all his possessions and 'hated' his parents and other relatives, we shall need to understand both these verbs as dramatic figures of speech. We are not to hate our parents literally, nor to renounce all our possessions literally. What we *are* summoned to is to put Jesus Christ first, above even our family and our goods.

3. *The early church of Jesus.*   Luke writes of the first Christian community of Jerusalem that they 'had everything in common,'

that 'no one claimed that any of his possessions was his own,' that 'they shared everything they had' and 'gave to anyone as he had need,' and that in consequence 'there were no needy persons among them.'[42]

Is Luke setting their common life before us as an example for every church to copy? In the sense that the early Spirit-filled believers loved and cared for one another, and eliminated poverty within their fellowship, yes. But is he also advocating the common ownership of goods? Among the Essene groups, especially in their central community at Qumran, this was obligatory, and every novice entering the order had to hand over his property.[43] But it is plain from Luke's narrative that the Christians' selling and sharing were neither universal nor compulsory. For some believers still had houses in which they met. The sin of Ananias and Sapphira was not that they were selfish to withhold some of their property, but that they were deceitful to pretend they had given it all. Peter said to them: 'Didn't it belong to you before it was sold? And after it was sold, wasn't the money at your disposal?' (Acts 5.4) Thus the Christian's right to property is affirmed, together with the voluntary nature of Christian giving.

The example, teaching, and early church of Jesus all challenge us to renounce covetousness, materialism, and luxury, and to care sacrificially for the poor. But they do not establish the case that all Christians must actually become poor.

If the first option for affluent Christians is to become poor, the second and opposite option is to *stay rich*. Some seek to defend this stance by an appeal to biblical arguments. Human beings were commanded in the beginning (they rightly say) to subdue and develop the earth, that is, to extract its animal, vegetable, and mineral wealth and to harness it for their use. Wealth, moreover, was a sign of God's blessing, and they intend to claim and enjoy it. 'The Lord will send a blessing on your barns and on everything you put your hand to. The Lord your God will bless you in the land he is giving you. . . . You will lend to many nations but will borrow from none' (Deuteronomy 28.8,12). What could be clearer than that? they ask.

The most shameless example of this reasoning which I have come across was in the literature of a certain Pentecostal evangelist. He was appealing for funds to enable him to send Christian materials to the Third World. 'There's no better way to insure your own financial security,' he argued, all in capital letters, 'than to plant some seed-money in God's work. His law of sowing and reaping guarantees you a harvest of much more than you sow. . . . Have you limited God to your present income, business, house or car? There's no limit to God's plenty! . . . Write on the enclosed slip what you need from God—the salvation of a loved one, healing, a raise in pay, a better job, newer car or home, sale or purchase of property, guidance in business or investment. . . , *whatever you need*. . . . Enclose your slip with your seed-money. . . . Expect God's material blessings in return. . . .'

Our first response to this is vigorously to deny what such Christians are affirming. When God's people were a nation, he did indeed promise to reward their obedience with material blessings, but in Christ he has blessed us 'with every spiritual blessing' (Ephesians 1.3). Our second response is to draw attention to what they are omitting, for there are other biblical principles which they have overlooked. The earth was to be developed for the common good, and its riches shared with all mankind. The Old Testament economy which promised wealth also commanded the care of the poor. And the rich man in the parable of Jesus found himself in hell not because of his wealth but because of his neglect of the beggar at his gate. That is, Dives indulged himself at the very time when Lazarus was starving.

In the light of these additional biblical truths, and of the contemporary destitution of millions, it is not possible for affluent

Christians to 'stay rich,' in the sense of accepting no modification of economic life-style. We cannot maintain a 'good life' (of extravagance) and a 'good conscience' simultaneously. One or other has to be sacrificed. Either we keep our conscience and reduce our affluence, or we keep our affluence and smother our conscience. We have to choose between God and mammon.

Consider Paul's instruction to Timothy regarding rich people:

> Command those who are rich in this present world not to be arrogant nor to put their hope in wealth, which is so uncertain, but to put their hope in God, who richly provides us with everything for our enjoyment. Command them to do good, to be rich in good deeds, and to be generous and willing to share. In this way they will lay up treasure for themselves as a firm foundation for the coming age, so that they may take hold of the life that is truly life.
>
> 1 Timothy 6.17–19

We observe at once that the apostle does not tell 'those who are rich in this present world' to 'become poor.' But he does not allow them to 'stay rich' either. Instead, he first warns them of the spiritual dangers of wealth (as Jesus said, it is not impossible but it is hard for the rich to enter God's kingdom), and then tells them to be generous with their wealth, which will inevitably result in a lowering of their own standard of living.

The first danger of wealth is pride: 'command those who are rich . . . not to be arrogant.' For wealth makes people feel self-important and so 'contemptuous of others' (PHILLIPS). Rich people are tempted to boast of their home, car, possessions, and gadgets. It is easy for wealthy people to become snobs, to emphasise their social 'class' and despise others. James pictures the situation when first a rich man enters a Christian assembly wearing fine clothes, and then a poor man in rags comes in. If we behave obsequiously to the rich person and show him to one of the best seats, while rudely telling the poor person to stand on one side or sit on the floor, we have been guilty of class distinctions and so have disrupted the fellowship. It is not difficult to tell whether our affluence has alienated us from our less well-to-do brothers and sisters. If it has, we find ourselves embarrassed in each other's company.

If wealth's first peril is pride, its second is materialism: 'Command those who are rich . . . not . . . to put their hope in wealth which is so uncertain, but to put their hope in God. . . .' 'Materialism' is not the mere possession of material things, but an unhealthy obsession with them. It is but a short step from wealth to materialism, from having riches to putting our trust in them, and many take it. But it is foolish. There is no security in wealth. It is not for nothing that Paul writes of 'uncertain riches.' Burglars, pests, rust, and inflation all take their toll. Many have gone to bed rich and woken up poor, or like the Rich Fool in Jesus' parable have not woken up at all.

Trust in wealth is not only foolish; it is also unworthy of human beings, since our trust should not be in a thing but a Person, not in money but in God 'who richly provides us with everything for our enjoyment.' This is an important addition, for the Christian antidote to materialism is not asceticism; austerity for its own sake is to reject the good gifts of the Creator.

Here then are the two main dangers to which rich people are exposed—pride (looking down on the poor) and materialism (enjoying the gift and forgetting the Giver). Wealth can spoil our two noblest relationships. It can make us forget God and despise our fellow human beings. These negative warnings prepare us for the positive instruction which follows.

After considering and rejecting the opposite options of becoming poor and staying rich, we come to the third, which is to *be generous and contented.* The apostle summons Christian believers to be both. We do not claim that these things by themselves will solve the problem of world poverty, but at least they are an appropriate expression of solidarity with the poor.

Take generosity. The skeleton of verses 17 and 18 is striking: 'Command those who are rich . . . to be rich.' More precisely, 'command those who are rich in this present world . . . to be rich in good deeds.' In other words, let them add one kind of wealth to another. Tell them 'to do good, to be rich in good deeds, and to be generous and willing to share.' Then they will be imitating our generous God 'who richly provides us with everything for our enjoyment.' They will also store up treasure in heaven (v.19), as Jesus urged us to do.

Next, contentment needs to be added to generosity, for it would be anomalous if generous giving to others resulted in discontent with what we have left. Paul exhorts to contentment in 1 Timothy 6.6–10, as follows:

> *But godliness with contentment is great gain. For we brought nothing into the world, and we can take nothing out of it. But if we have food and clothing, we will be content with that. People who want to get rich fall into temptation and a trap and into many foolish and harmful desires that plunge men into ruin and destruction. For the love of money is a root of all kinds of evil. Some people, eager for money, have wandered from the faith and pierced themselves with many griefs.*

We notice that, whereas the other paragraph we considered relates to 'those who are rich' (v.17), this one is addressed to 'people who want to get rich' (v.9), that is, the covetous. Paul sets covetousness and contentment in contrast to one another. Covetousness is a self-destructive passion, a craving which is never satisfied, even when what had been craved is now possessed. As Schopenhauer said, 'gold is like sea water—the more one drinks of it, the thirstier one becomes.'[44] 'Beware of covetousness,' warned Jesus. 'Covetousness is idolatry,' added Paul.[45] It seduces the heart from love for God and imprisons it in love for money. It brings much pain and many sorrows, for 'the love of money is a root of all kinds of evil' (v.10).

Contentment, on the other hand, is the secret of inward peace. It remembers the stark truth that 'we brought nothing into the world, and we can take nothing out of it' (v.7). Life, in fact, is a pilgrimage from one moment of nakedness to another. So we should travel light, and live simply. Bishop John V. Taylor has put it well: 'The word "poverty" has come to sound so negative and extreme in our ears that I prefer the word "simplicity," because it puts the emphasis on the right points. . . . Our enemy is not possessions but excess. Our battle cry is not "nothing!" but "enough!" '[46] Simplicity says 'if we have food and clothing, we will be content with that' (v.8). Christian contentment is coupled with godliness, the knowledge of God in Jesus Christ, and 'godliness with contentment is great gain' (v.6).

We have looked at the three options which confront all affluent Christians. Should we become poor? No, not necessarily. Though Jesus Christ still calls some like the Rich Young Ruler to a life of total voluntary poverty, it is not the vocation of all his disciples. Then should we stay rich? No, this is not only unwise (because of the perils of conceit and materialism) *but actually impossible* (because we are to give generously, which will have the effect of reducing our wealth). Instead of these two, we are to cultivate generosity on the one hand and simplicity with contentment on the other.

At this point the temptation is to lay down rules and regulations, whether for ourselves or others, and so lapse into pharisaism. It is yet another 'ism' to avoid—materialism (an obsession with things), asceticism (an austerity which denies the good gifts of the Creator), and pharisaism (binding one another with rules). Instead, we would be wise to stick to principles.

The principle of simplicity is clear. Its first cousin is contentment. It concentrates on what we need, and measures this by what we use. It rejoices in the Creator's gifts, but hates waste, greed, and clutter. It says with the Book of Proverbs, 'give me neither poverty nor riches, but give me only my daily bread,' for to have either too much or too little may lead to disowning or dishonouring God (30.8f.). It wants to be free of anything and everything which distracts from the loving service of God and others.

One of the most controversial sections of the Lausanne Covenant, adopted at the conclusion of the International Congress on World Evangelization in 1974, relates to the need for more simple living. It goes like this: 'All of us are shocked by the poverty of millions and disturbed by the injustices which cause it. Those of us who live in affluent circumstances accept our duty to develop a simple life-style, in order to contribute more generously to both relief and evangelism.'[47] It was to elucidate the implications of these sentences that an International Consultation on Simple Life-style was held in 1980. It issued 'An Evangelical Commitment to Simple Life-style,' whose nine paragraphs deserve careful study.

Paragraph 5 is entitled 'Personal Life-style' and develops the concept of 'simplicity.' It includes a general resolve to 'renounce waste and oppose extravagance in personal living, clothing and housing, travel and church buildings.' But it betrays no negative asceticism. On the contrary, it picks up from Dr. Ronald Sider's paper 'Living More Simply for Evangelism and Justice' a number of important distinctions: 'We also accept the distinction between necessities and luxuries, creative hobbies and empty status symbols, modesty and vanity, occasional celebrations and normal routine, and between the service of God and slavery to fashion.'[48] The point is that simple living is not incompatible with carefree enjoyment.

The principle of generosity is clear too. John expresses it in these terms; 'If anyone has material possessions and sees his brother in need but has no pity on him, how can the love of God be in him?' (1 John 3.17). Our God is a generous God. If his love indwells us, we shall relate what we 'have' (possessions) to what we 'see' (need) and take action.

May God help us to simplify our life-style, grow in generosity, and live in contentment!

Part II

Sexual Issues

Chapter Five

Women, Men, and God

A SCHOOLGIRL WAS ONCE ASKED TO WRITE AN ESSAY ON WHY women outnumber men in the world. 'God made Adam first,' she wrote. 'When he had finished, he looked at him and said to himself "Well, I think I could do better than that if I tried again." So then he made Eve. And God liked Eve so much better than Adam that he has been making more women than men ever since.'

The self-confident feminism of that young girl stands out in strong relief against the prevailing attitudes of the centuries. For there is no doubt that in many cultures women have habitually been despised and demeaned by men. They have often been treated as mere playthings and sex objects, as unpaid cooks, housekeepers, and child-minders, and as brainless simpletons incapable of engaging in rational discussion. Their gifts have been unappreciated, their personality smothered, their freedom curtailed, and their service in some areas exploited, in others refused.

The Rise of Feminism

This record of the oppression of women has been so longstanding and widespread that there is an evident need for reparation by male-dominated society. Yet in presuming to include a chapter on this topic, I immediately find myself in an unfavourable position. Indeed my maleness, some will say, is more than an initial disadvantage; it constitutes a total disqualification. They may be right. How far can men understand women, let alone make pronouncements about them? Let me make two points in self-defence. First, I have tried to listen carefully to what feminists (both secular and Christian) are saying, have read some of their books, and have struggled to understand their hurts, frustration, and even rage. At the same time, secondly, I am concerned, on this as on every subject, to listen to what Scripture says. This double listening is painful. But it should save us both from denying the teaching of Scripture in a determination to be modern, and from affirming it in a way that ignores the modern challenges and is insensitive to the people most deeply affected by them.

The ancient world's scorn for women is well known. Plato, who believed that the soul is both imprisoned in the body and released only to be reincarnated, went on to suggest that a bad man's fate would be reincarnation as a woman.[1] Aristotle, although respected as the father of biology because of his two works *The History of Animals* and *The Generation of Animals*, regarded a female as 'a kind of mutilated male.' He wrote: 'Females are imperfect males, accidentally produced by the father's inadequacy or by the malign influence of a moist south wind.'[2]

Such crude male chauvinism was not, unfortunately, limited to the pagan world. Even Jewish writers, whose knowledge of the Old Testament should have given them a better understanding, made derogatory remarks about women. Josephus expressed his opinion that 'the woman is inferior to the man in every way.'[3] William Barclay sums up the low view of women expressed in the Talmud in these words: 'In the Jewish form of morning prayer . . . a Jewish man every morning gave thanks

that God had not made him "a Gentile, a slave or a woman"....
In Jewish law a woman was not a person, but a thing. She had
no legal rights whatsoever; she was absolutely in her husband's
possession to do with as he willed."[4]

It is a further tragedy that some of the early church fathers,
influenced more by Greek and Talmudic perspectives than by
Scripture, also sometimes spoke disparagingly of women. Tertullian, for example, wrote: 'You are the devil's gateway; you
are the unsealer of that (forbidden) tree; you are the first de-
serter of the divine law; you are she who persuaded him whom
the devil was not valiant enough to attack. You destroyed so
easily God's image, man. On account of your desert—that is,
death—even the Son of God had to die.'[5]

This kind of exaggerated language is incongruous from the
pen of a follower of Jesus, to whom the contemporary liberation
of women is largely due. The shame is that it did not come earlier, and that the initiative was not taken more explicitly in his
name.

At least during this century the status and service of women
have been rapidly changing, especially in the West. Women
have now been emancipated from nearly all the restrictions
which had previously been imposed upon them. They have obtained the franchise, thanks to the courageous agitation of the
suffragettes. In many countries (at least in theory) they receive
equal pay for equal work. In Britain the *Sex Disqualification (Removal) Act* of 1919 opened to them virtually every public function, profession, and civil post. By the 1960s only two
professions were still closed to them, the London Stock Exchange and the ordained ministry of the historic churches.
In 1973, however, the Stock Exchange capitulated. Now it
is only ordination which, in some churches, is denied to
women.

As the feminist movement gathered momentum, especially in
the sixties, the utterances of some of its leaders became more

strident. Take Germaine Greer as an example, the Australian lecturer and authoress. She regarded her book *The Female Eunuch* (which *Newsweek* called 'a dazzling combination of erudition, eccentricity and eroticism') as part of 'the second feminist wave.' The first had been that of the suffragettes, but their movement had failed because they had never taken advantage of the freedoms they had won. 'The cage door had opened, but the canary had refused to fly out.'[6] The suffragettes had been content with reform by participation in the existing political system; Germaine Greer called for revolution. She has a chapter entitled 'The Middle-class myth of love and marriage,' in which she 'hints that women ought not to enter into socially sanctioned relationships, like marriage, and that once unhappily in, they ought not to scruple to run away.' Women 'are the true proletariat, the truly oppressed majority'; they should rebel, and withdraw their labour.[7]

Extreme statements like this can be counterproductive, however. They may alienate the very people who recognise that feminists have a strong case which deserves to be heard and weighed. This includes Germaine Greer herself. Christians are put off by her tendency to vulgarity of expression. Even the title of her first book they found somewhat shocking. Yet doubtless she needed to shock in order to gain a hearing. For what she was rebelling against was the stereotype of 'the Eternal Feminine,' 'the Sexual Object sought by all men,' whose value is not in herself but in the demand she excites in others. 'She is not a woman. . . . She is a doll. . . . She is an idol. . . . Her essential quality is her castratedness.'[8] In other words, all that is required of 'the female eunuch' is a sexless submission to the sexual desires of men. Is it not right to revolt against this demeaning of women?

The most persuasive presentation which I have read is Janet Radcliffe Richards' *The Sceptical Feminist*. She begins by describing her book as 'a battle on two fronts,' since she is combating on the one hand the position which says 'there is no justification for the existence of a feminist movement' and on the other 'a good deal of common feminist dogma and practice.'[9] She calls her thesis 'a philosophical enquiry,' as befits a lecturer in philosophy, and she develops her arguments with incisive logic. Feminism to her is not an irrational movement by women for women, in which on every single issue (however indefensible) women side with women against men. Instead, it arises from the conviction that 'women suffer from systematic social injustice because of their sex,' and therefore it is 'a movement for the elimination of sex-based injustice.'[10]

Every complaint of injustice and every cry for justice should make the Christian sit up and take notice, for justice is concerned with God-given rights. We need therefore to ask several questions: What are women's rights? Wherein lies a woman's essential identity, and how is it either discovered or destroyed? What according to Scripture is the status which God gives to women, and what is the work to which he calls them? In seeking to summarise and synthesise the biblical teaching on these sensitive topics, I shall focus on four crucial words—equality, complementarity, responsibility, and ministry.

Equality

It is essential to begin at the beginning, namely with the first chapter of Genesis:

> Then God said, 'Let us make man in our image, in our likeness, and let them rule over the fish of the sea and the birds of the air, over the livestock, over all the earth, and over all the creatures that move along the ground.'
>
> So God created man in his own image, in the image of God he created him; male and female he created them.
>
> God blessed them and said to them, 'Be fruitful and increase in number; fill the earth and subdue it. Rule over the fish of the sea and the birds of the air and over every living creature that moves on the ground.'
>
> Genesis 1.26–28

Putting together the divine resolve ('let us make man . . . and let them rule . . .'), the divine creation ('so God created . . .') and the divine blessing ('Be fruitful . . . fill the earth and subdue it . . .'), the emphasis seems to be on three fundamental truths about human beings, namely that God made (and makes) them in his own image, that he made (and makes) them male and female, giving them the joyful task of reproducing, and that he gave (and gives) them dominion over the earth and its creatures. Thus from the beginning man was 'male and female,' and men and women were equal beneficiaries both of the divine image and of the earthly rule. There is no suggestion in the text that either sex is more like God than the other, or that either sex is more responsible for the earth than the other. No. Their resemblance to God and their stewardship of his earth (which must not be confused, although they are closely related) were from the beginning shared equally, since both sexes were equally created by God and like God.

More than this. The threefold affirmation of God's creation in verse 27 is not just poetic parallelism. There is surely a deliberate emphasis here, which we are intended to grasp. Twice it is asserted that God created man in his own image, and the third time the reference to the divine image is replaced by the words 'male and female.' We must be careful not to speculate beyond what the text warrants. Yet, if both sexes bear the image of God (as is forcefully asserted), then this seems to include not only our humanity (authentic humanness reflecting divinity), but our plurality (our relationships of love reflecting those which unite the persons of the Trinity) and even, at least in the broadest sense, our sexuality. Is it too much to say that since God, when he made man in his own image, made him male and female, there must be within the being of God himself something which corresponds to the 'feminine' as well as the 'masculine' in humankind?

If so, is the National Council of Churches of Christ (USA)

justified in publishing *An Inclusive Language Lectionary*, from which all 'sexist' or 'exclusive' vocabulary has been eliminated? We can certainly applaud their desire 'to express the truth about God and about God's inclusive love for all persons' and 'to provide to both reader and hearer a sense of belonging to a Christian faith community in which truly all are one in Christ.' They were right, therefore, to translate 'brethren' as 'sisters and brothers,' and the generic 'man' as 'human being' or 'human-kind,' for in so doing they simply clarified what these words have always meant. I do not think they had the liberty, however, actually to change the biblical text, on the ground that they regarded its language as sometimes 'male-biased or otherwise inappropriately exclusive.' To designate God 'the Father (*and Mother*)' and Jesus Christ his 'only Child' is to set aside the experience and instruction of Jesus, who addressed God as 'Abba Father,' knew himself as 'the Son,' and taught us to call God 'our Father in heaven.'[11]

What we should do, however, is give full weight to those passages of Scripture which speak of God in feminine—and especially maternal—terms, for these texts help to illumine the nature and quality of his 'fatherhood.' For example, in the Song of Moses, Yahweh is not only 'the Rock who fathered you' but also 'the God who gave you birth.' It is a remarkable statement that he is simultaneously Israel's Father and Mother. In consequence, Israel may be sure of God's persevering faithfulness. For though a human mother may 'forget the baby at her breast and have no compassion on the child she has borne,' yet, Yahweh promises, 'I will not forget you!' Instead, he will unfailingly love and console his people: 'As a mother comforts her child, so will I comfort you. . . .' Moreover, if Yahweh in these texts revealed himself as the mother of his people Israel, the individual Israelite felt at liberty to enter into this relationship. The psalmist dared even to liken his quiet confidence in God to the humble trustfulness of a breast-fed child. Then Jesus himself on occasion used feminine imagery, likening God to a woman who had lost a coin, as well as to a father who had lost a son, and likening himself in his anguish over impenitent Jerusalem to a hen wanting to gather her chicks under her wings.[12]

So then, returning to the creation story, it is clear that from the first chapter of the Bible onwards, the fundamental equality of the sexes is affirmed. Whatever is essentially human in both male and female reflects the divine image which we equally bear. And we are equally called to rule the earth, to cooperate with the Creator in the development of its wealth for the common good.

This primeval sexual equality was, however, distorted by the Fall. Part of God's judgment on our disobedient progenitors was his word to the woman: 'Your desire will be for your husband, and he will rule over you.' Thus the sexes would experience a measure of alienation from one another. In place of the equality of the one with the other, and of the complementarity of the one to the other (which we have yet to consider), there would come the rule of one over the other. Sexual complementarity was intended from the beginning to include masculine 'headship,' as Paul argued, but by reason of the Fall 'headship' degenerated into 'domination.'

The fact is that men have exploited this judgment of God, and have brutally oppressed and subjugated women in ways God never intended. Examples could be given from many cultures. Let me give three. First, from Gandhi's *Autobiography*: 'A Hindu husband regards himself as lord and master of his wife, who must ever dance attendance upon him.'[13] Next, consider Sura 4 of the Koran, entitled 'Women': 'Men have authority over women because Allah has made the one superior to the other. . . . As for those from whom you fear disobedience, admonish them and send them to beds apart and beat them. . . .'[14] My third example comes from the Eskimos. Raymond de Coccola spent twelve years among the *krangmalit* in the Canadian Arctic, as a Roman Catholic missionary, and got to know them well. He was shocked when an Eskimo hunter used a word of a woman which was also applied to a she-wolf or a bitch. 'Trained to do all manner of mean tasks,' he reflected, 'the Eskimo woman is used to enduring the weaknesses and appetites of men. But I still could not get used to what appeared to be a master-and-slave relationship between the hunter and his wife.'[15]

These are examples of the unlawful exploitation of women, however. In the Old Testament the husband was certainly patriarch of his clan, and their *baal* (lord or ruler). Yet their women folk were not despised or ill-treated. They were regarded as an integral part of the covenant community, so that 'men, women and children' were together assembled to listen to the public reading of Torah and to share in the worship (e.g. Deuteronomy 31.12). Marriage was held in high honour, modelled on Yahweh's covenant love to Israel; the beauty of sexual love was celebrated (as in the Song of Songs); the capabilities of a good wife were praised (e.g. Proverbs 31); godly and enterprising women like Hannah, Abigail, Naomi and Ruth, and Esther were held up for admiration, and it was constantly emphasised that widows must be cared for.

Yet the prophets looked forward to the days of the New Covenant in which the original equality of the sexes would be reaffirmed. For God would pour out his Spirit on all flesh, including sons and daughters, menservants and maidservants. There would be no disqualification on account of sex.

Then Jesus came in the fulness of time, born of a woman (Galatians 4.4). Although Protestants are anxious to avoid the exaggerated veneration of the Virgin Mary accorded to her in the Roman Catholic and Orthodox Churches, we should also avoid the opposite extreme of failing to honour her. If the angel Gabriel addressed her as 'highly favoured,' and if her cousin Elizabeth called her 'blessed . . . among women,' we should not be shy to think and speak of her in the same terms, because of the greatness of her Son.[16]

It was not only his birth of a woman, however, which restored to women that measure of dignity lost by the Fall, but his attitude to them. In addition to his apostles, who were all men, Jesus was accompanied on his travels by a group of women, whom he had healed and who now provided for him out of their means. Next, he spoke to one at Jacob's Well who, as woman, Samaritan, and sinner had a threefold disability, but Jesus actually engaged in a theological discussion with her. It was similar with the woman who had been caught in the act of adultery; he was gentle with her and refused to condemn her. Then he allowed a prostitute to come behind him as he reclined at table, to wet his feet with her tears, wipe them with her hair, and cover them with kisses. He accepted her love, which he interpreted as gratitude for her forgiveness. In doing so, he risked his reputation and ignored the silent indignation of his host. He was probably the first man to treat this woman with dignity; previously men had only used her.[17]

Here were three occasions on which *in public* he received a sinful woman. A Jewish male was forbidden to talk to a woman on the street, even if she were his wife, daughter or sister. It was also regarded as impious to teach a woman the law; it would be better for the words of the law to be burned, said the Talmud, than that they should be entrusted to a woman. But Jesus broke these rules of tradition and convention. When Mary of Bethany sat at his feet listening to his teaching, he commended her as doing the one thing that was needed, and he honoured another Mary as the very first witness of the Resurrection.[18] All this was unprecedented. Without any fuss or publicity, Jesus terminated the curse of the Fall, reinvested woman with her partially lost nobility, and reclaimed for his new kingdom community the original creation blessing of sexual equality.

That the apostle Paul had grasped this is plain from his great charter statement of Christian freedom: 'There is neither Jew nor Greek, slave nor free, male nor female, for you are all one in Christ Jesus' (Galatians 3.28).

This does not mean that Jews and Greeks lost their physical differences, or even their cultural distinctives, for they still spoke, dressed and ate differently; nor that slaves and free people lost their social differences, for most slaves remained slaves and free people free; nor that men lost their masculinity and women their femininity. It means rather that *as regards our standing before God*, because we are 'in Christ' and enjoy a common relationship to him, racial, national, social, and sexual distinctions are irrelevant. People of all races and classes, and of both sexes, are equal before him. The context is one of justification by grace alone through faith alone. It affirms that all who by faith are in Christ are equally accepted, equally God's children, without any distinction, discrimination or favouritism according to race, sex or class. So, whatever needs later to be said about sexual roles, there can be no question of one sex being superior or inferior to the other. Before God and in Christ 'there is neither male nor female.' We are equal.

Sexual equality, then, established by creation but perverted by the Fall, was recovered by the redemption that is in Christ. What redemption remedies is the Fall; what it recovers and reestablishes is the Creation. Thus men and women are absolutely equal in worth before God—equally created by God like God, equally justified by grace through faith, equally regenerated by the outpoured Spirit. In other words, in the new community of Jesus we are not only equally sharers of God's image, but also equally heirs of his grace in Christ (1 Peter 3.7) and equally indwelt by his Spirit. This Trinitarian equality (our common participation in Father, Son, and Holy Spirit) nothing can ever destroy. Christians and churches in different cultures have denied it; but it is an indestructible fact.

Complementarity

At the same time, although men and women are equal, they are not the same. Equality and identity are not to be confused. We are different from one another, and we complement one an-

other in the distinctive qualities of our own sexuality, psychological as well as physiological. This fact forms the basis of our
different and appropriate roles in society. As J. H. Yoder has
written, 'equality of *worth* is not identity of *role.*'[19]

When we investigate male and female roles, however, we
must be careful not to acquiesce uncritically in the stereotypes
which our particular culture has developed, let alone imagine
that Moses brought them down from Mt. Sinai along with the
Ten Commandments. This would be a serious confusion of
Scripture and convention.

It is the expectation that women must fit into a predeter-
mined role against which feminists are understandably rebelling. For who fixed the mould but men? This is what the
American psychologist Betty Friedan meant by 'the feminine
mystique' in her book of that title. It is the image to which
women feel compelled to conform, and which has been imposed on them by a male-dominated society. 'It is my thesis,'
she wrote, 'that the core of the problem for women today is
not sexual but a problem of identity—a stunting or evasion
of growth that is perpetuated by the feminine mystique. . . .
Our culture does not permit women to accept or gratify their
basic need to grow and fulfill their potentialities as human beings. . . .'[20] Motherhood is indeed a divine vocation, and calls
for great sacrifices. But it is not woman's only vocation. There
are other equally serious and equally unselfish forms of service
to society which she may be called to give.

There is nothing in Scripture to suggest, for example, that
women should not pursue their own career or earn their own
living; or that married women should do all the shopping, cooking, and cleaning, while their husbands remain noncon-
tributing beneficiaries of their labour; or that baby-rearing is an
exclusively feminine preserve into which men may not trespass.
The German saying which restricts the province of women to
'Kinder, Küche, und Kirche' (children, kitchen, and church)

is an example of blatant male chauvinism. Scripture is silent about this kind of division of labour. Does it then say anything about sexual roles and relationships?

It is without doubt by a deliberate providence of God that we have been given two distinct creation stories, Genesis 2 supplementing and enriching Genesis 1:

> The Lord God said, 'It is not good for the man to be alone. I will make a helper suitable for him.'
>
> Now the Lord God had formed out of the ground all the beasts of the field and all the birds of the air. He brought them to the man to see what he would name them; and whatever the man called each living creature, that was its name. So the man gave names to all the livestock, the birds of the air and all the beasts of the field.
>
> But for Adam no suitable helper was found. So the Lord God caused the man to fall into a deep sleep; and while he was sleeping, he took one of the man's ribs and closed up the place with flesh. Then the Lord God made a woman from the rib he had taken out of the man, and he brought her to the man.
>
> Genesis 2.18–22

What is revealed in this second story of creation is that, although God made male and female *equal*, he also made them *different*. In Genesis 1, masculinity and femininity are related to God's image, while in Genesis 2 they are related to each other, Eve being taken out of Adam and brought to him. Genesis 1 declares the equality of the sexes; Genesis 2 clarifies that 'equality' means not 'identity' but 'complementarity' (including, as we shall soon see, a certain masculine headship). It is this 'equal but different' which we find it hard to preserve. Yet the two parts of it are not incompatible; they belong to each other.

Because men and women are equal (by creation and in Christ), there can be no question of the inferiority of either to the other. But because they are complementary, there can be no question of the identity of one with the other. Further, this double truth throws light on male-female relationships and roles. Because they have been created by God with *equal* dignity, men and women must respect, love, serve, and not despise, one another. Because they have been created *complementary* to each other, men and women must recognise their differences and not try to eliminate them or usurp one another's distinctives.

Commenting on the special creation of Eve, Matthew Henry writes with quaint profundity that she was 'not made out of his head to top him, nor out of his feet to be trampled upon by him, but out of his side to be equal with him, under his arm to be protected, and near his heart to be beloved.' Perhaps he got this idea from Peter Lombard who in about A.D. 1157, just before becoming Bishop of Paris, wrote in his *Book of Sentences*: 'Eve was not taken from the feet of Adam to be his slave, nor from his head to be his lord, but from his side to be his partner.'[21]

It is when we begin to elaborate the meaning of complementarity, to explain in what ways the two sexes complement each other, and to define the distinctives of masculinity and feminity, that we find ourselves in difficulties. Feminists become uncomfortable. They are suspicious of attempts to define femininity, partly because the definitions are usually made by men, who have (or at least may have) vested interests in securing a definition congenial to them, and partly because many sexual distinctives, as we have seen, are not intrinsic but established by social pressures. As Janet Radcliffe Richards puts it, feminists consider it is 'not by *nature* that women are so different from men, but by *contrivance*.'[22]

But inherent sexual differences remain, however much some people wish to abolish them. One author who has emphasised their importance is George F. Gilder in his book *Sexual Suicide*. 'The feminists refer often . . . to "human beings," ' he writes, 'but I do not care to meet one. I am only interested in men and women.'[23] Again, 'there are no human beings; there are just men and women, and when they deny their divergent sexuality, they reject the deepest sources of identity and love. They commit sexual suicide.'[24] They also succeed in 'exalting the sexual eccentric—the androgyne.'[25] George Gilder quotes Margaret Mead that 'if any human society . . . is to survive, it must have a pattern of social life that comes to terms with the differences between the sexes.' For, he continues, 'the differences between the sexes are the single most important fact of human society.'[26]

Responsibility

All students of Genesis agree that chapter 1 teaches sexual equality and chapter 2 sexual complementarity. To these, however, the apostle Paul adds masculine 'headship.' He writes both that 'the husband is the head of the wife' (Ephesians 5.23) and, more generally, that 'the head of every man is Christ, and the head of the woman is man, and the head of Christ is God' (1 Corinthians 11.3). How, is it asked, can male headship be reconciled with sexual equality and complementarity?

Some immediately reply that it cannot—for example, Dr. Paul Jewett in his otherwise admirable book *Man as Male and Female*. His thesis can be simply stated. The original 'partnership' which God intended for men and women was replaced in Old Testament days by a hierarchical model derived from Israel's cultural milieu. But then with Jesus 'a new thing happened: he spoke of women and related to women as being fully human and equal in every way to men. In this respect Jesus was truly a revolutionary.'[27] This dialectic between the Old Testament and Jesus was embodied in Paul, who expressed now the one viewpoint, now the other. As the apostle of Christian liberty he 'spoke the most decisive word . . . in favour of woman's liberation' (namely Galatians 3.28 'there is neither male nor female'), but as the former Jewish rabbi, following rabbinic interpretations of Genesis 2, he spoke 'the most decisive word . . . in favour of woman's subjection' (namely 1 Corinthians 11.3 'the head of the woman is the man').[28]

'These two perspectives,' Dr. Jewett continues 'are incompatible, there is no satisfying way to harmonize . . . them.'[29] Indeed, 'female subordination' is 'incompatible with (a) the biblical narratives of man's creation, (b) the revelation which is given us in the life of Jesus, and (c) Paul's fundamental statement of Christian liberty' (i.e. Galatians 3.28).[30] This incongruity, he concludes, is due to the fact that Scripture is human as well as divine, and that Paul's own 'insight' has 'historical limitations.'[31] In other words, Paul was mistaken. He did not grasp the full implications of his own assertion that in Christ there is neither male nor female. He did not know his own mind. We have to choose between the apostle of Christian liberty and the unreformed rabbi, and, says Dr. Jewett, we greatly prefer the former.

Now there is much in Dr. Jewett's book which is excellent, especially his exposition of the attitudes and teaching of Jesus. But to abandon the task of harmonisation and declare the apostle Paul to be double-minded and mistaken is a counsel of despair. It is better to give him credit for consistency of thought. The truth is that submission does not imply inferiority, and that distinct sexual identities and roles are not incompatible with equality of worth.

Others reject Paul's teaching about headship on the ground that it was culturally conditioned, and that therefore it may have been valid for his generation but cannot be regarded as binding on ours. The attempt is sometimes made to strengthen this cultural argument by a reference to slavery, for if Paul told wives to submit to their husbands, he also told slaves to submit to their masters. Slaves have long since been liberated; is it not high time that women were liberated too? This parallel between slaves and women, and between abolitionism and feminism, was made as long ago as 1837, when two American books were published, namely, *The Bible Against Slavery* by Theodore Weld and *Letters on the Equality of the Sexes* by Sarah Grimke, his sister-in-law. The key text in their argument was Galatians 3.28, since in it Paul wrote that in Christ on the one hand 'there is neither slave nor free' and on the other 'there is neither male nor female.'[32]

The argument is flawed, however. For the analogy between women and slaves is extremely inexact on two counts. First, women are not chattel property, bought and sold in the marketplace, as slaves were. And secondly, though Paul sought to regulate the behaviour of slaves and masters, he nowhere appealed to Scripture in defence of slavery, whereas he did base his teaching about masculine headship on the biblical doctrine of creation. He drew his readers' attention to the *priority* of creation ('Adam was formed first, then Eve,' 1 Timothy 2.13), the *mode* of creation ('man did not come from woman, but woman from man,' 1 Corinthians 11.8) and the *purpose* of creation ('neither was man created for woman, but woman for man,' 1 Corinthians 11.9).

Thus, according to Scripture, although 'man is born of woman' and the sexes are interdependent (1 Corinthians 11.11f), yet woman was made after man, out of man, and for man. These three arguments cannot be haughtily dismissed (as some writers attempt to dismiss them) as 'tortuous rabbinic exegesis.' On the contrary, as Dr. James B. Hurley demonstrates in his *Man and Woman In Biblical Perspective*, they are exegetically well founded: (a) by right of primogeniture 'the firstborn inherited command of resources and the responsibility of leadership,' (b) when Eve was taken out of Adam and brought to him, he named her 'woman,' and 'the power to assign . . . a name was connected with control,' and (c) she was made for him neither as an afterthought, nor as a plaything, but as his companion and fellow worker, to share with him 'in the service of God and in the custodial ruling of the earth.'[33]

It is essential to note that Paul's three arguments are taken from Genesis 2, not Genesis 3. That is to say, they are based on the Creation, not the Fall. And, reflecting the facts of our human creation, they are not affected by the fashions of a passing culture, for what creation has established, no culture is able to destroy. The wearing of a veil or of a particular hairstyle was indeed a cultural expression of submission to masculine headship,[34] and may be replaced by other symbols more appropriate to the twentieth century, but the headship itself is creational, not cultural.

How, then, shall we interpret headship?

Some scholars point out that in classical Greek *kephalē* ('head') could mean 'source' or 'beginning,' and argue from this that Paul meant only that man is woman's 'origin,' referring to the priority of creation. Even if this were so, however, it cannot be used to contradict the notion of leadership.[35] Headship definitely implies some kind of authority, to which submission is necessary, as when 'God placed all things under his (sc. Christ's) feet and appointed him to be head over everything for the church' (Ephesians 1.22). But we must be careful not to overpress this. It is true that the same requirement of submission is made of wives to husbands, children to parents, slaves to masters, and citizens to the state. There must therefore be a common denominator between these attitudes. Yet I cannot believe that anybody conceives the wife's submission to her husband to be *identical* with the obedience expected of children, slaves or citizens. A very different relationship is in mind. Besides, the word *authority* is not used in the New Testament to describe the husband's role, nor *obedience* the wife's. Nor does *subordination* seem to me to be the right word to describe her submission. Although it would be a formally correct translation of the Greek *hupotagē*, it has in modern parlance unfortunate overtones of inferiority, even of military rank and discipline.[36] Instead, I suggest that the word *responsibility* conveys more accurately the kind of headship Paul envisages. I base my case not on the word itself so much as on the two models Paul uses in Ephesians 5 to illustrate the head's attitude to the body. The first is Christ's attitude to his body, the church, and the second is our personal concern for the welfare of our own body.

First, 'the husband is the head of the wife as Christ is head of the church, his body, of which he is the Saviour' (v.23). Those last words are revealing. Christ is 'head' of the church in the sense that he is its 'Saviour.' Changing the metaphor, he loved the church as his bride, 'and gave himself up for her to make her holy . . . and to present her to himself . . . holy and blameless' (vv.25–27). Secondly, 'husbands ought to love their wives as their own bodies. He who loves his wife loves himself. After all, no one ever hated his own body, but he feeds and cares for it (RSV 'nourishes and cherishes it'), just as Christ does the church—for we are members of his body' (vv.28–30). The ancient world did not think of the head's relationship to the body in modern neurological terms, for they did not know about the central nervous system. They thought rather of the head's integration and nurture of the body. So Paul wrote elsewhere of Christ as head of the church, from whom the whole body is 'joined and held together' and 'grows' (Ephesians 4.16; Colossians 2.19).

The husband's headship of his wife, therefore, is a headship more of care than of control, more of responsibility than of authority. As her 'head,' he gives himself up for her in love, just as Christ did for his body, the church. And he looks after her, as we do our own bodies. His concern is not to crush her, but to liberate her. As Christ gave himself for his bride, in order to present her to himself radiant and blameless, so the husband gives himself for his bride, in order to create the conditions within which she may grow into the fulness of her femininity.

But what is 'femininity' that it needs conditions to be created for its flowering? Can 'masculinity' and 'femininity' be defined in terms of certain invariable distinctives? Many scholars say not, adding that different cultures have arbitrarily assigned different qualities and therefore different roles to their men and women. Margaret Mead, for example, in her classic *Male and Female*, 'a study of the sexes in a changing world,' compares the perceptions of sexuality in seven South Sea peoples with each other and with contemporary America. She shows that the diversity of masculine and feminine traits is enormous, the differences and similarities, the vulnerabilities, handicaps and potentialities, all varying from culture to culture. Yet there are some regularities, she adds, which seem to go back ultimately to the basic physiological distinctions between male and female, and relate to the tension between activity and passivity, initiative and response, potency and receptivity.[37] Janet Radcliffe Richards is understandably concerned with the same question. She has a chapter entitled 'The Feminist and the Feminine,' and asks: 'What is it that people are afraid of, when they say they are opposed to feminism because it will result in women's ceasing to be feminine?'[38]

At the risk of causing offence, I think it is necessary for us to face the apostle Peter's description of women as 'the weaker sex' (1 Peter 3.7). Of course we know that women can be extremely strong. In some cultures they perform all the heavy manual jobs. They are capable of astonishing feats of physical endurance. And there were the Amazons, the women warriors of Greek mythology. Yet even such an ardent feminist as Janet Richards feels bound to concede that 'presumably women must in some sense tend to be weaker than men.'[39] And Margaret Mead writes: 'Still in every society men are by and large bigger than women, and by and large stronger than women.'[40] The reason we feel some embarrassment in saying this is that 'weakness' is not a quality which twentieth-century westerners normally admire, because we have absorbed something of the power philosophy of Nietzsche. In consequence, we tend like him to despise weakness, whereas Peter tells us that it is to be honoured. Moreover, a recognition that the woman is 'weaker' is not incompatible with Peter's other statement in the same verse that she and her husband are equally 'heirs . . . of the gracious gift of (eternal) life.'

Under the rubric of 'weakness' we should probably include those characteristically feminine traits of gentleness, tenderness, sensitivity, patience, and devotion. These are delicate plants, which are easily trodden under foot, and which wither and die if the climate is unfriendly. I cannot see that it is demeaning to women to say that masculine 'headship' is the God-given means by which their femininity is protected and enabled to blossom. Of course men need women ('it is not good for the man to be alone'), but women also need men. Masculine headship is intended not to smother but to serve them, and to ensure that they are—and may more fully become—themselves.

The heartfelt cry of the feminist is for 'liberation.' She feels inhibited by male dominance from discovering her true identity. Letha Scanzoni and Nancy Hardesty, for example, who follow Dr. Paul Jewett in his treatment of the biblical material, write near the beginning of their book *All We're Meant To Be:* 'The liberated Christian woman . . . is free to know herself, be herself, and develop herself in her own special way, creatively using to the full her intellect and talents.' Then towards the end they write: 'What are the basic issues of women's liberation? Do women want to become men? No, we simply want to be full human beings. . . . We only want to be persons, free to give the world all that our individual talents, minds and personalities have to offer.'[41]

The resolute desire of women to know, be and develop themselves, and to use their gifts in the service of the world, is so obviously God's will for them, that to deny or frustrate it is an extremely serious oppression. It is a woman's basic right and responsibility to discover herself, her identity, and her vocation. The fundamental question is in what relationship with men will women find and be themselves? Certainly not in a subordination which implies inferiority to men and engenders low self-esteem. Instead, Letha Scanzoni and Nancy Hardesty insist on 'a fully equal partnership.' Equality and partnership between the sexes are sound biblical concepts. But not if they are pressed into denying a masculine headship of protective care. It is surely a distorted headship of domination which has convinced women that they cannot find themselves that way. Only the biblical ideal of headship, which because it is selflessly loving may justly be called 'Christlike,' can convince them that it will facilitate, not destroy, their true identity.

Does this truth apply only to married women, whose caring head is their husband? What about single women? Perhaps the reason why this question is not directly addressed in Scripture is that in those days unmarried women were under their father's protective care, as married women were under their husband's. Today, however, at least in the West, it is usual for unmarried women to leave their parents and set up their own home independently. I see no reason to resist this. But I think it would be unnatural for such women to isolate themselves from men altogether, for men and women need each other. It would therefore be more conducive to the full flowering of their femininity if in some context, whether among relatives and friends, or at work, or (if they are Christians) at church, they could experience the supportive care of a man or men. If it is 'not good for man to be alone,' without feminine companionship, it is not good for woman to be alone either, without masculine headship.

Ministry

That women are called by God to ministry hardly needs any demonstration. 'Ministry' is 'service' (*diakonia*), and every Christian, male and female, young and old, is called to follow in the footsteps of him who said he had not come to be served, but to serve (Mark 10.45). The only question is what form women's ministry should take, whether any limits should be placed on it, and in particular whether women should be ordained.

The Roman Catholic and Eastern Orthodox Churches have no women priests; they have set themselves firmly against this development. Many Lutheran Churches now have them, for example in Scandinavia, although serious disagreement on this issue continues. The French Reformed Church accepted women ministers in 1965 and the Church of Scotland in 1966. Among the British Free Churches, the Congregationalists have had female ministers since 1917, while Methodists and Baptists have followed suit more recently. In the Anglican Church the pattern is uneven. Bishop R. O. Hall of Hong Kong was the first to ordain a woman priest (that is, presbyter) in 1944. In 1968 the Lambeth Conference (of Anglican bishops) declared that 'the theological arguments as at present presented for and against the ordination of women to the priesthood are inconclusive.' In 1975, however, the Church of England's General Synod expressed the view that there are 'no fundamental objections to the ordination of women to the priesthood,' although no women have yet been ordained in the Church of England. Then at the 1978 Lambeth Conference the bishops recognised that some Anglican provinces now had women clergy, and agreed to respect each other's discipline in this matter. Nevertheless, a deep division remains, which is partly theological and partly ecumenical, namely the damage which women's ordination would do to Anglican relationships with the Roman Catholic and Orthodox Churches. A sizeable group has broken away from the American Episcopal Church on this issue, and a similar split is threatened in the Church of England if women are ever ordained. In other spheres, however, for example as deaconesses and as pioneer missionaries, women have an outstanding record of dedicated service.

Some Christians, anxious to think and act biblically, will immediately say that the ordination of women is inadmissible.

Not only were all the apostles and the presbyters of New Testament times men, but the specific instructions that women must be 'silent in the churches' and 'not teach or have authority over a man'[42] settle the matter.

That is only one side of the argument, however. On the other side, a strong *prima facie* biblical case can be made for active female leadership in the church, including a teaching ministry. In the Old Testament there were prophetesses as well as prophets, who were called and sent by God to be bearers of his word, women like Huldah, in the time of King Josiah. Before her, Miriam, Moses' sister, was described as a 'prophetess,' while Deborah was more; she also 'judged' Israel for a number of years, settling their disputes, and actually led them into battle against the Canaanites.[43] In the New Testament, although indeed Jesus had no women apostles, it was to women that he first revealed himself after the Resurrection and entrusted the good news of his victory.[44] In addition, the Acts and the Epistles contain many references to women speakers and women workers. Philip the evangelist's four unmarried daughters all had the gift of prophecy, and Paul refers to women who prayed and prophesied in the Corinthian church. He seems to have stayed on several occasions with Aquila and Priscilla ('my fellow workers in Christ,' he called them), and Priscilla was evidently active for Christ in their married partnership, for twice she is named before her husband, and it was together that they invited Apollos into their home and 'explained to him the way of God more adequately.'[45] Paul seems to have had women helpers in his entourage, as Jesus had had in his. It is impressive to see the number of women he mentions in his letters. Euodia and Syntyche in Philippi he describes as 'fellow workers' (a word he also applied to men like Timothy and Titus), who had 'contended' at his side 'in the cause of the gospel.' And in Romans 16 he refers appreciatively to eight women. He begins by commending 'our sister Phoebe, a servant (or perhaps 'deacon') of the church in Cenchrea,' who had been 'a great help to many people' including Paul himself, and then sends greetings (among others) to Mary, Tryphena, Tryphosa, and Persis, all of whom, he says, have worked 'hard' or 'very hard' in the Lord's service.[46]

It is true that all the biblical examples in the preceding paragraph are of women's ministries which were either 'charismatic' (e.g. prophetesses) or informal and private (e.g. Priscilla teaching Apollos in her home), and that none was 'institutional' (e.g. presbyters). Nevertheless, if God saw no impediment against calling women into a teaching role, the burden of proof lies with the church to show why it should not appoint women to similar responsibilities.

There is a more general presumption in favour of women's ministry (including leadership and teaching) than these specific references, however. It is that on the Day of Pentecost, in fulfilment of prophecy, God poured out his Spirit on 'all flesh,' including 'sons and daughters' and his 'servants, both men and women.' If the gift of the Spirit was bestowed on all believers of both sexes, so were his gifts. There is no evidence, or even hint, that the *charismata* were restricted to men. On the contrary, the Spirit's gifts were distributed to all for the common good, making possible what is often called an 'every member ministry of the Body of Christ.'[47] We must conclude, therefore, not only that Christ gives *charismata* (including the teaching gifts) to women, but that alongside his gifts he issues his call to develop and exercise them in his service and in the service of others, for the building up of his body.

This much is clear. But now we return to the double command to women to be silent in the public assembly. How shall we handle these texts? Attempts have been made to restrict the application of both of them to particular local circumstances. Certainly the context of 1 Corinthians 14 is the building up of the church (e.g. vv. 3ff and 26) and so was the requirement that 'everything should be done in a fitting and orderly way' (v.40).

It may well be, therefore, as some commentators have suggested, that just as tongue-speakers should 'keep quiet in the church' if there is no interpreter (v.28), and a prophet should stop talking if a revelation is given to somebody else (v.30), so too, talkative women should 'remain silent in the churches' and, if they have questions, put them to their husbands when they get home (vv. 34f). For (and this is the principle which seems to govern all public behaviour in church) 'God is not a God of disorder but of peace' (v.33).[48] It can hardly be a prohibition of *all* talking by women in church, since Paul has earlier referred to prophetesses (11.5) and here allows 'everyone' to contribute 'a hymn, or a word of instruction, a revelation, a tongue or an interpretation' (v. 26), without limiting these to men.

The attempt has also been made by some to understand 1 Timothy 2.11ff as alluding to some particular, heretical, feminist movement.[49] But I do not myself think it has been successful. The apostle's instruction sounds quite general: 'A woman should learn in quietness and full submission. I do not permit a woman to teach or to have authority over a man; she must be silent.'

What strikes me about these sentences (and about 1 Corinthians 14.34), and has not been adequately considered by commentators, is that Paul expresses two antitheses, the first between to 'learn in quietness' or 'be silent' and 'to teach,' and the second between 'full submission' and 'authority.' The latter is the substantial point, confirms Paul's constant teaching about female submission to male headship, and is firmly rooted in the biblical account of creation ('for Adam was formed first, then Eve'). But the other instruction (the requirement of silence and the prohibition of teaching), in spite of the controversial reference to the fact that Eve was 'deceived' not Adam, seems to be an *expression* of the authority-submission syndrome, rather than an *addition* to it. There does not appear to be anything inherent

in our distinctive sexualities which makes it universally inap-
propriate for women to teach men. So is it possible, I want to
ask, whether, although the requirement of 'submission' is of
permanent and universal validity, because grounded in creation, the requirement of 'silence,' like that of head-covering of 1
Corinthians 11, was a first-century cultural application of it? Is
it possible, then, that the demand for female silence was not an
absolute prohibition of women teaching men, but rather a prohibition of any kind of teaching which infringes the principle of
male headship?

My tentative answer to my own two questions is in the affir-
mative. I believe that there are situations in which it is entirely
proper for women to teach, and to teach men, because in so
doing they are not usurping an improper authority over them.
For this to be so, three conditions need to be fulfilled, relating to
the content, context, and style of the teaching.

First, the *content*. Jesus chose, appointed and inspired his
apostles as the infallible teachers of his church. And they were
all men, presumably because their foundational teaching required a high degree of authority. The situation today is entirely different. The canon of Scripture has long ago been
completed, and there are no apostles in the church. Instead, the
primary function of Christian teachers is to 'guard the deposit'
of apostolic doctrine in the New Testament and expound it.
They do not therefore claim authority for themselves, but put
themselves and their teaching under the authority of Scripture.
This being so, may not women be numbered among them?

Secondly, there is the *context* of teaching, which should be a
team ministry in the local church. Whether directly or in-
directly, Paul appointed 'elders' (plural) in every church.[50]
Many local churches in our day are repenting of an unbiblical
one-man ministry and returning to the healthy New Testament
pattern of a plural pastoral oversight. Members of a team can
capitalize the sum total of their gifts, and in it there should

surely be a woman or women. But, in keeping with biblical teaching on masculine headship, I think a man should be the team leader. The practice of 'cultural transposition' seeks to clothe the unchanged essence of revelation in new and appropriate cultural dress. In the first century, masculine headship was expressed in the requirement of female head coverings and the prohibition of women teaching men; could it not be expressed today, in a way that is both faithful to Scripture and relevant to the twentieth century, in terms of female participation in team ministries of which men are leaders? The team concept should also take care of the problem of ecclesiastical discipline. Discipline involves authority, it is rightly said, and should therefore not be exercised by a woman. But then it should not be exercised by a man on his own either. Discipline (especially in its extreme form of excommunication) should ideally be administered by the whole local church membership, and before the ultimate is reached by a team of leaders or elders together.[51]

The third condition of acceptable teaching by women concerns its *style*. Christian teachers should not be swashbucklers, whether they are men or women. The humility of Christian teachers is to be seen both in their submission to the authority of Scripture and in their spirit of personal modesty. Jesus warned his apostles against imitating either the vainglorious authoritarianism of the Pharisees or the power-hungry bossiness of secular rulers.[52] And the apostle Peter, sensitive to the temptation to pride which all Christian leaders face, urged his fellow elders to put on the apron of humility, not lording it over those entrusted to their pastoral care, but rather being examples to Christ's flock.[53] This instruction to men will be even more clearly exemplified in women who come to terms with their feminine identity and are not trying to be, or behave like, men.

It seems then to be biblically permissible for women to teach men, provided that the content of their teaching is biblical, its context a team, and its style humble. For in such a situation they would be exercising their gift without claiming a 'headship' which is not theirs.

Does this mean, then, that women could and should be ordained? The difficulty I have in giving a straight answer to this question is due to the layers of muddle which have been wrapped round it. What is 'ordination'? And to what kind of 'ministry' is it the gateway? Christians of 'Catholic' persuasion tend to say that women cannot be 'priests.' But since I do not believe the pastoral ministry to be 'priestly' in a 'Catholic' sense, that is not my problem. Christians of Reformed persuasion tend to see the presbyterate as a fixed office which necessarily involves both authoritative teaching and the exercise of discipline, and is therefore not open to women. But it is doubtful if the New Testament gives us a rigid blueprint of ministry in which all pastors are 'teaching elders' in the Reformed mould.

Supposing the oversight envisaged in the New Testament is not priestly in the 'Catholic' sense but pastoral; and supposing it is not necessarily presbyteral either in the fixed Reformed sense of authority and discipline, but more fluid, modest and varied, offering different kinds and degrees of ministry; and supposing ordination involves the public recognition of God-given gifts, together with the public authorisation to exercise them in a team—are 'ministry' and 'ordination' conceived in these ways to be denied to women? I cannot see why. It is true that local church pastors are described as 'over' the congregation in the Lord, and that the congregation is told 'obey your leaders and submit to their authority.'[54] If all ordained Christian ministry inevitably has this flavour of authority and discipline about it, then indeed I think we would have to conclude that it is for men only. But if there are circumstances in which the pastoral care of people is a much more modest ministry, and the style of exercising it is humble, then no biblical principle is infringed if women are welcomed to share in it. I hope it is clear that the fundamental issue before the church is neither 'priest-hood,' nor 'ordination,' but the degree of authority which necessarily inheres in the presbyterate. The practical problem, at least from an Anglican perspective, is whether women could be ordained to the presbyterate, and their ministry then restricted by licence to membership of a pastoral team. I still do not think it biblically appropriate for a woman to become a Rector or a Bishop.

I conclude with some central simplicities. If God endows women with spiritual gifts (which he does), and thereby calls them to exercise their gifts for the common good (which he does), then the church must recognise God's gifts and calling, must make appropriate spheres of service available to women, and should 'ordain' (that is, commission and authorise) them to exercise their God-given ministry, at least in team situations. Our Christian doctrines of creation and redemption tell us that God wants his gifted people to be fulfilled not frustrated, and his church to be enriched by their service.

Chapter Six

Marriage and Divorce

ALTHOUGH IN ALL SOCIETIES MARRIAGE IS A RECOGNISED AND regulated human institution, it is not a human invention. Christian teaching on this topic begins with the joyful affirmation that marriage is God's idea, not man's. As the Preface to the 1662 Marriage Service says, it was 'instituted by God himself in the time of man's innocency'; it was 'adorned and beautified' by Christ's presence when he attended the wedding at Cana; and it symbolises 'the mystical union betwixt Christ and his church.' In these ways God has shaped, endorsed and ennobled marriage. True, he calls some people to forego it and remain single in this life,[1] and in the next world after the Resurrection it will be abolished.[2] Nevertheless, while the present order lasts, marriage is to be 'honoured by all'; those who 'forbid people to marry' are false teachers who have been misled by deceiving spirits.[3] Moreover, because it is a 'creation ordinance,' preceding the Fall, it is to be regarded as God's gracious gift to all humankind.

Classical theology has followed the biblical revelation in identifying three main purposes for which God ordained marriage. It has also usually listed them in the order in which they are mentioned in Genesis 1 and 2, while commenting that prior-

157

ity of order does not necessarily signify priority of importance. The first command to the male and female whom God had made in his own image was, 'Be fruitful and increase in number' (Genesis 1.28). So the procreation of children has normally headed the list, though adding their upbringing within the love and discipline of the family.[4]

Secondly, God said ' "It is not good for the man to be alone. I will make a helper suitable for him" ' (Genesis 2.18). Thus God intended marriage (to quote the 1662 Book of Common Prayer again) for 'the mutual society, help and comfort that the one ought to have of the other both in prosperity and in adversity.' Dr. Jack Dominian uses more modern phraseology when he writes that husband and wife can give each other 'sustenance' (supporting and 'cherishing' one another), 'healing' (for married life is the best context in which early childhood hurts may be healed by love), and 'growth' or self-realization (stimulating each other to fulfil their individual potential and so become mature persons).[5]

Thirdly, marriage is intended to be that reciprocal commitment of self-giving love which finds its natural expression in sexual union, or becoming 'one flesh' (Genesis 2.24).

These three purposes have been strengthened by the Fall. The loving discipline of family life has become all the more necessary because of the waywardness of children, mutual support because of the sorrows of a broken world, and sexual union because of temptations to immorality. But all three purposes existed before the Fall and must be seen as part of God's loving provision in the institution of marriage.

The higher our concept of God's original ideal for marriage and the family, the more devastating the experience of divorce is bound to be. A marriage which began with tender love and rich expectations now lies in ruins. Marital breakdown is always a tragedy. It contradicts God's will, frustrates his purpose, brings to husband and wife the acute pains of alienation, disillusion, recrimination, and guilt, and precipitates in any children of the marriage a crisis of bewilderment, insecurity, and often anger.[6]

Changing Attitudes

Yet, in spite of the suffering involved, the number of divorces continues to increase. In 1980 in Britain there were 409,000 marriages (35 percent of which were remarriages) and 159,000 divorces. The previous year it was calculated that a marriage took place every 85 seconds and a divorce every 180. The total number of divorced people in Britain is now over two million, and there is an alarming number of one-parent families. The British divorce rate, which has increased by 600 percent during the last twenty-five years, is now one of the highest in the western world. In the UK one in every three marriages breaks up; in the USA it is more than one in every two.[7]

The sociological reasons for the growth in the divorce rate are many and varied. They include the emancipation of women, changes in the pattern of employment (both parents working), the pressures on family life exerted by unemployment and financial anxiety, and of course the provisions of the civil law for easier divorce. But undoubtedly the greatest single reason is the decline of Christian faith in the West, together with the loss of commitment to a Christian understanding of the sanctity and permanence of marriage, and the growing non-Christian assault on traditional concepts of sex, marriage, and family. A clear indication of secularisation in this area is the fact that, whereas in 1850 only 4 percent of British marriages took place in a Register Office (as opposed to a church, chapel or synagogue), by 1979 the percentage had risen to 51.

Consider as an example of changed attitudes the book by George and Nena O'Neill entitled *Open Marriage: a new lifestyle for couples.* They confidently declare that monogamous marriage is obsolete, and urge their readers to replace an 'archaic, rigid, outmoded, oppressive, static, decaying, Victorian' institution with one that is 'free, dynamic, honest, spontaneous, creative.' They refuse to glorify either traditional marriage or motherhood, and regard partners as equal, independent individuals who enjoy complete and unfettered role reversibility.[8]

In a letter to *The Times* on 14 July 1983 Dr. Jack Dominian expressed his conviction that society is now witnessing 'a profound change in the nature of marriage.' 'The name remains the same,' he wrote, 'but its inner world is changing from being primarily a permanent contract, in which the children and their welfare were its main concern, to a relationship intended to be permanent, in which companionship, equity and personal fulfilment are becoming just as important as the welfare of children.'

Dr. Dominian was too polite to call this shift in perception by its proper name 'selfishness,' but surely that is what it is. If each partner comes to regard marriage as primarily a quest for his or her self-fulfilment, rather than as an adventure in reciprocal self-giving, through which parents and children grow into maturity, the outcome is likely to be bleak. Yet, it is this self-centred attitude to marriage which is being put forward by many today. Here is an unabashed quotation from the book *Divorce: how and when to let go* by John H. Adam and Nancy Williamson Adam (Prentice-Hall, 1979). It appeared in the June 1982 issue of *New Woman*, which claims more than eight million readers: 'Yes, your marriage can wear out. People change their values and lifestyles. People want to experience new things. Change is a part of life. Change and personal growth are traits for you to be proud of, indicative of a vital searching mind. You must accept the reality that in today's multi-faceted world it is especially easy for two persons to grow apart. Letting go of your marriage—if it is no longer good for you—can be the most successful thing you have ever done. Getting a divorce can be a positive, problem-solving, growth-oriented step. It can be a personal triumph.' Here is the secular mind in all its shameless perversity. It celebrates failure as success, disintegration as growth, and disaster as triumph.

Not only is the Christian view of marriage as a lifelong commitment or contract now a minority view in the West, but the church is in danger of giving in to the world. Among Christian people too marriages are no longer as stable as they used to be, and divorces are becoming almost commonplace. Even some Christian leaders divorce their spouse and remarry, the while retaining their position of Christian leadership. In this area also the Christian mind is showing signs of capitulating to secularism.

My concern in this chapter is with the Christian understanding of marriage as set forth in Scripture. Politico-legal issues (like the place of matrimonial offence in the concept of irretrievable breakdown, justice in financial settlements, custody of and access to children) are very important. So are social and psychological questions, some of which I have already mentioned. And I shall come to personal and pastoral matters at the end. But of primary importance for the Christian mind are the biblical questions. Even the painful trauma of a failed marriage cannot be made an excuse for avoiding these.

What has God revealed to be his will in regard to marriage, and the possibility of divorce and remarriage? And how can we frame our policies and practice in accordance with biblical principles? To be sure, there are no easy answers. In particular, the church feels the tension between its prophetic responsibility to bear witness to God's revealed standards and its pastoral responsibility to show compassion to those who have been unable to maintain his standards. John Williams is right to bid us remember that 'the same God who said through Malachi "I hate divorce" (2.16) also said through Hosea (whose partner had been blatantly immoral) "I will heal their waywardness and

love them freely, for my anger has turned away from them"
(14.4).'[9]

Old Testament Teaching

The nearest the Bible comes to a definition of marriage is Genesis 2.24, which Jesus himself was later to quote, when asked about permissible grounds for divorce, as a word of God (Matthew 19.4,5). Immediately after Eve has been created and brought to Adam, and Adam has recognised her (in an outburst of love poetry) as his God-given spouse, the narrator comments: 'For this reason a man will leave his father and mother and be united to his wife, and they will become one flesh.'

From this we may deduce that a marriage exists in God's sight when a man leaves his parents with a view to 'cleaving' to his wife and becomes one flesh with her. The 'leaving' and the 'cleaving' belong together, and should take place in that order. They denote the replacement of one human relationship (child-parent) by another (husband-wife). There are some similarities between these relationships, for both are complex and contain several elements. These are physical (in one case conception, birth, and nurture, in the other sexual intercourse), emotional ('growing up' being the process of growing out of the dependence of childhood into the maturity of partnership), and social (children inheriting an already existent family unit, parents creating a new one). Yet there is an essential dissimilarity between them too. The biblical expression 'one flesh' clearly indicates that the physical, emotional, and social unity of husband and wife is more profoundly and mysteriously personal than the relationship of children to parents. It is increasingly recognised that development as a human being necessitates a measure of emotional separation from parents, and that, as Dr. Dominian has put it, 'the failure to achieve a minimum of emotional independence is one of the main causes of marital breakdown.'[10]

So Genesis 2.24 implies that the marriage union is exclusive ('a man . . . . his wife . . .'), publicly acknowledged ('leaves his parents'), permanent ('cleaves to his wife'), and consummated by sexual intercourse ('become one flesh'). A biblical definition of marriage might then be as follows: 'Marriage is an exclusive heterosexual covenant between one man and one woman, ordained and sealed by God, preceded by a public leaving of parents, consummated in sexual union, issuing in a permanent mutually supportive partnership, and normally crowned by the gift of children.' This is not to affirm that marriage is literally 'indissoluble' in the sense that nothing is able to disrupt it, since divorce (which is a dissolution of the marriage bond) is permissible in certain extreme circumstances, as we shall see. Yet even when permissible, dissolution is always a departure from the divine intention and ideal. In principle, marriage is a lifelong union, what John Murray called 'originally and ideally indissoluble,'[11] and divorce is a breach of covenant, an act of 'treachery,' which God says he 'hates' (Malachi 2.13ff).

This brings us to Deuteronomy 24.1–4, which is of particular importance because it is the only Old Testament passage which refers to grounds or procedures for divorce.

> [1]*If a man marries a woman who becomes displeasing to him because he finds something indecent about her, and he writes her a certificate of divorce, gives it to her and sends her from his house,*[2] *and if after she leaves his house she becomes the wife of another man,*[3] *and her second husband dislikes her and writes her a certificate of divorce, gives it to her and sends her from his house, or if he dies,*[4] *then her first husband, who divorced her, is not allowed to marry her again after she has been defiled. That would be detestable in the eyes of the Lord. Do not bring sin upon the land the Lord your God is giving you as an inheritance.*

The first point to clarify concerns the thrust of this legislation. It neither requires, nor recommends, nor even sanctions divorce. Its primary concern is not with divorce at all, nor even with certificates of divorce. Its object is to forbid a man to re-marry his former spouse, if he has divorced her, since this would be 'detestable in the eyes of the Lord.' It is thought that the purpose of the ruling was to protect the woman from an unpredictable and perhaps cruel former husband. At all events, the first three verses are all the protasis or conditional part of the sentence; the apodosis or consequence does not begin until verse 4. The law is not approving divorce; what it says is that *if* a man divorces his wife, and *if* he gives her a certificate, and *if* she leaves and remarries, and *if* her second husband dislikes and divorces her, or dies, *then* her first husband may not marry her again.

Secondly, although divorce is not encouraged, yet if it happens, the ground on which it takes place is that the husband finds 'something shameful' (NEB, RSV) or 'something indecent' (NIV) in his wife. This cannot refer to adultery on her part, for this was punishable by death, not divorce.[12] So what was it? During the first century B.C. the rival pharisaic parties led by Rabbi Shammai and Rabbi Hillel were debating this very thing. Shammai was strict and understood 'something indecent' (whose Hebrew root alludes to 'nakedness' or 'exposure') as a sexual offence of some kind which, though left undefined, fell short of adultery or promiscuity. Rabbi Hillel, by contrast, was lax. He picked on the phrases that the wife 'becomes displeasing' to her first husband (v.1) or that her second husband 'dislikes' her (v.3). He interpreted them as including even the most trivial misdemeanours, for example, if she spoiled the food she was cooking for him, or was quarrelsome, or if he came across a woman more beautiful than she, and so lost interest in her.[13] In fact, 'anything which caused annoyance or embarrassment to a husband was a legitimate ground for a divorce suit.'[14]

A third point from these Deuteronomy verses, which is note-worthy, is that if divorce was allowed, so evidently was remarriage. The text presupposes that, once the woman had received her certificate of divorce and been sent from the house, she was free to remarry, even though in this case she was the guilty party, having done 'something indecent' on account of which she had been divorced. In fact, so far as is known, the cultures of the ancient world all understood that divorce carried with it the permission to remarry; *divortium a thoro et mensa* (from bed and board), namely a legal separation, without being also *a vinculo matrimonii* (from the marriage bond itself), was not contemplated. Dr. James B. Hurley summarises the marriage and divorce laws of the Code of Hammurabi, who was king of Babylon in the early eighteenth century B.C. when Abraham left Ur, and of the harsher Assyrian laws at the time of Israel's exodus from Egypt.[15] And Dr. Gordon Wenham has added information from the fifth-century B.C. papyri at Elephantine, a small Jewish garrison town in southern Egypt, as well as from Philo, Josephus, and the Greek and Roman worlds.[16] All these cultures supply evidence for divorce by the husband, and in some cases by the wife as well, with liberty to remarry. Usually the divorced wife had her dowry returned to her, and received some divorce money as well. If divorce was comparatively infrequent in the ancient world, it was because the termination of one marriage and the arrangement of a second would have been financially crippling.

The Teaching of Jesus

Our Lord's instruction on marriage and divorce was given in response to a question from the Pharisees. Mark says they posed their question in order to 'test' him (10.2), and Matthew elaborates what the test question was: ' "Is it lawful for a man to divorce his wife for any and every reason?" ' (19.3). Perhaps behind their question was the public scandal of Herodias, who had left her husband Philip in order to marry King Herod Antipas. John the Baptist had courageously denounced their union as 'unlawful' (Mark 6.17ff), and had been imprisoned as a result. Would Jesus be equally outspoken, especially when, as seems probable, he was at the time within the jurisdiction of Herod (Mark 10.1)? Certainly the Pharisees wanted to embroil him in the Shammai-Hillel debate, already mentioned. Hence the emphasis in their question on the 'reasons' or 'causes' which justify divorce.

> [3] *Some Pharisees came to him to test him. They asked, 'Is it lawful for a man to divorce his wife for any and every reason?'* [4] *'Haven't you read,' he replied, 'that at the beginning the Creator "made them male and female,"* [5] *and said, "For this reason a man will leave his father and mother and be united to his wife, and the two will become one flesh"?* [6] *So they are no longer two, but one. Therefore what God has joined together, let man not separate.'* [7] *'Why then,' they asked, 'did Moses command that a man give his wife a certificate of divorce and send her away?'* [8] *Jesus replied, 'Moses permitted you to divorce your wives because your hearts were hard. But it was not this way from the beginning.* [9] *I tell you that anyone who divorces his wife, except for marital unfaithfulness, and marries another woman commits adultery.'* [10] *The disciples said to him, 'If this is the situation between a husband and wife, it is better not to marry.'* [11] *Jesus replied, 'Not everyone can accept this teaching, but only those to whom it has been given.* [12] *For some are eunuchs because they were born that way; others were made that way by men; and others have renounced marriage because of the kingdom of heaven. The one who can accept this should accept it.'*
>
> Matthew 19.3–12

It is clear that Jesus disassociated himself from the laxity of Rabbi Hillel. He had already done so in the Sermon on the Mount. His teaching on divorce in that passage was given as one of his six antitheses, introduced by the formula 'you have heard that it was said . . . but I tell you. . . .' What he was opposing in these antitheses was not Scripture ('it has been written') but tradition ('it has been said'), not the revelation of God but the perverse interpretations of the Scribes. The object of their distortions was to reduce the demands of the law and make them more comfortable. In the divorce antithesis the scribal quotation ('It has been said, "Anyone who divorces his wife must give her a certificate of divorce" ') appears to be a deliberately misleading abbreviation of the Deuteronomy 24 passage. It gives the impression that divorce was readily permissible, even for trivial reasons (as Hillel taught), provided only that a certificate was given. Jesus categorically rejected this. What did he teach?

First, *Jesus endorsed the permanence of marriage.* It is significant that he did not give the Pharisees a direct answer to their question about divorce. Instead, he spoke to them about marriage. He referred them back to Genesis 1 and 2, and asked incredulously if they had not read these chapters. He drew their attention to the two facts that human sexuality was a divine creation and human marriage a divine ordinance, for he bracketed two texts (Genesis 1.27 and 2.24) and made God the author of both. The same Creator who 'at the beginning . . . "made them male and female" ' also said [in the biblical text] 'For this reason a man will leave his father and mother and be united to his wife, and they will become one flesh.' 'So,' Jesus went on, adding his own explanatory assertion, 'they are no longer two, but one.' And 'therefore,' adding his own prohibition, 'what God has joined together [literally, 'yoked together'], let man not separate.'

The teaching is unambiguous. The marriage bond is more than a human contract: it is a divine yoke. And the way in which God lays this yoke upon a married couple is not by creating a kind of mystical union but by declaring his purpose in his Word. Marital breakdown, and even the so-called 'death' of a relationship, cannot then be regarded as being in itself a ground for dissolution, for the basis of the union is not fluctuating human experience ('I love you, I love you not') but the divine will and word (they 'become one flesh').

Secondly, *Jesus declared the Mosaic provision of divorce to be a temporary concession to human sin.* The Pharisees responded to his quotations from Genesis by asking a second question: 'Why then did Moses command that a man give his wife a certificate of divorce and send her away?' To this Jesus replied: 'Moses permitted you to divorce your wives because your hearts were hard. But it was not this way from the beginning.' Thus, what they had termed a 'command' Jesus called a 'permission,' and a reluctant permission at that, due to human stubbornness rather than divine intention.[17]

Since Jesus referred to the Mosaic provision as a concession to human sin, which was also intended to limit its evil effects, it cannot possibly be taken as indicating God's approval of divorce. To be sure, it was a *divine* concession, for according to Jesus whatever Moses said, God said. Yet the divine concession of divorce was contrary to the divine institution of marriage 'from the beginning.' The Rabbis' error lay in ignoring the distinction between God's absolute will (Genesis 1 and 2) and his legal provision for human sinfulness (Deuteronomy 24). 'Human conduct which falls short of the absolute command of God is sin and stands under the divine judgment. The provisions which God's mercy has designed for the limitation of the consequences of man's sin must not be interpreted as divine approval for sinning.'[18]

Thirdly, *Jesus called remarriage after divorce 'adultery.'* Putting together his teaching from the Synoptic Gospels, and leaving aside for the moment the exceptive clause, we may summarize it as follows: a man who divorces his wife, and then remarries, both commits adultery himself[19] and, because it is assumed that his divorced wife will also remarry, causes her to commit adultery as well (Matthew 5:32). A woman who divorces her husband and remarries similarly commits adultery (Mark 10.12). Further, a man (and presumably a woman too, assuming reciprocity in this situation as in others) who marries a divorcee commits adultery.[20] These are hard sayings. They expose with candour the logical consequences of sin. If a divorce and remarriage take place, which have no sanction from God, then any new union which follows, being unlawful, is adulterous.

Fourthly, *Jesus permitted divorce and remarriage on the sole ground of immorality.* It is well known that Matthew 5.32 and 19.9 both contain an 'exceptive clause,' whose purpose is to exempt one category of divorce and remarriage from being branded 'adultery.' Much controversy has raged round this clause. I do not think I can do more than indicate three conclusions which I have reached about it.

1. *The exceptive clause should be accepted as an authentic utterance of Jesus.*

Because it does not occur in the parallel sayings in Mark and Luke, many scholars have been too ready to dismiss it. Some suggest that it was an early scribal interpolation and no part of Matthew's original text. But there is no manuscript evidence that it was a gloss; even the alternative reading of Codex Vaticanus, retained in the RSV margin, does not omit the clause. Other scholars attribute the clause to Matthew himself, and/or to the church in which he was writing, but deny that Jesus ever spoke it. But its omission by Mark and Luke is not in itself a sufficient ground for rejecting it as an editorial invention or interpretation by the first evangelist. It is perfectly possible to suppose that Matthew included it for his Jewish readership who were very concerned about the permissible grounds for divorce, whereas Mark and Luke, writing for Gentile readers, did not have the same concern. Their silence is not necessarily due to their ignorance; it may equally well be that they took the clause for granted. Pagan cultures regarded adultery as a ground for divorce. So did both the Jewish schools of Hillel and Shammai, in spite of their disagreements on other points. This was not in dispute.

2. *The word 'porneia' means sexual immorality.*

In deciding how to translate *porneia*, we need to avoid both extremes of too much laxity and too much rigidity. Several 'rigid' views have been held, which identifty *porneia* as one particular sexual sin—either fornication in the sense of the discovery of premarital immorality, or a marriage within the prohibited degrees, or postmarriage adultery. The main reason for rejecting any of these translations is that, although *porneia* could mean all of them, it would not be understood as referring to any one of them if there were no further qualification. *Porneia* was, in fact, a generic word for sexual infidelity or 'marital unfaithfulness' (NIV) and included, 'every kind of unlawful sexual intercourse' (Arndt-Gingrich).

The 'lax' view is that *porneia* includes offences which may be regarded as 'sexual' not in physical terms, but because they undermine the foundations of married unity, for example cruelty, and even a basic temperamental incompatibility. It may be possible to use other arguments for the legitimacy of divorce on such grounds as these, but it is not possible to do so from the meaning of the word *porneia*. *Porneia* means physical sexual immorality; the reason why Jesus made it the sole permissible ground for divorce must be that it violates the 'one flesh' principle which is foundational to marriage as divinely ordained and biblically defined.

3. *Divorce for immorality is permissible, not mandatory.*

Jesus did not teach that the innocent party *must* divorce an unfaithful partner, still less that sexual unfaithfulness *ipso facto* dissolves the marriage. He did not even encourage or recommend divorce for unfaithfulness. On the contrary, his whole emphasis was on the permanence of marriage in God's purpose and on the inadmissibility of divorce and remarriage. His reason for adding the exceptive clause was to clarify that the only divorce and remarriage which is not tantamount to adultery is that of an innocent person whose partner has been unfaithful, for in this case the unfaithfulness has already been committed by the guilty partner. Jesus' purpose was emphatically not to encourage divorce for this reason, but rather to forbid it for every other reason. As John Murray wrote: 'It is the *one* exception that gives prominence to the illegitimacy of every other reason. Preoccupation with the one exception should never be permitted to obscure the force of the negation of all others.'[21]

At this point I need to mention the extreme view which has been plausibly argued by Dr. Gordon Wenham in the *Third Way* articles already mentioned. He believes that Jesus' exceptive clause permitted divorce in the sense of separation, but that he forbade all remarriage. He bases his case on two main arguments. First, that for five centuries (with the sole exception of Ambrosiaster in the fourth century) the church fathers denied all right of remarriage after divorce, insisting that nothing can dissolve marriage except death, and that this remained the standard position of the western Church until Erasmus defended the innocent party's right to remarry after divorce, and the Protestant Reformers followed him. Secondly, Gordon Wenham argues that only such a total ban on remarriage can account for the astonishment of the disciples. Their response was, 'If this is the situation between a husband and wife, it is better not to marry' (Matthew 19.10). Moreover, Jesus replied to this by referring to three kinds of 'eunuch,' meaning 'celibate.'

Dr. Wenham's case is strong but not conclusive. First, the early church fathers could have been mistaken in this matter, as they were in others. Secondly, the statement in Matthew 5.32 that a husband who illegitimately divorces his wife, 'causes her to commit adultery' can be true only if after the divorce she re-marries. Thirdly, the disciples' astonishment leading to the teaching on celibacy could have had another cause. Their perception must certainly have been of the strictness of Jesus. Not only did he reject the trivial laxity of the Hillel school, but also Shammai's interpretation, and indeed Moses' own reference to 'something indecent,' as being too imprecise. Only sexual infidelity could be admitted as a ground for breaking the marriage bond. This had been clearly recognised in the Old Testament because it was punishable by death. But the death sentence for adultery had fallen into disuse, and in any case the Romans did not permit the Jews to administer it. So when Joseph suspected Mary of unfaithfulness, he thought of divorce, not death (Matthew 1.18f). And Jesus refused to be trapped by those who asked if the woman caught in adultery should be stoned (John 8.3ff). It seems, then, that he abrogated the death penalty for sexual infidelity, and made this the only legitimate ground for dissolving the marriage bond, by divorce not death, and then only as a permission. The original creation ordinance of a life-long union is the better way, and will be accepted by citizens of his kingdom. James B. Hurley sums it up well:

> We can now see why the disciples were so surprised at Jesus' teaching. He was far stricter than the rabbis. He disallowed divorce for all of the reasons which had been adduced in connection with Deuteronomy 24.1, and permitted it only on grounds which were unknown in the Old Testament. He permitted it only for sexual violations of the marriage bond, violations which, under the Old Testament, would have meant a death sentence. According to Jesus only illicit sexual relations (porneia: adultery, homo-sexuality, bestiality) provide reason to terminate a marriage.[22]

The Teaching of Paul

The teaching of Paul which we have to consider occurs in 1 Corinthians 7.10–16, and concerns in particular the so-called 'Pauline privilege':

¹⁰ To the married I give this command (not I, but the Lord): A wife must not separate from her husband. ¹¹ But if she does, she must remain unmarried or else be reconciled to her husband. And a husband must not divorce his wife.

¹² To the rest I say this (I, not the Lord): If any brother has a wife who is not a believer and she is willing to live with him, he must not divorce her. ¹³ And if a woman has a husband who is not a believer and he is willing to live with her, she must not divorce him. ¹⁴ For the unbelieving husband has been sanctified through his wife, and the unbelieving wife has been sanctified through her believing husband. Otherwise your children would be unclean, but as it is, they are holy.

¹⁵ But if the unbeliever leaves, let him do so. A believing man or woman is not bound in such circumstances: God has called us to live in peace. ¹⁶ How do you know, wife, whether you will save your husband? Or, how do you know, husband, whether you will save your wife?

We need to observe, first, that *Paul is giving authoritative, apostolic instruction.* The antithesis he makes between verse 10 ('I give this command [not I but the Lord])' and verse 12 ('To the rest I say this [I, not the Lord])' has been much misunderstood. It is quite mistaken to imagine that he is setting Christ's teaching and his own in opposition to each other, with the further implication that Christ's has authority, whereas his has not. No, his contrast is not between divine, infallible teaching (Christ's) and human, fallible teaching (his own), but between two forms of divine and infallible teaching, the one dominical (the Lord's) and the other apostolic (his own). There can be no doubt that this is correct, for Paul continues to use the authoritative apostolic *ego* 'I' in this chapter, in verse 17 ('this is the rule I lay down in all the churches'), verse 25 ('I have no command from the Lord,' i.e. no recorded saying of Jesus, 'but I give a judgment as one who by the Lord's mercy is trustworthy') and verse 40 ('I think that I too have the Spirit of God'). Later and similarly, he puts his authority above that of prophets and declares his instruction to be the Lord's command: 'If anybody thinks he is a prophet or spiritually gifted, let him acknowledge that what I am writing to you is the Lord's command' (14.37).

Secondly, *Paul echoes and confirms Jesus' prohibition of divorce*. In verses 10 and 11, as in his teaching in Romans 7.1–3, and as in the Lord's teaching recorded by Mark and Luke, the prohibition of divorce is stated in absolute terms. 'A wife must not separate from her husband. . . . And a husband must not divorce his wife.' This is because he is expressing the general principle. It is not necessary to suppose that he knew nothing of the Lord's exceptive clause.

In verse 11 he adds an important parenthesis to the effect that if a wife does separate from her husband, 'she must remain unmarried or else be reconciled to her husband.' The verb Paul uses for separate (*chōrizo*) could refer to divorce and was so used both in marriage contracts in the papyri and by some early church fathers (Arndt-Gingrich). But the context suggests that Paul is not referring to divorce. He seems rather to be envisaging a situation in which the husband has not been sexually unfaithful and the wife is therefore not at liberty to divorce him. Some other reason (unstated) has prompted her to 'separate' from him. So Paul emphasises that in this case she is not free to remarry. Her Christian calling is either to remain single or to be reconciled to her husband, but not to remarry.

Thirdly, *Paul permits divorce on the desertion of an unbelieving partner*. He addresses three successive paragraphs 'to the unmarried and the widows' (vv. 8, 9), 'to the married' (vv. 10, 11), and 'to the rest' (vv. 12–16). The context reveals that by 'the rest' he has in mind a particular kind of mixed marriage. He gives no liberty to a Christian to marry a non-Christian, for a Christian woman 'is free to marry anyone she wishes, but he must belong to the Lord' (v. 39). And the converse is equally true of Christian men (2 Corinthians 6.14ff). Paul is rather handling the situation which arises when two non-Christians marry, one of whom is subsequently converted. The Corinthians had evidently sent him questions about this. Was the marriage unclean? Should the Christian partner divorce the non-Christian? What was the status of the children? Paul's reply is clear.

If the unbelieving partner 'is willing to live with' the believing, then the believer must not resort to divorce. The reason given is that the unbelieving partner 'has been sanctified' through his or her believing spouse, and so have the children. The 'sanctification' in mind is clearly not a transformation of character into the likeness of Christ. As John Murray puts it, 'the sanctification of which Paul speaks ... must be the sanctification of privilege, connection and relationship.'[23]

But if, on the other hand, the unbelieving partner is unwilling to stay, and decides to leave, then 'let him do so. A believing man or woman is not bound in such circumstances.' The reasons given are that God has called us to live in peace, and that the believer cannot guarantee to win the unbeliever by insisting on perpetuating a union which the unbeliever is not willing to continue.

It is important to grasp the precise situation which the apostle envisages, and not to draw unwarrantable deductions from his teaching. He affirms that, if the unbeliever refuses to stay, the believer 'is not bound,' that is, bound to hold on to him or her, indeed, bound to the marriage itself.[24] Several negative points need to be made about the freedom which the believing partner is here given.

1. The believer's freedom is not due to his or her conversion, but rather to the partner's nonconversion and unwillingness to remain. Christians sometimes plead for what they call 'gospel realism,' arguing that because conversion makes all things new, a marriage contracted in preconversion days is not necessarily still binding, and in its place a new beginning may be made.

This is dangerous reasoning, however. Are all preconversion contracts cancelled by conversion, including all one's debts? No, Paul's teaching lends no possible support to such a view. On the contrary, he contradicts it. His teaching is not that after conversion the believing partner is defiled by the unbeliever, and should therefore extricate himself from the relationship. It is the opposite, that the unbelieving partner has been 'sanctified' by the believer, and that therefore the believer should not seek to escape. Further, Paul urges in verses 17–24 that Christians should remain in the state in which they were when God called them, and that we are able to do so because now we are there 'with God.'

2. The believer's freedom is not due to any resolve of his own to begin divorce proceedings, but only to his reluctant acquiescence in his partner's 'desertion,' or unwillingness to stay. The initiative must not be the believer's. On the contrary, if the unbelieving partner is willing to remain, 'he must not divorce her' and 'she must not divorce him' (vv. 12, 13). The furthest Paul goes is to say that if the unbeliever insists on leaving, 'let him do so' (v. 15).

3. The believer's freedom is not due to 'desertion' of any and every kind, nor to desertion for any form of unbelief (e.g. the Roman Catholic Church's view that marriage is not *ratum* if a partner is unbaptised), but only to the specific unwillingness of an unconverted person on religious grounds to continue living with his or her now converted partner. The 'Pauline privilege' provides no basis, therefore, for divorce on the ground of desertion; this is not a Christian option.

Summing up what Scripture teaches in the passages so far considered, we may make the following three affirmations:

1. God created man male and female in the beginning, and himself instituted marriage. His intention was and is that

human sexuality will find fulfilment in marriage, and that marriage will be an exclusive, loving, and lifelong union. This is his ideal.

2. Divorce is nowhere commanded, and never even encouraged, in Scripture. On the contrary, even if biblically justified, it remains a sad and sinful declension from the divine ideal.

3. Divorce and remarriage are permissible (not mandatory) on two grounds. First, an innocent person may divorce his or her partner if the latter has been guilty of serious sexual immorality. Secondly, a believer may acquiesce in the desertion of his or her unbelieving partner, if the latter refuses to go on living with him or her. In both cases, however, the permission is given in negative or reluctant terms. Only if a person divorces his partner on the ground of marital unfaithfulness is his remarriage not adulterous. Only if the unbeliever insists on leaving, is the believer 'not bound.'

The Covenant Principle

An earlier and shorter version of what I have written above appeared in *Churchman* in the autumn of 1971 and was published the following year as a Falcon booklet. My position was criticised by Dr. David Atkinson in his book *To Have and To Hold* (1979). He called it 'legislative' and expressed his uneasiness in the following terms: 'The difficulty with this view is that in pastoral practice it *can* lead to the sort of casuistry which can become negatively legalistic. It concentrates on physical adultery but neglects other "unfaithfulness," and can mean that the Church's blessing for second marriage is reserved only for those who are fortunate (!) enough to have had their former partner commit adultery against them. It raises the question as to what breaks the marriage bond.'[25]

It is, indeed, because of the practical problems which beset us when we insist on a 'matrimonial offence' as the only legitimate ground for divorce, that an alternative and more flexible approach has been sought. The Church of England report *Putting Asunder* (1966) recommended the concept of 'irretrievable breakdown' as an alternative, and the 1969 Divorce Reform Act was based upon it. Then the Church of England Commission which was presided over by Canon Professor Howard Root, and which reported in *Marriage, Divorce and The Church* (SPCK, 1971), investigated further the concept that some marriages do in fact 'die' even while both married partners are still alive. And a few years later the Commission chaired by Bishop Kenneth Skelton of Lichfield, which reported in *Marriage and the Church's Task* (CIO, 1978), took a similar line. Can some biblical basis be found for this abandonment of the 'matrimonial offence' as the ground for divorce?

It is clear that Scripture regards marriage as a covenant, indeed—although between two human beings—as a 'covenant of God' (Proverbs 2.17 literally), instituted and witnessed by him. In a letter which I received some years ago Roger Beckwith, Warden of Latimer House, summarised what he saw to be the five terms of the marriage covenant: (1) Love (as in every covenant), but married love involving specific obligations; (2) living together as a single household and family; (3) faithfulness to the marriage bed; (4) provision for the wife by the husband; and (5) submission to the husband by the wife. He suggested further that if one of these five fundamental terms of the marriage covenant is violated, the injured party is similarly released from his own undertakings.

In David Atkinson's book *To Have and To Hold,* subtitled 'the Marriage Covenant and the Discipline of Divorce,' he develops the covenant idea further. He defines a covenant as 'an agreement between parties based on promise, which includes these four elements: (1) an undertaking of committed faithfulness made by one party to the other (or by each to the other); (2) the acceptance of that undertaking by the other party; (3) public knowledge of such an undertaking and its acceptance; and (4) the growth of a personal relationship based on and expressive of such a commitment.'[26] It is not difficult to apply such a definition of 'covenant' to marriage, especially because human marriage is used in Scripture as a model of God's covenant with his people, and God's covenant as a model for human marriage.[27] David Atkinson goes on to quote Professor G.R. Dunstan's development of this analogy, in that God's covenant and human marriage both have (1) an *initiative of love*, inviting a response, and so creating a relationship, (2) a *vow of consent*, guarding the union against the fitfulness of emotion, (3) *obligations of faithfulness*, (4) the *promising of blessing* to those who are faithful to their covenant obligations, and (5) *sacrifice*, the laying down of life in death, especially in this case death to the old independence and self-centredness.[28]

David Atkinson goes on to argue that 'the covenant structure of marriage lends weight to the view . . . that marriage is not a metaphysical status which cannot be destroyed; it is rather a moral commitment which should be honoured.'[29] Yet a covenant can be broken. 'Covenants do not just "break down," ' however, 'they are broken; divorce expresses sin as well as tragedy.' So then 'from a biblical moral perspective, we cannot dissolve the category of "matrimonial offence" without remainder into the less personally focused concept of "irretrievable breakdown." '[30] Instead, 'the covenant model for marriage places the question of divorce in the area of moral responsibility.[31] And his conclusion is that 'any action which constitutes unfaithfulness to the marriage covenant so persistent and unrepentant that reconciliation becomes impossible may be sufficient to break the bond of marriage and so may release the other partner from their covenant promise.'[32]

There is much in the covenant model of marriage which is compelling. To begin with, it is a thoroughly biblical notion. It also emphasises the great solemnity both of covenant making and of covenant breaking—in the former case emphasising love, commitment, public recognition, exclusive faithfulness, and sacrifice, and in the latter the sin of going back on promises and rupturing a relationship of love. I confess, however, that my problem is how to fuse the two concepts of covenant loyalty and matrimonial offence. I can understand the reasons for not wanting to build permission to divorce on two offences. But if Scripture regards the marriage covenant as capable of being broken in several ways, how shall we explain the single offence mentioned in our Lord's exceptive clause? Certainly the covenant relationship envisaged in marriage (the 'one flesh' union) is far deeper than other covenants, whether a suzerainty treaty, a business deal or even a pact of friendship. May it not be, therefore, that nothing less than a violation (by sexual infidelity) of this fundamental relationship can break the marriage covenant?

God's marriage covenant with 'Jerusalem' (personifying his people), described at length in Ezekiel 16, is germane to this issue. God says to her: 'I gave you my solemn oath and entered into a covenant with you. . . , and you became mine' (v.8). But Jerusalem 'played the harlot,' or rather (because she gave hire rather than receiving it), was a wife guilty of promiscuous adultery (vv. 15–34). Therefore, God said he would sentence her to 'the punishment of women who commit adultery . . .' (v. 38). Nevertheless, although her behaviour was worse even than her 'younger sister . . . Sodom' (vv. 46–52), and although she had despised God's oath 'by breaking the covenant' (v. 59), yet God said: 'I will remember the covenant I made with you in the days of your youth, and I will establish an everlasting covenant with you' (v. 60), bringing forgiveness and penitence.

It seems to me that we must allow these perspectives of God's covenant to shape our understanding of the marriage covenant. The marriage covenant is not an ordinary human contract which, if one party to it reneges, may be renounced by the other. It is more like God's covenant with his people. In this analogy (which Scripture develops) only fundamental sexual unfaithfulness breaks the covenant. And even this does not lead automatically or necessarily to divorce; it may rather be an occasion for reconciliation and forgiveness.

Personal and Pastoral Realities

This has been a long chapter. Some readers will have been provoked by it, finding it drily academic, or unfeeling towards the profound sufferings of those whose marriages break down, or remote from the realities of the contemporary Western world, or all three. I can understand their reactions. Yet it has been necessary to give the biblical material a thorough examination. For this book is about developing a Christian mind on current issues. Conscientious disciples of Jesus know that Christian action is impossible without Christian thought; they resist the temptation to take short cuts. At the same time, the process of 'making up one's mind' means reaching a decision which has practical consequences. What then are these likely to be? Because of the great seriousness with which Scripture views both marriage and divorce, I conclude with four urgent pastoral needs.

First, there is *the need for thorough biblical teaching about marriage and reconciliation.* Pastors must give positive instruction on both these subjects. In sermons, Sunday School and Confirmation classes we have to hold before the congregation we serve the divine intention and ideal of exclusive, committed, lifelong faithfulness in marriage. We ought also to give clear and practical teaching on the duty and the way of forgiveness, for reconciliation lies at the very heart of Christianity. For some years now I have followed a simple rule, that whenever anybody asks me a question about divorce, I refuse to answer it until I have first talked about two other subjects, namely, marriage and reconciliation. This is a simple attempt to follow Jesus in his own priorities. When the Pharisees asked him about the grounds for divorce, he referred them instead to the original institution of marriage. If we allow ourselves to become preoccupied with divorce and its grounds, rather than marriage and its ideals, we lapse into pharisaism. God's purpose is marriage not divorce, and his gospel is good news of reconciliation. We need to see Scripture as a whole, and never isolate the topic of divorce.

Secondly, there is *the need for preparation for marriage*. Couples preparing for marriage usually cherish high ideals for the future, and are ready, even anxious, for help. Yet hard-pressed clergy can often manage to give each couple no more than a single interview during which time legal and social questions sometimes crowd out the spiritual and moral dimensions of marriage. Some clergy arrange courses for groups of engaged couples. Others give couples a book or a short annotated list of recommended reading. Best of all, perhaps, is the resolve to harness the services of mature lay couples in the congregation, who would be willing to spend several evenings with an engaged couple, meet them again after the wedding, and continue to keep in touch with them during the early days of adjustment.

Thirdly, there is *the need for a reconciliation service*. In the UK probation officers appear to be more involved than anybody else in married couples and families who need help. Then there are voluntary organisations like the National Marriage Guidance Council, the Catholic Marriage Advisory Council, and the Family Discussion Bureau. I wish the churches were yet more actively involved in this ministry, especially at the local level. Christians are supposed to be in the reconciliation business. Many more people would seek help, and seek it *early* when it is most needed, if they knew where they could turn for sympathy, understanding, and advice. Sometimes expert marital therapy will be necessary, but at other times a listening ear may be enough. As Dr. Jack Dominian writes, 'marital reconciliation ultimately depends on the ability of the spouses to change sufficiently to meet each other's minimal needs.'[33] But a friend can often be the catalyst to help people see the need for change and want it.

American Christians are in advance of Britain in this area. Partly as a result of the current epidemic of suing (in 1982, 22,000 lawsuits were being filed every day), the Christian Legal Society took the initiative in 1977 to set up 'the Christian Conciliation Service.' Responding to Christ's call to his followers to be peacemakers, to his teaching in Matthew 18.15–17 and to Paul's in 1 Corinthians 6.1–8, they are seeking to resolve conflicts and settle disputes (in business, marriage, and other fields) out of court. So they offer mediation, reconciliation, and (if these fail) arbitration, as alternatives to the adversarial approach of the civil courts.[34]

Fourthly, there is *the need for pastoral ministry to the divorced*. Because marriage is a 'creation ordinance,' God's purposes for it do not vary; they are the same for the world as for the church. The non-Christian world will often be unable and unwilling to fulfil them because of the hardness of human hearts, and so is likely to have its own legislation for divorce. It is right, however, to expect higher standards in the new community of Jesus. He repeatedly told his followers not to follow the way of the world. 'It shall not be so among you,' he said. In marriage, therefore, the church's calling is not to conform to popular trends, but to bear witness to God's purpose of permanence.

Nevertheless, 'hardness of heart' is not confined to the non-Christian world. As with the Old Testament people of God, so with the people of the New Covenant, some concession to human fallibility and failure will be needed, and each church or denomination will have to make its own regulations. The sustained policy of the Church of England for several decades has been to refuse to marry in church any person who has a previous spouse still living, while at the same time seeking to offer a ministry of pastoral compassion and care to those who have been divorced. In 1981, however, reversing a vote taken in 1978, the General Synod resolved that 'there are circumstances in which a divorced person may be married in church during the lifetime of a former partner.' So means are now being sought by which some divorced people may be married in church. This seems right, for if Jesus and his apostle Paul did allow divorce and remarriage in certain circumstances, then this permission of a new beginning needs what Professor Oliver O'Donovan has called 'institutional visibility.'[35]

What 'institutional arrangements' should the church make? Professor O'Donovan continues: 'The primary question is how it may find *some* arrangement that will give adequate form both to its beliefs about the permanence of marriage and to its beliefs about the forgiveness of the penitent sinner.'[36] It could express the ambivalence either by permitting the remarriage in church (emphasising the gospel of redemption), while adding some kind of discipline (recognising God's marriage ideal), or by refusing the remarriage in church (emphasising the ideal,) while adding some expression of acceptance (recognising the gospel). I myself incline to the former. But before any church service for the marriage of a divorced person is permitted, the church must surely exemplify its adherence to the revelation of God in two ways. It must satisfy itself first that the remarriage comes within the range of the biblical permissions, and secondly that the couple concerned accept the divine ideal of marriage permanence.

In this case the church service could not with integrity be identical with a normal marriage ceremony. Some expression of penitence should be included, either in private preliminary to the ceremony or in the public service itself. Either way would be an acknowledgment that every divorce, even when biblically permissible, is a declension from the divine ideal. This is not to stand in judgment on the people concerned in any proud or paternalistic way; it is rather to confess the universal taint of sin, in which we ourselves, as well as they, are personally involved.

In all this we continue to be caught in the tension between law and grace, witness and compassion, prophetic ministry and pastoral care. On the one hand, we need the courage to resist the prevailing winds of permissiveness and to set ourselves to uphold marriage and oppose divorce. The state will continue to frame its own divorce laws, and the church may have been right to propose the 'irretrievable breakdown' concept as the least unsatisfactory basis for legislation in a secular society. But the church also has its own witness to bear to the teaching of its divine Lord, and must exercise its own discipline.

On the other hand, we shall seek to share with deep compassion in the suffering of those whose marriage has failed, and especially of those whom we cannot conscientiously advise to seek an escape by divorce. We may on occasion feel at liberty to advise the legitimacy of a separation without a divorce, or even a divorce without a remarriage, taking 1 Corinthians 7.11 as our warrant. But we have no liberty to go beyond the permissions of our Lord. He knew his Father's will and cared for his disciples' welfare. Wisdom, righteousness, and compassion are found in following him.

Chapter Seven

The Abortion Dilemma

THE DEBATE OVER ABORTION IS ADMITTEDLY COMPLEX. IT HAS MED-
ical, legal, theological, ethical, social, and personal aspects. It is
also a highly emotional subject, for it touches on the mysteries
of human sexuality and reproduction, and often involves
acutely painful dilemmas.

Yet Christians cannot opt out of personal decision making or
public discussion regarding this topic merely because of its
complexity. Instead, two factors should bring it to the top of our
agenda.

First, what is involved in the abortion issue is nothing less
than our Christian doctrines of both God and man, or, more
precisely, the sovereignty of God and the sanctity of human life.
All Christian people believe that Almighty God is the only
giver, sustainer and taker-away of life. On the one hand 'he
himself gives all men life and breath and everything else,' and
'in him we live and move and have our being.' On the other, as
the psalmist says to God, 'when you take away their breath,
they die and return to the dust.' Indeed, whenever anybody
dies, Christian faith struggles to affirm with Job: 'The Lord gave
and the Lord has taken away; may the name of the Lord be
praised.'[1] To the Christian, then, both life-giving and life-taking

are divine prerogatives. And although we cannot interpret 'you shall not kill' as an absolute prohibition, since the same law which forbade killing also sanctioned it in some situations (e.g. capital punishment and holy war), yet the taking of human life is a divine prerogative which is permitted to human beings only by specific divine mandate. Without this, to terminate human life is the height of arrogance. Hence Mother Teresa's strong feelings about the evil of abortion:

> . . . only God can decide life and death. . . . That is why abortion is such a terrible sin. You are not only killing life, but putting self before God; yet people decide who has to live and who has to die. They want to make themselves almighty God. They want to take the power of God in their hands. They want to say, 'I can do without God. I can decide.' That is the most devilish thing that a human hand can do . . .'[2]

Next, the question of abortion concerns our doctrine of man as well as of God. For, however undeveloped the embryo may still be, everybody agrees that it is living and human. And in whatever way we decide to formulate the relationship between newborn and unborn children, our evaluation of human being is inevitably involved. Therefore the present practice of almost indiscriminate abortion reflects a rejection of the biblical view of human dignity. This aspect of the situation most concerned Francis Schaeffer and Everett Koop in their book and film *Whatever Happened to the Human Race?*, which related to infanticide and euthanasia as well as abortion. They rightly traced 'the erosion of the sanctity of human life' to 'the loss of the Christian consensus.'[3]

So then, if both divine sovereignty and human dignity are being challenged by the abortion debate, no conscientious Christian can stand aside from it.

The Revolution in Public Attitudes

The second reason for taking the issue seriously concerns the revolution which has recently taken place in public attitudes. Whether or not doctors have actually subscribed to the ancient Hippocratic Oath (fifth century B.C.), it has been generally assumed that they took its main undertakings for granted:

> I will follow that method of treatment which, according to my ability and judgment, I consider for the benefit of my patients, and abstain from whatever is deleterious and mischievous. I will give no deadly drug to anyone if asked, nor suggest any such counsel; and in like manner I will not give to a woman a pessary to procure abortion.

Since some other clauses of the Oath are decidedly antiquated, the Declaration of Geneva (1948) updated it, while at the same time taking care to include the promise: 'I will maintain the utmost respect for human life from the time of conception.'

One would not necessarily expect a country like Japan, whose Christian population numbers less than 1 percent, to reflect a biblical view of the sanctity of human life (although of course the Buddhist tradition professes all life to be sacred). So we are not altogether surprised by the statistics which followed their liberalisation of abortion legislation in 1948. In the first eight years no fewer than five million abortions were performed, and in the year 1972 the number had increased to one and a half millions annually.[4]

But in the West, the heir of many centuries of Christian tradition, one's expectations are naturally higher. In England abortion remained illegal until the Infant Life (Preservation) Act of 1929 provided that no action would be punishable 'when done in good faith with the intention of saving the life of the mother.' David Steel's 1967 Abortion Act appeared to many to be only a cautious extension of this. Two registered medical practitioners were required to express their opinion, 'formed in good faith,' that the continuance of the pregnancy would involve either (1) risk to the life of the pregnant woman, or (2 and 3) risk of injury to her or her existing children's physical or mental health, 'greater than if the pregnancy were terminated,' or (4) 'substantial risk that if the child were born it would suffer from such physical or mental abnormalities as to be seriously handicapped.'

Whatever the intentions were of the Abortion Law Reform Association (who masterminded the bill), it seems clear that its catastrophic consequences were not foreseen by its parliamentary sponsors. Before the Act became law, the number of legal abortions carried out annually in the hospitals of the National Health Service in England and Wales crept up slowly to 6,100 (1966).[5] In 1968, however, the number was already 24,000, and the peak of 167,000 was reached in 1973.[6] By 1983 over two million legal abortions had been performed since the 1967 Act was passed.

The situation in the United States is even worse. In 1970 a Texas lady (who used the pseudonym Jane Roe) became pregnant and decided to fight the antiabortion legislation of her state. She took Henry Wade, the Dallas district attorney, to court. In January 1973 in the now notorious *Roe v. Wade* case, the United States Supreme Court declared by 7 votes to 2 that the Texas law was unconstitutional.[7] Its judgment inhibited all regulation of abortion during the first three months of pregnancy, and during the second and third trimesters regulated it only in relation to the mother's physical or mental health. This ruling implicitly permitted abortion on demand at every stage of pregnancy. The number of legal abortions in the United States in 1969 was less than 20,000. In 1975 it passed the million mark, and in 1980 had reached more than one and a half millions. This means that in 1980 for every 1000 'births' (natural and induced) in the United States, 300 were abortions. In fact, over 4,250 babies are aborted daily, 177 hourly, or three every minute. In Washington D.C., the nation's capital, abortions now outnumber live births by three to one.[8]

The total number of legal and illegal abortions throughout the world was estimated in 1968 at between thirty and thirty-five millions.[9] It must have increased further by now.

These figures are so staggering as to defy the imagination. I do not think Francis Schaeffer and Everett Koop are exaggerating when they write of 'The Slaughter of the Innocents,' or John Powell, S.J. when he entitles his moving book *Abortion: The Silent Holocaust*.[10] To make his point yet more forcefully, he introduces his book with a chart of 'war casualties,' on which each cross represents 50,000 American combatants killed. The Korean and Vietnam wars have only one cross each. World War I has two and a half, and World War II eleven. But 'the War on the Unborn' has no fewer than 240 crosses, representing the 12 million legal American abortions up to the beginning of 1981.

Any society which can tolerate these things, let alone legislate for them, has ceased to be civilised. One of the major signs of decadence in the Roman Empire was that its unwanted babies were 'exposed,' that is, abandoned and left to die. Can we claim that contemporary western society is any less decadent because it consigns its unwanted babies to the hospital incinerator instead of the local rubbish dump? Indeed modern abortion is even worse than ancient exposure in this respect that it has been commercialised, and has become, at least for some doctors and clinics, an extremely lucrative practice.[11] But reverence for human life is an indispensable characteristic of a humane and civilised society.

The Key Issue

Those who campaign for a lax policy on abortion, and those who campaign for a strict one, begin their argument from opposite positions.

Proabortionists emphasise the rights of the mother, and especially her right to choose; antiabortionists emphasise the rights of the unborn child, and especially his or her right to live. The first see abortion as little more than a retroactive contraceptive, the second as little less than prenatal infanticide. The appeal of proabortionists is usually to compassion (though also to the justice of what they see as a woman's rights); they cite situations in which the mother and/or the rest of the existing family would suffer intolerable strain if an unwanted pregnancy were allowed to come to term. The appeal of antiabortionists is usually also and especially to justice; they stress the need to defend the rights of the unborn child who is unable to defend himself.

Those who oppose easy abortion are not lacking in compassion, however. They recognise the hardships, and even tragedies, which the arrival of an unplanned baby often brings. For example, an expectant mother is already worn out by a large and demanding family. Their home is already over-crowded and their budget over-stretched. It would be financially crippling to have another mouth to feed. The family simply could not cope with another child. Or the mother is herself the wage-earner (because she is widowed or divorced, or her husband is sick or unemployed); to have another child would ruin the family. Or the husband is violent or cruel, perhaps an alcoholic or even a psychopath, and his wife dare not allow another child to come under his influence. Or she is unmarried and feels she cannot face either the stigma or the disadvantage which she and her child would have to endure in a single-parent family. Or she is a schoolgirl or student, and a continued pregnancy would interfere with her education and her career. Or perhaps her pregnancy is due to adultery or incest or rape, and these tragedies are great enough in themselves without adding to them an unplanned, unwanted child. Or she has contracted rubella, or had a prenatal scan, and fears that her child will be a mongol or defective in some other way.

All these cases, and many more, cause great personal suffering, and arouse our sincere Christian compassion. It is easy to understand why some women in such situations opt for the abortion which seems to them the only escape, and why some doctors interpret the law as liberally as they can, in order to justify one.

But Christians who confess Jesus as Lord, and who desire to live under the authority of his truth, justice, and compassion, can never be pure pragmatists. We have to ask ourselves what principles are involved. Our compassion needs both theological and moral guidelines. If it is expressed at the expense of truth or justice, it ceases to be genuine compassion.

The key issue, then, is a moral and theological one. It concerns the nature of the fetus (*fetus* is Latin for 'offspring'). How are we to think of the embryo in the mother's womb? Our evaluation of the fetus will largely determine our attitude to abortion. Furthermore, although other questions of principle are involved in genetic engineering, *in vitro* fertilisation, and embryo experimentation, and I am not intending to address these issues in this chapter, yet in these areas too the main question is the same: what is the status before God of a fertilised ovum, whether in the womb or in a test tube?

We reject as totally false and utterly abhorrent the notion that the fetus is merely a lump of jelly or blob of tissue, or a growth in the mother's womb, which may therefore be extracted and destroyed like teeth, tumours or tonsils. Yet some appear to adopt this extreme position. For example, K. Hindell and Madelaine Simms (pro-abortion campaigners) have written that 'medically and legally the embryo and fetus are merely parts of the mother's body, and not yet human.'[12] Such people insist that the fetus belongs to the woman who bears it; that it cannot be regarded as in any sense independent of her or as human in its own right; that to have it removed is no more significant than the surgical removal of some other unwanted tissue; and that the decision to abort or not to abort rests entirely with the woman. Since it is her body, it is also her choice. Nobody else (and certainly no man, feminists would add) has any say in the matter. A liberated woman cannot be forced to bear a child; she has absolute control over her own reproductive powers and processes.

After a mass rally in Hyde Park, arranged by the Society for the Protection of Unborn Children in June 1983, we were walking to 10 Downing Street, in order to present a petition to the Prime Minister, when at the top of Whitehall a group of young women started chanting—

> Not the Church, not the State,
> Let the woman decide her fate.

I went over to talk to them, and quietly remonstrated that it was not the woman's fate we were concerned about in our rally and march, so much as her unborn child's. Their only reply was to shout unprintable obscenities at me, and to make the rather obvious point that I would not be able to give birth to a child in a million years. I am not saying that they were wholly wrong, for I recognise that abortion is more a woman's issue than a man's. It is she who has been made pregnant, perhaps without her consent, who has to bear the pregnancy, and who will carry the burden of early child care. It is all too easy for a man to forget these facts. Nevertheless, her child has independent rights both before and after birth, and it is these rights which those young women in Whitehall did not acknowledge.

That an embryo, though carried within the mother's body, is nevertheless not a part of it, is not only a theological but a physiological fact. This is partly because the child has a genotype distinct from the mother's, but also because the whole process of gestation, from ovulation to birth, may be seen as a kind of 'expulsion' of the child with a view to its ultimate independence.

A second group of people seek the decisive moment of the

embryo's 'humanisation' at some point between conception and birth. Some opt for implantation when the egg, four or five days after fertilisation, descends the fallopian tube and becomes attached to the wall of the uterus. And it is true both that implantation is an indispensable stage in the development of the fetus, and that the greatest number of spontaneous abortions (often due to fetal abnormality) takes place before this moment. Nevertheless, implantation changes only the environment of the fetus, not its constitution.

In former generations 'quickening' was regarded by many as the moment of, or at least the evidence for, the 'ensoulment' of the embryo, but we now know that this new beginning is not of the child's movement but of the mother's perception of it.

A third option is 'viability,' the time when the fetus, if born prematurely, would be able to survive. But modern medical techniques are constantly bringing this moment forward. The fourth option is to regard birth itself as the crucial moment. This was the position adopted by Rex Gardner in his *Abortion: The Personal Dilemma* (1972). 'My own view,' he wrote, 'is that while the fetus is to be cherished increasingly as it develops, we should regard its first breath at birth as the moment when God gives it not only life, but the offer of Life.' He quoted Genesis 2.7 as biblical evidence, when God breathed into man's nostrils 'the breath of life.' He appealed also to common human experience: 'an audible sigh of relief goes round the delivery room when the baby gives that first gasp.'[13] It is certainly true that no funeral is held for a stillborn child, and that Scripture usually speaks of 'new life' beginning at 'new birth.' Yet this does not settle the matter, since Scripture also speaks of God 'begetting' us and of the implanted 'seed' which leads to new birth.[14] In addition, pictures of the child just before birth reveal that there is no fundamental difference between the unborn and the newly born: both are dependent on their mother, although in a different way.

The third group of people, which I think should include all

Christians, although they use different formulations and draw different deductions, looks back to conception or fusion as the decisive moment when human being begins. This is the official position of the Roman Catholic Church. Pope Pius XII, for example, in his address to the Italian Catholic Society of Midwives in 1951, said: 'the baby, still not born, is a man in the same degree and for the same reason as the mother.'[15] Similarly, many Protestants, although some find difficulty with the nonrecognition of 'degree,' yet similarly affirm that there is no point between conception and death at which we can say 'after that point I was a person, but before it I was not.' Certainly the conceptus is alive, and certainly the life it possesses is human life.

Indeed, many medical people who make no Christian profession recognise this fact. Thus the First International Conference on Abortion, meeting in 1967 in Washington D.C., declared: 'We can find no point in time between the union of sperm and egg and the birth of an infant at which point we can say that this is not a human life.'[16]

The Biblical Basis

To me the firmest foundation in Scripture for this view is to be found in Psalm 139, in which the author marvels at God's omniscience and omnipresence, and in the course of his meditation makes important statements about our prenatal existence. To be sure, Psalm 139 makes no claim to be a textbook on embryology. It employs poetical imagery and highly figurative language, (e.g. verse 15 'I was woven together in the depths of the earth'). Nevertheless, the psalmist is affirming at least three important truths.

The first concerns his *creation*. 'You created my inmost being; you knit me together in my mother's womb' (verse 13). Two homely metaphors are used to illustrate God's creative skill, namely the potter and the weaver. God is like a skilled artisan, who 'created' (or better 'formed') him as the potter works the clay. The same thought recurs in Job 10.8, where Job affirms that God's hands had 'fashioned and made' him (RSV) or 'shaped' and 'modelled' him (JB). The other picture is that of the weaver who 'knit' him together (verse 13), which the NASB renders 'thou didst weave me.' Similarly Job asks: 'Did you not . . . clothe me with skin and flesh and knit me together with bones and sinews?' (10.10,11). In consequence, the psalmist goes on: 'For all these mysteries I thank you: for the wonder of myself, for the wonder of your works' (verse 14, JB).

Though not intending to give a scientific account of fetal development, the biblical authors are nevertheless affirming (in the familiar imagery of the ancient Near East) that the process of embryonic growth is neither haphazard nor even automatic, but a divine work of creative skill.

The psalmist's second emphasis is on *continuity*. He is now an adult, but he looks back over his life until before he was born. He refers to himself both before and after birth by the same personal pronouns 'I' and 'me,' for he is aware that during his antenatal and postnatal life he was and is the same person. He surveys his existence in four stages.

First (v.1), 'you have searched me' (the past). Secondly (verses 2,3), 'you know when I sit and when I rise, . . . you are familiar with all my ways' (the present). Thirdly (verse 10), 'your hand will guide me, your right hand will hold me fast' (the future). And fourthly (verse 13), 'you knit me together in my mother's womb' (the prenatal stage). Yet in all four stages (before birth, from birth to the present, at the present moment, and in the future) he refers to himself as 'I.' He who is thinking and writing as a grown man has the same personal identity as the fetus in the womb. He is aware of no discontinuity between his antenatal and postnatal being. On the contrary, in and out of his mother's womb, before and after his birth, as embryo, baby, youth, and adult, he is conscious of being the same person.

The third truth the psalmist expresses I will term *communion*, for he is conscious of a very personal and particular communion between God and himself. It is the same God who created him, who now sustains him, knows him, and loves him, and who will forever hold him fast. Psalm 139 is perhaps the most radically personal statement in the Old Testament of God's relationship to the individual believer. The 'I-you' relationship is expressed in almost every line. Either the pronoun or the possessive in the first person ('I-me-my') comes forty-six times in the psalm, and in the second person ('you-your') thirty-two times. More important than the 'I-you' relationship is his awareness of the 'you-me' relationship, of God knowing him, surrounding him, holding him (verses 1–6), and of God sticking to him in covenant faithfulness and never leaving him or letting him go (verses 7–12).

Indeed, *communion* may not be the best description of this third awareness, because the word implies a reciprocal relationship, whereas the psalmist is bearing witness to a relationship which God has established and which God sustains. Perhaps therefore *covenant* would be a better word, indeed a unilateral covenant, or covenant of 'grace' which God initiated and which God maintains. For God our Creator loved us and related himself to us long before we could respond in a conscious relationship to him. What makes us a person, then, is not that we know God, but that he knows us; not that we love God but that he has set his love upon us. So each of us was already a person in our mother's womb, because already then God knew us and loved us.

These three words (*creation, continuity,* and *communion* or *covenant*) give us the essential biblical perspective from which to think. The fetus is neither a growth in the mother's body, nor even a potential human being, but already a human life who, though not yet mature, has the potentiality of growing into the fulness of the individual humanity he *already* possesses.

Other biblical passages express the same sense of personal continuity due to divine grace. Several times in the Wisdom Literature of the Old Testament the conviction is expressed that it is God who 'made me in the womb' (Job 31.15; Psalms 119.73), even though we do not know how (Ecclesiastes 11.5), who 'brought me out of the womb,' and who therefore 'from my mother's womb' has been my God (Psalms 22.9,10; 71.6).

The prophets shared the same belief, whether of the individual like Jeremiah ('before I formed you in the womb I knew you,' 1.5), or of 'the Servant of the Lord' (whom the Lord both formed and called in the womb, Isaiah 49.1,5) or by analogy of the nation of Israel (Isaiah 46.3,4).

The implications of these texts for personal continuity cannot be avoided by analogy with New Testament assertions that God 'chose' us in Christ and 'gave' us his grace in Christ 'before the creation of the world' (e.g. Ephesians 1.4; 2 Timothy 1.9). The argument would then be that, just as we did not exist before the beginning of time except in the mind of God, so we had no personal existence in the womb, although God is said to have 'known' us in both cases. The analogy is inexact, however, for the situations are different. In passages which relate to *election*, the emphasis is on salvation by grace not works, and therefore on God's choice of us before we existed or could do any good works. In passages which relate to *vocation*, however (whether the calling of prophets like Jeremiah or of apostles like Paul— cf. Galatians 1.16—), the emphasis is not only on God's gracious choice but on his 'forming' or 'fashioning' them for their particular service. This was not 'before the creation of the world,' nor even 'before conception,' but rather 'before birth,' before they were yet fully 'formed,' that is, while they were still being 'fashioned' in the womb. Personal continuity before and after birth is integral to this teaching.

There is only one Old Testament passage which some interpreters have thought to devalue the human fetus, namely Exodus 21.22–25.[17] The situation envisaged is not in dispute. While two men are fighting, they accidentally hit a pregnant woman with the result that she either miscarries or 'gives birth prematurely' (NIV). The penalty laid down depends on the seriousness of any injury sustained. If the injury is not serious, a fine is to be imposed; if it is serious, there is to be exact retribution, 'life for life' etc. Some have argued that the first category (no serious injury) means the death of the child, while the second is serious harm to the mother, and that therefore the mere imposition of a fine in the former case indicates that the fetus was regarded as less valuable than the mother. This is a gratuitous interpretation, however. It seems much more probable that the scale of penalty was to correspond to the degree of injury, whether to the mother or to her child, in which case mother and child are valued equally.

Turning to the New Testament, it has often been pointed out not just that when Mary and Elizabeth met, both being pregnant, Elizabeth's baby (John the Baptist) 'leaped in her womb' in salutation of Mary's baby, Jesus, but that Luke here uses the same word *brephos* of an unborn child (1.41, 44) as he later uses of the newborn baby (2.12, 16) and of the little ones whom people brought to Jesus to bless (18.15).

Fully in keeping with all this implied continuity, Christian tradition affirms of Jesus Christ in the Apostles' Creed that he was 'conceived by the Holy Spirit, born of the Virgin Mary, suffered under Pontius Pilate, was crucified, dead, and buried, and on the third day he rose again. . . .' Throughout these events, from beginning to end, Jesus was and is the same person. The Jesus who lived, died, and rose again is the very same Jesus who was conceived in the womb of his virgin mother.

Modern medical science appears to confirm this biblical teaching. It was only in the 1960s that the genetic code was unravelled. Now we know that the moment the ovum is fertilised by the penetration of the sperm, the twenty-three pairs of chromosomes are complete, the zygote has a unique genotype which is distinct from both parents, and the child's sex, size and shape, colour of skin, hair and eyes, temperament and intelligence are already determined. Each human being begins as a single ferti-lised cell, while an adult has about thirty million million cells. Between these two points (fusion and maturity) forty-five gen-erations of cell division are necessary, and forty-one of them occur *before birth*.

Prenatal medical photography has further disclosed the mar-vels of fetal development. I have in mind particularly the strik-ingly beautiful pictures in the Swedish photographer Lennart Nilsson's book *A Child is Born*.[18] At three to three and a half weeks the tiny heart begins to beat. At four, though the fetus is only about a quarter of an inch long, the head and body are distinguishable, as are also the rudimentary eyes, ears, and mouth. At six or seven weeks brain function can be detected, and at eight (the time abortions begin to be performed) all the child's limbs are apparent, including fingers, fingerprints, and toes. At nine or ten weeks the baby can use its hands to grasp and its mouth to swallow, and can even suck its thumb. By thirteen weeks, the completion of the first trimester, the embryo is completely organised, and a miniature baby lies in the mother's womb; he can alter his position, respond to pain, noise, and light, and even get a fit of hiccups. From then on the child merely develops in size and strength. By the end of the fifth month and the beginning of the sixth (before the second trimester is complete, and while the pregnancy is not yet two-thirds complete), the baby has hair, eyelashes, nails, and nip-ples, and can cry, grip, punch, and kick (which sometimes hap-pens after an abortion has been performed by hysterotomy, to the extreme distress of the medical team).

Expectant mothers endorse from their own experience their sense of bearing a living child. True, parents sometimes give their little one a humorous nickname, especially if they do not know which sex it will turn out to be. But they also say with pride 'we have a baby on the way.' During pregnancy one mother said she 'felt herself to be the mother of a person, with certain motherly responsibilities before birth, and others after birth.' Another wrote: 'My feelings know that this is a person, and thus has his or her own independent rights before God.'

A Contemporary Christian Debate

It would not be honest to claim that all Christians see eye to eye on this issue, even all Christians who seek to submit to the authority of Scripture. An apparently sharp difference of opinion has surfaced since an interdisciplinary seminar of theologians and doctors was held in 1983, jointly sponsored by the London Institute for Contemporary Christianity and the Christian Medical Fellowship. The keynote address was given by Canon Oliver O'Donovan, Regius Professor of Moral and Pastoral Theology at Oxford, under the title 'And who is a Person?' His starting point was the Parable of the Good Samaritan. Just as Jesus declined to answer the question 'and who is my neighbour?' by providing a set of criteria, so there are no criteria (whether self-consciousness or reason or responsive love) by which to decide who is a 'person.' Instead, the Good Samaritan identified his neighbour by caring for him, since 'the truth of neighbourhood is known in engagement.' Just so, the question 'who is a person?' cannot be answered speculatively. Instead, we come to *recognise* someone as a person 'only from a stance of prior moral commitment to treat him or her as a person.' Then later we come to *know* him or her as a person, as he or she is disclosed to us in personal relationships. It is not that personhood is *conferred* on someone by our resolve to treat him as a person, but that personhood is *disclosed* that way. Personhood becomes apparent in personal relationships, although it is not established by them. At the same time, before we commit ourselves to the service of a person, it is right to look for evidence that it is appropriate to do so, either by appearance or (in the case of a fetus) by our scientific knowledge of its unique geno-type.

There are thus three stages. First, there must be recognition, making it appropriate to engage with a person as person. Next follows commitment, caring for him as a person. And thirdly there comes encounter: 'those whom we *treat* as persons when they are yet unborn, become *known* to us as persons when they are children.' These three stages acknowledge the gradualness of development into personal encounter, while affirming the re-ality of personhood from the moment of conception.[19]

In an unpublished essay entitled 'The Logic of Beginnings,' Professor Donald MacKay, director of the Research Depart-ment of Communication and Neuroscience at Keele University, takes issue with Professor O'Donovan's argument. 'Things come into existence in various ways,' he writes. For example, artifacts (like a car) are assembled piece by piece, rain clouds form by condensation, an explosive mixture of gas and air de-velops gradually, while plants and animals grow. Each of these processes has an end product (a car, a raincloud, an explosion, a mature plant or an animal), but it is difficult for us to perceive either the exact moment when this comes into being or the exact nature of the change which takes place when it does. This leads Donald MacKay to criticise the language of 'potentiality.' To be sure, the beginning of every process has the potentiality to reach the end product, granted the enabling conditions, but this does not justify ontological assertions about the earlier stages. For example, various components will become a car, if they are assembled properly, but we do not refer to them as a 'potential car,' because they might instead end up on the scrap heap.

May we then refer to a fertilised ovum as a 'potential human being'? Yes, in the sense that it will lead to maturity if gestation proceeds normally, but no if this leads us to attribute to the ovum the specific properties of the end product. The value of 'potentiality' language is that it emphasises the importance of beginnings, expectations, and resulting obligations; its danger is to imagine that all the attributes and rights of the end product already belong to the beginning. They do not, even if there is a direct line of continuity between the two.

In particular, Donald MacKay concludes, before the fetus may rightly be considered a 'conscious personal agency,' there are certain information-processing requirements which are necessary for human self-supervision. This is not to reduce a person to a brain, but to say that a person cannot be embodied in a structure which lacks a self-supervisory system because it lacks adequate brain development. 'The capacity to sustain conscious personhood is a systemic property of the central nervous system.' On the one hand, the fertilised ovum is a 'physical structure with the richest and most strangely mysterious repertoire known to man,' for it can develop into 'the embodiment of a new human being in the image of God, loved by God, replete with potentialities of not merely earthly but eternal significance.' On the other, to treat it as 'a person with the rights of a person' is a conspicuous example of 'thin-end-of-the-wedgery.'[20]

In summary, Oliver O'Donovan insists that the fetus has 'personhood' from the moment of fusion, and that therefore we must commit ourselves to its care, although only later will its personhood be revealed in personal relationships. Donald MacKay agrees that from the moment of fusion the conceptus has biological life and a marvellous repertoire of potentiality, but only becomes a person possessing rights and demanding care when brain development makes self-supervision possible.

The conflict between the two learned professors sounds irreconcilable. Yet I believe that there may be more common ground between them than appears at first sight, and I do not believe that either is altogether denying what the other affirms.

Donald MacKay emphasizes the development of the fetus, while not denying that already the fertilised ovum has a rich repertoire. Oliver O'Donovan emphasises that from the very beginning the conceptus has a unique and complete genotype, and indeed personhood, while not denying that its destiny is to reach human maturity. Is this not at base the old tension (with which the New Testament has made us familiar) between the 'already' and the 'not yet'? Tertullian expressed it as early as the end of the second century: 'he also is a man who is about to be one; you have the fruit already in its seed.'[21] In our own day Paul Ramsey has put it like this: 'The human individual comes into existence as a minute informational speck. . . . His subsequent prenatal and postnatal development may be described as *a process of becoming what he already is* from the moment he was conceived.'[22] Lewis Smedes calls the status of a fetus a 'deep ontological ambiguity—the ambiguity of not being something yet and at the same time having the makings of what it will be.'[23]

This brings me back to Psalm 139 and to the reason for the psalmist's sense of continuity of being, namely God's steadfast love. Indeed, it is God's loving, personal commitment to the unborn child which makes me uncomfortable with Donald MacKay's nonpersonal analogies (material artifacts, clouds, gases, plants, and animals). The sovereign initiative of God in creating and loving is the biblical understanding of grace. Donald MacKay declines to attribute personhood to the newly conceived fetus because as yet it has no brain to sustain either self-supervision or conscious relationships. But supposing the vital relationship which confers personhood on the fetus is God's conscious, loving commitment to him, rather than his to God? Such a one-sided relationship is seen in parents who love their child, and commit themselves to its care and protection, long before it is able to respond. A unilateral initiative is what makes grace to be grace. It is, in fact, God's grace which confers on the unborn child, from the moment of its conception, both the unique status which it already enjoys and the unique destiny which it will later inherit. It is grace which holds together this duality of the actual and the potential, the already and the not yet.

Implications and Conclusions

How will our evaluation of the uniqueness of the human fetus (however we decide to formulate it) affect our thinking and acting?

To begin with, it will change our attitudes. Since the life of the human fetus is a human life, with the potential of becoming a mature human being, we have to learn to think of mother and unborn child as two human beings at different stages of development. Doctors and nurses have to consider that they have two patients, not one, and must seek the well-being of both. Lawyers and politicians need to think similarly. As the United Nations' 'Declaration of the Rights of the Child' (1959) put it, the child needs 'special safeguards and care, including appropriate legal protection, before as well as after birth.' Christians would wish to add 'extra care before birth,' for the Bible has much to say about God's concern for the defenceless, and the most defenceless of all people are unborn children. They are speechless to plead their own cause and helpless to protect their own life. So it is our responsibility to do for them what they cannot do for themselves.

All Christians should therefore be able to agree that the human fetus is in principle inviolable. Baron Michael Ramsey, when as Archbishop of Canterbury he was addressing the Church Assembly in 1967, said: 'We have to assert as normative the general inviolability of the fetus. . . . We shall be right to continue to see as one of Christianity's great gifts to the world the belief that the human fetus is to be reverenced as the embryo of a life capable of coming to reflect the glory of God. . . .'

It is this combination of what the human fetus already is and

one day could be which makes the realities of abortion so hor-
rific. How can anybody conceivably reconcile the brutal techniques of abortion with the concept of the abortus as a potential
mirror of God's glory? The oldest method is 'D and C,' dilation
and curettage. The cervix is dilated to facilitate the insertion of
an implement, either a 'curette' with which the wall of the
womb is scraped until the fetus is cut into pieces, or a suction
tube by which it is torn into pieces. In either case a violent and
bloody dismemberment takes place. The second method (employed between twelve and sixteen weeks after conception) is
to inject a toxic (usually saline) solution by a long needle in-
serted through the mother's abdomen into the amniotic sac en-
veloping the fetus, which is thus poisoned, burned, and killed,
and then 'spontaneously' ejected. At a later stage of pregnancy
surgery is used, either a hysterotomy which resembles a Cae-
sarean section (except that in this case the baby is taken from
the womb to be killed, not saved) or a complete hysterectomy
by which womb and fetus are removed together and discarded
together. A fourth method, an alternative to surgery, is the use
of prostaglandin, a hormone which induces immediate prema-
ture delivery, often of a live baby.

A factual knowledge of these procedures should lead us to
revise our vocabulary, for the popular euphemisms make it easier for us to conceal the truth from ourselves. The occupant of
the mother's womb is not a 'product of conception' or 'gametic
material,' but an unborn child. Even 'pregnancy' tells us no
more than that a woman has been 'impregnated,' whereas the
truth in old-fashioned language is that she is 'with child.' How
can we speak of 'the termination of a pregnancy' when what is
terminated is not just the mother's pregnancy but the child's
life? And how can we describe the average abortion today as
'therapeutic' (a word originally used only when the mother's
life was at stake), when pregnancy is not a disease needing therapy, and what abortion effects nowadays is not a cure but a

killing? And how can people think of abortion as no more than a kind of contraceptive, when what it does is not prevent conception but destroy the conceptus? We need to have the courage to use accurate language. Induced abortion is feticide, the deliberate destruction of an unborn child, the shedding of innocent blood.

Is abortion, then, never justified? To answer this question in a way that is both faithful and realistic, theologians and doctors need each other. More interdisciplinary consultation is necessary. Doctors are understandably impatient with theologians because they tend to be unpractical, making ivory-tower pronouncements unrelated to painful clinical dilemmas. Theologians, on the other hand, are understandably impatient with doctors because they tend to be pragmatists, making clinical decisions uncontrolled by theological principle. The principle on which we should be able to agree is well expressed as the first aim of the Society for the Protection of Unborn Children, namely 'that human life ought not to be taken except in cases of urgent necessity.'

Professor G. R. Dunstan is probably right that there is an ethic of 'justifiable feticide,' by analogy with 'justifiable homicide.'[24] But if we accept the general inviolability of the human fetus, then every exception has to be rigorously and specifically argued. Ever since the Infant Life (Preservation) Act (1929) an abortion to save the mother's life has been legal in England, though not condoned by the Roman Catholic Church. With improved modern medical techniques, however, this case hardly ever arises, although one could imagine a borderline situation in which an unwanted pregnancy threatened an overburdened and neurotic mother with such a complete breakdown, that she would become 'a physical and mental wreck,[25] or seems to be in imminent danger of taking her own life. According to Scripture human life may be taken only to protect and preserve another life, e.g. in self-defence; we have no liberty to introduce death into a situation in which it does not exist or is not threatened.

What about the 'substantial risk' of the child to be born being 'seriously handicapped,' which is the fourth clause of the 1967 Abortion Act? Antenatal screening and amniocentesis (tapping and testing the amniotic fluid) can now reveal abnormalities in the fetus at about the fourth month. Is an abortion then morally justified? Many think so. Dr. Glanville Williams has expressed himself forcefully on this issue: 'to allow the breeding of defectives is a horrible evil, far worse than any that may be found in abortion.'[26] In discussing the tragic predicament of a mother who gives birth to 'a viable monster or an idiot child,' he even wrote: 'an eugenic killing by a mother, exactly paralleled by the bitch that kills her misshapen puppies, cannot confidently be pronounced immoral.'[27]

How should a Christian conscience react to this possibility? Surely with horror. The only exception would be an anencephalic child (born without a brain) or a child so completely malformed as to be incapable of independent survival; these could be allowed to die, for in such cases the fetus is recognised as being non-human and is generally referred to as a 'monster.'

But there are at least three reasons why such a drastic procedure must be reserved for only the most exceptional cases and must not be extended to other—even severe—abnormalities. First, it is now frequently said that the issue is not the 'sanctity' of life but the 'quality' of life, and that the life of a severely handicapped person is not worth living. But who can presume to decide this? To me the most moving speech at the Hyde Park Rally in June 1983, which I have already mentioned, was made by Alison Davis, who described herself as 'a happy spina bifida adult' and spoke from a wheelchair. 'I can think of few concepts more terrifying,' she said, 'than saying that certain people are better off dead, and may therefore be killed *for their own good*.' One doctor, on hearing her say that she was glad to be alive, 'made the incredible observation that no one can judge their own quality of life, and that other people might well consider a life like mine miserable!' On the contrary, she insisted, 'most handicapped people are quite contented with the quality of their lives.' After all, it is love which gives quality to life and makes it worth living, and it is we—their neighbours—who can choose whether to give love to the handicapped or withhold it. The quality of their life is in our hands.

Secondly, once we accept that a handicapped child may be destroyed before birth, why should we not do it also after birth? Indeed, the practice of infanticide has already begun. Doctors of course do not use this word, and some try to persuade themselves that starving babies to death is not killing them, but 'I'd like to bet they'd change their minds,' said Alison Davis, 'if we did it to them!' The solemn fact is that if society is prepared to kill an unborn child on the sole ground that it will be handicapped, there is no logical reason why we should not go on to kill the deformed newborn, the comatose victim of a car crash, the imbecile, and the senile. The handicapped become disposable when their lives are judged 'worthless' or 'unproductive,' and we are back in Hitler's horrible Third Reich.

Christians will rather agree with Jean Rostan, the French biologist, who wrote: 'For my part I believe that there is no life so degraded, debased, deteriorated or impoverished that it does not deserve respect and is not worth defending with zeal and conviction. . . . I have the weakness to believe that it is an honour for our society to desire the expensive luxury of sustaining life for its useless, incompetent, and incurably ill members. I would almost measure society's degree of civilisation by the amount of effort and vigilance it imposes on itself out of pure respect for life.'[28]

A third reason for not aborting the handicapped is that to do so would be for fallible mortals to play God. We do not have that authority, and those who arrogate it to themselves are bound to make grave mistakes. Maurice Baring used to tell the story of one doctor who asked another: 'About the termination of a pregnancy, I want your opinion. The father was syphilitic, the mother tuberculous. Of the four children born the first was blind, the second dead, the third was deaf and dumb, and the fourth also tuberculous. What would you have done?' 'I would have ended the pregnancy.' 'Then you would have murdered Beethoven.'[29]

In this whole discussion we have to be on our guard against selfish rationalisations. I fear that the real reason why we say that serious handicap would be an unbearable burden for a child, if it were allowed to be born, is that it would be an unbearable burden for us. But Christians must remember that the God of the Bible has expressed his special protective care for the handicapped and weak.

What then shall we do? First, *we need to repent.* I agree with Raymond Johnston, the director of CARE Trust, when he wrote in a newspaper article: 'I personally am convinced that the destruction of the unborn on this massive, deliberate scale is the greatest single offence regularly perpetrated in Britain today, and would be the *first* thing an Old Testament prophet *redivivus* would reproach us for.' Dr. Francis Schaeffer and Dr. Everett Koop dedicated their book and film *Whatever Happened to the Human Race?* 'to those who were robbed of life, the unborn, the weak, the sick, the old, during the dark ages of madness, selfishness, lust and greed for which the last decades of the twentieth century are remembered.' Were they right to condemn our 'enlightened' western civilisation as 'the dark ages'? At least in this matter I think they were, and I for one am ashamed that we Christians have not been 'the light of the world' which Jesus intended us to be.

Secondly, *we must accept full responsibility for the effects of a tighter abortion policy,* if it can be secured. To agitate for it without being prepared to bear its cost would be sheer hypocrisy. We must not occasion an increase of illegal 'back street' abortions. Instead, we shall want to help the pregnant woman to overcome any reluctance she feels to have her baby, and see that she is given every possible personal, medical, social, and financial support. God tells us to 'carry each other's burdens, and in this way . . . fulfil the law of Christ' (Galatians 6.2). We shall want to ensure that, although some babies are unwanted (and even unloved) by their parents, no baby is unwanted by society in general and by the church in particular. We should not hesitate to oppose the abortion, and urge the birth, of every child. Pregnancy is a time of emotional instability, so that the minds and feelings of expectant mothers sometimes change. Rex Gardner refers to two reports about women who have been refused an abortion. In one case 73 percent of them, in the other 84 percent, said they were glad the pregnancy had not been terminated. He also quotes Sir John Stallworthy that some of the happiest people he knows are those who have said to him: 'You don't remember, but the first time I came wanting an abortion. Thank God you did not agree, because this child has brought the greatest joy into our home that we have ever known.'[30] As for those who would find the strain of keeping their child too great, there is a lengthy queue of married but infertile couples who are longing for the chance to adopt. As Mother Teresa says, 'we are fighting abortion by adoption.'

I thank God for the organisations which have been pioneering a supportive ministry for pregnant women, like Birthright in Canada and the United States, Alternatives to Abortion International (whose publication is called *Heartbeat*), and LIFE and SPUC (Society for the Protection of Unborn Children) in England.[31] In different ways they are offering a caring service, such as counselling women with an unplanned pregnancy, offering emergency help to those in despair, giving advice on practical problems, finding accommodation for mothers both before and after their child's birth, helping to secure employment for them, granting financial help, and providing personal support groups. As Louise Summerhill, founder of Birthright has written, 'we help rather than abort, we believe in making a better world for babies to come into, rather than killing them.'[32]

Thirdly, *we need to support a positive educational and social campaign*. Christians must not be shy to teach thoroughly and constantly the biblical understanding of humanness and of the value, indeed the sacredness, of human life. We have to recognise that all abortions are due to unwanted pregnancies, and that all unwanted pregnancies are due to a failure of some kind.

Often it is sexual failure, whether lack of sexual self-control (especially in men, who usually escape the tragic consequences of their action) or lack of a responsible use of contraceptives. The Church of England General Synod's Board for Social Responsibility has called for 'a major effort at social education' (and moral education too, we might add), in order 'to reduce the number of unwanted pregnancies,' 'to undermine the habit of mind which leads straight from the recognition of pregnancy to resort to an abortionist,' and to move the public 'to find a better solution.'[33] This is 'The Better Way' of which Rex Gardner writes in his chapters 28 and 29.[34]

Unplanned pregnancies are also often due to social failure, to such conditions as poverty, unemployment, and overcrowding. So for this reason too we should be working for a better society. Social evils are to be fought; they will not be solved by more abortions.

More important in the end than either social education or social action, vital as they both are, is the good news of Jesus Christ. He came to bind up the brokenhearted and support the weak. He calls us to treat all human life with reverence, whether in the unborn, the infant, the handicapped or the senile.

I have no desire to stand in personal judgment either on the women who have resorted to an abortion, or on the men whose sexual self-indulgence is responsible for most unwanted pregnancies. I want to say to them instead 'there is forgiveness with God' (Psalms 130.4), for Christ died for our sins and offers us a new beginning. He rose again and lives, and by his Spirit can give us a new, inward power of self-control. He is also building a new community characterised by love, joy, peace, freedom, and justice. A new beginning. A new power. A new community. This is the gospel of Christ.

Chapter Eight

Homosexual Partnerships?

BECAUSE OF THE EXPLOSIVE NATURE OF THIS TOPIC, LET ME BEGIN BY describing the proper context for our thinking about it and by affirming a number of truths about my readers and myself which I am taking for granted as I write.

The Context for Discussion

First, *we are all human beings.* That is to say, there is no such phenomenon as 'a homosexual.' There are only people, human persons, made in the image and likeness of God, yet fallen, with all the glory and the tragedy which that paradox implies, including sexual potential and sexual problems. However strongly we may disapprove of homosexual practices, we have no liberty to dehumanise those who engage in them.

Secondly, *we are all sexual beings.* Our sexuality, according to both Scripture and experience, is basic to our humanness. Angels may be sexless; we humans are not. When God made humankind, he made us male and female. So to talk about sex is to touch a point close to the centre of our personality. Our very identity is being discussed, and perhaps either endorsed or threatened. So the subject demands an unusual degree of sensitivity.

Moreover, not only are we all sexual beings, but we all have a particular sexual orientation. The American zoologist Alfred C. Kinsey's famous investigation into human sexuality led him to place every human being somewhere on a spectrum from 0 (an exclusively heterosexual bias, attracted only to the opposite sex) to 6 (an exclusively homosexual bias, attracted only to the same sex, whether homosexual males or 'lesbians,' as homosexual females are usually called). In between these poles Dr. Kinsey plotted varying degrees of bisexuality, referring to people whose sexual orientation is either dual or indeterminate or fluctuating. His researches led him to conclude that 4 percent of men (at least of white American men) are exclusively homosexual throughout their lives, that 10 percent are for up to three years, and that as many as 37 percent have some kind of homosexual experience between adolescence and old age. The percentage of homosexual women he found to be lower, although it rises to 4 percent between the ages of 20 and 35.[1] The numbers are high enough to warrant Dr. J. West's comment that 'homosexuality is an extremely common condition.'[2]

Thirdly, *we are all sinners*, indeed (among other things) sexual sinners. The doctrine of total depravity (which tends to be repudiated only by those who misunderstand it) asserts that every part of our human being has been tainted and twisted by sin, and that this includes our sexuality. Dr. Merville Vincent, of the Department of Psychiatry at Harvard Medical School, was surely correct when he wrote in 1972: 'In God's view I suspect we are all sexual deviants. I doubt if there is anyone who has not had a lustful thought that deviated from God's perfect ideal of sexuality.'[3] Nobody (with the sole exception of Jesus of Nazareth) has been sexually sinless. There is no question, therefore, of coming to this study with a horrid 'holier-than-thou' attitude of moral superiority. Being all of us sinners, we stand under the judgment of God and we are in urgent need of the grace of God. Besides, sexual sins are not the only sins, nor even necessarily the most sinful; pride and hypocrisy are surely worse.

Fourthly, in addition to being human, sexual, and sinful creatures, I take it that *we are all Christians.* At least the readers I have in mind in this chapter are not people who reject the lordship of Jesus Christ, but rather those who earnestly desire to submit to it, believe that he exercises it through Scripture, want to understand what light Scripture throws on this topic, and have a predisposition to seek God's grace to follow his will when it is known. Without this kind of commitment, it would be more difficult for us to find common ground. To be sure, God's standards for non-Christians are the same, but they are less ready to accept them.

Having delineated the context for our discussion, I am ready to ask the question: Are homosexual partnerships a Christian option? I phrase my question advisedly. It introduces us to three necessary distinctions.

First, at least since the Wolfenden Report of 1957 and the resultant Sexual Offences Act of 1967 in Britain, we have learned to distinguish between sins and crimes. Adultery has always (according to God's law) been a sin, but in most countries it is not an offence punishable by the state. Rape, by contrast, is both a sin and a crime. What the Sexual Offences Act of 1967 did was to declare that a homosexual act performed between consenting adults over 21 in private should no longer be a criminal offence. 'The Act did not in fact "legalise" such behaviour,' wrote Professor Sir Norman Anderson, 'for it is still regarded by the law as immoral, and is devoid of any legal recognition; all the Act did was to remove the criminal sanction from such acts when performed in private between two consenting adults.'[4]

Secondly, we have grown accustomed to distinguishing between a homosexual orientation or 'inversion' (for which people are not responsible) and homosexual physical practices (for which they are). The importance of this distinction goes beyond the attribution of responsibility to the attribution of guilt. We may not blame people for what they are, though we may for what they do. And in every discussion about homosexuality we must be rigorous in differentiating between this 'being' and 'doing,' that is, between a person's identity and activity, sexual preference and sexual practice, constitution and conduct.

But now we have to come to terms with a third distinction, namely between homosexual practices which are casual (and probably anonymous) acts of self-gratification and those which (it is claimed) are just as expressive of authentic human love as is heterosexual intercourse in marriage. No responsible homosexual person (whether Christian or not) is advocating promiscuous 'one night stands,' let alone violence or the corruption of young people and children. What some are arguing, however, especially in the so-called Gay Christian Movement, is that a heterosexual marriage and a homosexual partnership are 'two equally valid alternatives,'[5] being equally tender, mature, and faithful.

The question before us, then, does not relate to homosexual practices of a casual nature, but whether homosexual partnerships—lifelong and loving—are a Christian option. Our concern is to subject prevailing views (whether total revulsion or equally uncritical endorsement) to biblical scrutiny. Is our sexual 'preference' purely a matter of personal 'taste'? Or has God revealed his will regarding a norm? In particular, can the Bible be shown to sanction homosexual partnerships, or at least not to condemn them? What, in fact, does the Bible condemn?

The Biblical Prohibitions

The late Derrick Sherwin Bailey was the first Christian theologian to reevaluate the traditional understanding of the biblical prohibitions. His famous book, of which all subsequent writers on this topic have had to take careful account, namely *Homosexuality and the Western Christian Tradition*, was published in 1955. Although many have not been able to accept his attempted reconstruction, in particular his reinterpretation of the sin of

Sodom, other writers less cautious in scholarly standards than he regard his argument as merely preliminary and build on his foundations a much more permissive position. It is essential to consider this debate.

Four main biblical passages refer (or appear to refer) to the homosexual question negatively: (1) the story of Sodom (Genesis 19.1–13), with which it is natural to associate the very similar story of Gibeah (Judges 19); (2) the Levitical texts (Leviticus 18.22 and 20.13) which explicitly prohibit 'lying with a man as one lies with a woman'; (3) the apostle Paul's portrayal of decadent pagan society in his day (Romans 1.18–32); and (4) two Pauline lists of sinners, each of which includes a reference to homosexual practices of some kind (1 Corinthians 6.9–10 and 1 Timothy 1.8–11).

(1) The Stories of Sodom and Gibeah

The Genesis narrative makes it clear that 'the men of Sodom were wicked and were sinning greatly against the Lord' (13.13), and that 'the outcry against Sodom and Gomorrah' was 'so great and their sin so grievous' that God determined to investigate it (18.20, 21), and in the end 'overthrew those cities and the entire plain, including all those living in the cities' (19.25) by an act of judgment which was entirely consistent with the justice of 'the Judge of all the earth' (18.25). There is no controversy about this background to the biblical story. The question is: What was the sin of the people of Sodom (and Gomorrah) which merited their obliteration?

The traditional Christian view has been that they were guilty of homosexual practices, which they attempted (unsuccessfully) to inflict on the two angels whom Lot was entertaining in his home. Hence the word *sodomy*. But Sherwin Bailey challenged this interpretation on two main grounds. First, it is a gratuitous assumption (he argued) that the demand of the men of Sodom 'Bring them out to us, so that we may *know* them' meant 'so that we can have sex with them' (NIV). The Hebrew word for 'know' (*yāda'*) occurs 943 times in the Old Testament, of which only ten occurrences refer to physical intercourse, and even then only to heterosexual intercourse. It would therefore be better to translate the phrase 'so that we may get acquainted with them.' We can then understand the men's violence as due to their anger that Lot had exceeded his rights as a resident alien, for he had welcomed two strangers into his home 'whose intentions might be hostile and whose credentials . . . had not been examined.'[6] In this case the sin of Sodom was to invade the privacy of Lot's home and flout the ancient rules of hospitality. Lot begged them to desist because, he said, the two men 'have come under the protection of my roof' (v.8).

Bailey's second argument was that the rest of the Old Testament nowhere suggests that the nature of Sodom's offence was homosexual. Instead, Isaiah implies that it was hypocrisy and social injustice; Jeremiah makes it adultery, deceit, and general wickedness; and Ezekiel, arrogance, greed, and indifference to the poor.[7] Then Jesus himself (though Bailey does not mention this) on three separate occasions alluded to the inhabitants of Sodom and Gomorrah, declaring that it woud be 'more bearable' for them on the day of judgment than for those who reject his gospel.[8] Yet in all these references there is not even a whiff or rumour of homosexual malpractice! It is only when we reach the Palestinian pseudepigraphical writings of the second century B.C. that Sodom's sin is identified as unnatural sexual behaviour.[9] This finds a clear echo in the Letter of Jude, in which it is said that 'Sodom and Gomorrah and the surrounding towns gave themselves up to sexual immorality and perversion (v.7), and in the works of Philo and Josephus, Jewish writers who were shocked by the homosexual practices of Greek society.

Sherwin Bailey handled the Gibeah story in the same way, for they are closely parallel. Another resident alien (this time an anonymous 'old man') invites two strangers (not angels but a Levite and his concubine) into his home. Evil men surround the house and make the same demand as the Sodomites, that the visitor be brought out 'so that we may know him.' The owner of the house first begs them not to be so 'vile' to his 'guest,' and then offers his daughter and the concubine to them instead. The sin of the men of Gibeah, it is again suggested, was not their proposal of homosexual intercourse but their violation of the laws of hospitality.

Although Bailey must have known that his reconstruction of both stories was at most tentative, he yet made the exaggerated claim that 'there is not the least reason to believe, as a matter of either historical fact or of revealed truth, that the city of Sodom and its neighbours were destroyed because of their homosexual practices.'[10] Instead, the Christian tradition about 'sodomy' was derived from late, apocryphal Jewish sources.

But Sherwin Bailey's case is not convincing for a number of reasons: (1) The adjectives 'wicked,' 'vile,' and 'disgraceful' (Genesis 19.7; Judges 19.23) do not seem appropriate to describe a breach of hospitality; (2) the offer of women instead 'does look as if there is some sexual connotation to the episode.'[11]; (3) although the verb yāda' is used only ten times of sexual intercourse, Bailey omits to mention that six of these occurrences are in Genesis and one in the Sodom story itself (about Lot's daughters who had not 'known' a man, verse 8); (4) for those of us who take the New Testament documents seriously, Jude's unequivocal statement cannot be dismissed as merely an error copied from Jewish pseudepigrapha. To be sure, homosexual behaviour was not Sodom's only sin; but according to Scripture it was certainly one of them.

(2) The Leviticus Texts

Both texts in Leviticus belong to the 'Holiness Code' which is the heart of the book, and which challenges the people of God to follow his laws and not copy the practices either of Egypt (where they used to live) or of Canaan (to which he was bringing them). These practices included sexual relations within the prohibited degrees, a variety of sexual deviations, child sacrifice, idolatry, and social injustice of different kinds. In this context we must read the following two texts:

> 18.22   Do not lie with a man as one lies with a woman; that is detestable.

> 20.13   If a man lies with a man as one lies with a woman, both of them have done what is detestable. They must be put to death; their blood will be on their own heads.

'It is hardly open to doubt,' wrote Bailey, 'that both the laws in Leviticus relate to ordinary homosexual acts between men, and not to ritual or other acts performed in the name of religion.'[12] Others, however, affirm the very point which Bailey denies. They rightly point out that the two texts are embedded in a context preoccupied largely with ritual cleanness, and Peter Coleman adds that the word translated 'detestable' or 'abomination' in both verses is associated with idolatry.

'In English the word expresses disgust or disapproval, but in the Bible its predominant meaning is concerned with religious truth rather than morality or aesthetics.'[13] Are these prohibitions merely religious taboos, then? Are they connected with that other prohibition 'no Israelite man or woman is to become a temple prostitute' (Deuteronomy 23.17)? Certainly the Canaanitish fertility cult did include ritual prostitution, and therefore provided both male and female 'sacred prostitutes' (even if there is no clear evidence that either engaged in homosexual intercourse). The evil kings of Israel and Judah were constantly introducing them into the religion of Yahweh, and the righteous kings were constantly expelling them.[14] The homosexual lobby argues therefore that the Levitical texts prohibit religious practices which have long since ceased, and have no relevance to homosexual partnerships today.

(3) Paul's Statements in Romans 1

verse 26   *Because of this, God gave them over to shameful lusts. Even their women exchanged natural relations for unnatural ones.*

verse 27   *In the same way the men also abandoned natural relations with women and were inflamed with lust for one another. Men committed indecent acts with other men, and received in themselves the due penalty for their perversion.*

All are agreed that the apostle is describing idolatrous pagans in the Graeco-Roman world of his day. They had a certain knowledge of God through the created universe (verses 19, 20) and their own moral sense (verse 32). Yet they suppressed the truth they knew in order to practise wickedness. Instead of giving to God the honour due to him, they turned to idols, confusing the Creator with his creatures. In judgment upon them, 'God gave them over' to their depraved mind and their decadent practices (verses 24, 26, 28), including 'unnatural' sex. It seems at first sight to be a definite condemnation of homosexual behaviour. But two arguments are advanced on the other side: (1) although Paul knew nothing of the modern distinction between 'inverts' (who have a homosexual disposition) and 'perverts' (who, though heterosexually inclined, indulge in homosexual practices), nevertheless it is the latter he is condemning not the former. This must be so, because they are described as having 'abandoned' natural relations with women, whereas no exclusively homosexual male would ever have had them. (2) Paul is evidently portraying the reckless, shameless, profligate, promiscuous behaviour of people whom God has judicially 'given up'; what relevance has this to committed, loving homosexual partnerships?

(4) *The Other Pauline Texts*

1 Corinthians 6.9, 10   *Do you not know that the wicked will not inherit the kingdom of God? Do not be deceived: Neither the sexually immoral nor idolaters nor adulterers nor male prostitutes (malakoi) nor homosexual offenders (arsenokoitai) nor thieves nor the greedy nor drunkards nor slanderers nor swindlers will inherit the kingdom of God (Greek added).*

1 Timothy 1.9, 10   *We also know that law is made not for good men but for lawbreakers and rebels, the ungodly and sinful, the unholy and irreligious; for those who kill their fathers or mothers, for murderers, for adulterers and perverts (arsenokoitais), for slave traders and liars and perjurers—and for whatever else is contrary to the sound doctrine that conforms to the glorious gospel of the blessed God . . . (Greek added).*

Here are two ugly lists of sins which Paul affirms to be incompatible in the first place with the kingdom of God and in the second with either the law or the gospel. It will be observed that one group of offenders are called *malakoi* and the other (in both lists) *arsenokoitai*. What do these words mean?

To begin with, it is extremely unfortunate that in the original Revised Standard Version translation of 1 Corinthians 6.9 they were combined and translated 'homosexuals.' Bailey was right to protest, since the use of the word 'inevitably suggests that the genuine invert, even though he be a man of irreproachable morals, is automatically branded as unrighteous and excluded from the kingdom of God.'[15] Fortunately, the revisers heeded the protest, and the second edition (1973), though still combining the words, rendered them 'sexual perverts.' The point is that all ten categories listed in 1 Corinthians 6.9,10 (with the possible exception of 'the greedy') denote people who have offended by their *actions*, e.g. idolaters, adulterers, and thieves.

The two Greek words *malakoi* and *arsenokoitai* should not be combined, however, since they 'have precise meanings. The first is literally "soft to the touch" and metaphorically, among the Greeks, meant males (not necessarily boys) who played the passive role in homosexual intercourse. The second means literally "male in a bed" and the Greeks used this expression to describe the one who took the active role.'[16] The Jerusalem Bible follows James Moffatt in using the ugly words 'catamites and sodomites,' while among his conclusions Peter Coleman suggests that 'probably Paul had commercial pederasty in mind between older men and post-pubertal boys, the most common pattern of homosexual behaviour in the classical world.'[17] If this is so, then once again it can be (and has been) argued that the Pauline condemnations are not relevant to homosexual adults who are both consenting and committed to one another. Not that this is the conclusion with Peter Coleman himself draws. His summary is as follows: 'Taken together, St. Paul's writings repudiate homosexual behaviour as a vice of the Gentiles in Romans, as a bar to the Kingdom in Corinthians, and as an offence to be repudiated by the moral law in 1 Timothy.'[18]

Reviewing these biblical references to homosexual behaviour, which I have grouped, we have to agree that there are only four of them. Must we then conclude that the topic is marginal to the main thrust of the Bible? Must we further concede that they constitute a rather flimsy basis on which to take a firm stand against a homosexual life-style? Are those protagonists right who claim that the biblical prohibitions are 'highly specific'[19]—against violations of hospitality (Sodom and Gibeah), against cultic taboos (Leviticus), against shameless orgies (Romans) and against male prostitution or the corruption of the young (1 Corinthians and 1 Timothy), and that none of these passages alludes to, let alone condemns, a loving partnership between genuine homosexual inverts? This is the conclusion reached, for example, by Letha Scanzoni and Virginia Mollenkott in their book *Is The Homosexual My Neighbour?* They write:

> *The Bible clearly condemns certain kinds of homosexual practice (. . . gang rape, idolatry, and lustful promiscuity). However, it appears to be silent on certain other aspects of homosexuality— both the 'homosexual orientation' and 'a committed love-relationship analogous to heterosexual monogamy.'*[20]

But no, plausible as it may sound, we cannot handle the biblical material in this way. The Christian rejection of homosexual practices does not rest on 'a few isolated and obscure proof texts' (as is sometimes said), whose traditional explanation can be overthrown. And it is disturbing to me that those who write on this subject, and include in their treatment a section on the biblical teaching, all seem to deal with it in this way. For example, 'Consideration of the Christian attitude to homosexual practices,' wrote Sherwin Bailey 'inevitably begins with the story of the destruction of Sodom and Gomorrah.'[21] But this beginning is not at all 'inevitable.' In fact, it is positively mistaken, for the *negative* prohibitions of homosexual practices in Scripture make sense only in the light of its *positive* teaching in Genesis 1 and 2 about human sexuality and heterosexual marriage. Sherwin Bailey's book contains no allusion to these chapters at all. And even Peter Coleman, whose Christian *Attitudes to Homosexuality* is surely the most comprehensive biblical, historical, and moral survey which has yet been published, mentions them only in a passing reference to 1 Corinthians 6 where Paul quotes Genesis 2.24. Yet without the wholesome positive teaching of the Bible on sex and marriage, our perspective on the homosexual question is bound to be skewed.

Sex and Marriage in the Bible

The essential place to begin our investigation, it seems to me, is the institution of marriage in Genesis 2, although we have already looked at it in chapters 5 and 6. Since members of the Gay Christian Movement deliberately draw a parallel between heterosexual marriages and homosexual partnerships, it is necessary to ask whether this parallel can be justified.

We have seen that in his providence God has given us two distinct accounts of creation. The first (Genesis 1) is general, and affirms the *equality* of the sexes, since both share in the image of God and the stewardship of the earth. The second (Genesis 2) is particular, and affirms the *complementarity* of the sexes, which constitutes the basis for heterosexual marriage. In this second account of creation three fundamental truths emerge.

First, *the human need for companionship.* 'It is not good for the man to be alone' (2.18). True, this assertion was later qualified when the Apostle Paul (surely echoing Genesis) wrote: 'it is good for a man not to marry' (1 Corinthians 7.1). That is to say, although marriage is the good institution of God, the call to singleness is also the good vocation of some. Nevertheless, as a general rule, 'it is not good for the man to be alone.' For God has created us social beings. Since he is love, and has made us in his own likeness, he has given us a capacity to love and to be loved. He intends us to live in community, not in solitude. In particular, God continued, 'I will make a helper suitable for him.' Moreover, this 'helper' or companion, whom God pronounced 'suitable for him,' was also to be his sexual partner, with whom he was to become 'one flesh,' so that they might thereby both consummate their love and procreate their children.

Secondly, Genesis 2 reveals *the divine provision to meet this human need.* Having affirmed Adam's need for a partner, the search for a suitable one began. God first paraded the birds and beasts before him, and Adam proceeded to 'name' them, to symbolise his taking them into his service. But (v. 20) 'for Adam no suitable helper was found,' who could live 'alongside' or 'opposite' him, who could be his complement, his counterpart, his companion, let alone his mate. So a special creation was necessary.

The debate about how literally we are intended to understand what follows (the divine surgery under a divine anesthetic) must not prevent us from grasping the point. Something happened during Adam's deep sleep. A special work of divine creation took place. The sexes became differentiated. Out of the undifferentiated humanity of Adam, male and female emerged. And Adam awoke from his deep sleep to behold before him a reflection of himself, a complement to himself, indeed a very part of himself. Next, having created the woman out of the man, God himself brought her to him, much as today the bride's father gives the bride away. And Adam broke spontaneously into history's first love poem:

> Now at last [in contrast to the birds and beasts]
> This is now bone of my bones
>   and flesh of my flesh;
> She shall be called 'woman,'
>   for she was taken out of man.

There can be no doubting the emphasis of this story. According to Genesis 1 Eve like Adam was created in the image of God. But as to the manner of her creation, according to Genesis 2, she was made neither out of nothing (like the universe), nor out of 'the dust of the ground' (like Adam, verse 7), but out of Adam.

The third great truth of Genesis 2 concerns *the resulting institution of marriage.* Adam's love poem is recorded in verse 23. The 'therefore' or 'for this reason' of verse 24 is the narrator's deduction:

*For this reason a man will leave his father and mother and be
united to his wife, and they will become one flesh.*

Even the inattentive reader will be struck by the three references to 'flesh': 'this is . . . flesh of my flesh . . . they will become
one flesh.' We may be certain that this is deliberate, not acci-
dental. It teaches that heterosexual intercourse in marriage is
more than a union; it is a kind of reunion. It is not a union of
alien persons who do not belong to one another and cannot ap-
propriately become one flesh. On the contrary, it is the union of
two persons who originally were one, were then separated from
each other, and now in the sexual encounter of marriage come
together again.

It is surely this which explains the profound mystery of heterosexual intimacy, which poets and philosophers have celebrated in every culture. Heterosexual intercourse is much more
than a union of bodies; it is a blending of complementary personalities through which, in the midst of prevailing alienation,
the rich created oneness of human being is experienced again.
And the complementarity of male and female sexual organs is
only a symbol at the physical level of a much deeper spiritual
complementarity.

In order to become one flesh, however, and experience this
sacred mystery, certain preliminaries are necessary, which are
constituent parts of marriage. 'For this reason' (verse 24)

> *'a man' (the singular indicates that marriage is an exclusive
>   union between two individuals)*
> *'will leave his father and mother' (a public social occasion is in
>   view)*
> *'and be united to his wife' (marriage is a loving, cleaving com-
>   mitment or covenant, which is heterosexual and permanent)*
> *'and they will become one flesh' (for marriage must be consum-
>   mated in sexual intercourse, which is a sign and seal of the
>   marriage covenant, and over which no shadow of shame or
>   embarrassment had yet been cast, verse 25)*

Jesus himself later endorsed this teaching. He quoted Genesis 2.24, declared that such a lifelong union between a man and his wife was God's intention from the beginning, and added 'what God has joined together, let man not separate' (Mark 10.4-9).

Thus Scripture defines the marriage God instituted in terms of heterosexual monogamy. It is the union of one man with one woman, which must be publicly acknowledged (the leaving of parents), permanently sealed (he will 'cleave to his wife') and physically consummated ('one flesh'). And Scripture envisages no other kind of marriage or sexual intercourse, for God provided no alternative.

Christians should not therefore single out homosexual intercourse for special condemnation. The fact is that every sexual relationship or act which deviates from God's revealed intention is *ipso facto* displeasing to him and under his judgment. This includes polygamy and polyandry (which infringe the 'one man—one woman' principle), clandestine unions (since these have involved no decisive public leaving of parents), casual encounters and temporary liaisons, adultery and many divorces (which are incompatible with 'cleaving' and with Jesus' prohibition 'let man not separate'), and homosexual partnerships (which violate the statement that 'a man' shall be joined to 'his wife').

In sum, the only 'one flesh' experience which God intends and Scripture contemplates is the sexual union of a man with his wife, whom he recognises as 'flesh of his flesh.'

Contemporary Arguments Considered

Homosexual Christians are not, however, satisfied with this biblical teaching about human sexuality and the institution of heterosexual marriage. They bring forward a number of objections to it, in order to defend the legitimacy of homosexual partnerships.

(1) *The argument about Scripture and culture.*

Traditionally, it has been assumed that the Bible condemns all homosexual acts. But are the biblical writers reliable guides in this matter? Were there horizons not bounded by their own experience and culture? The cultural argument usually takes one of two forms.

First, the biblical authors were addressing themselves to questions relevant to their own circumstances, and these were very different from ours. In the Sodom and Gibeah stories they were preoccupied either with conventions of hospitality in the Ancient Near East which are now obsolete or (if the sin was sexual at all) with the extremely unusual phenomenon of homosexual gang rape. In the Levitical laws the concern was with antiquated fertility rituals, while Paul was addressing himself to the particular sexual preferences of Greek pederasts. It is all so antiquarian. The biblical authors' imprisonment in their own cultures renders their teaching on this topic irrelevant.

The second and complementary culture problem is that the biblical writers were not addressing themselves to *our* questions. Thus the problem of Scripture is not only with its teaching but also with its silence. Paul (let alone the Old Testament authors) knew nothing of post-Freudian psychology. They had never heard of 'the homosexual condition'; they knew only about certain practices. The difference between 'inversion' and 'perversion' would have been incomprehensible to them. The very notion that two men or two women could fall in love with each other and develop a deeply loving, stable relationship comparable to marriage simply never entered their heads. So then, just as slaves, blacks, and women have been liberated, 'gay liberation' is long overdue.

If the only biblical teaching on this topic were to be found in the prohibition texts, it might be difficult to answer these objections. But once those texts are seen in relation to the divine institution of marriage, we are in possession of a principle of divine revelation which is universally applicable. It was applicable to the cultural situations of both the Ancient Near East and the first-century Graeco-Roman world, and it is equally applicable to modern sexual questions of which the ancients were quite ignorant. The reason for the biblical prohibitions is the same reason why modern loving homosexual partnerships must also be condemned, namely that they are incompatible with God's created order. And since that order (heterosexual monogamy) was established by creation, not culture, its validity is both permanent and universal. There can be no 'liberation' from God's created norms; true liberation is found only in accepting them.

(2) *The argument about creation and nature*

I have sometimes read or heard this kind of statement: 'I'm gay because God made me that way. So gay must be good. I intend to accept, and indeed celebrate, what I am by creation.' Or again, 'You may say that homosexual practice is against nature and normality; but it's not against *my* nature, nor is it in the slightest degree abnormal for *me*.' Norman Pittenger was quite outspoken in his use of this argument a couple of decades ago. A homosexual person, he wrote, is 'not an "abnormal" person with "unnatural' desires and habits.' On the contrary, 'a heterosexually oriented person acts "naturally" when he acts heterosexually, while a homosexually oriented person acts equally "naturally" when he acts in accordance with his basic, inbuilt homosexual desire and drive.'[22]

Others argue that homosexual behaviour is 'natural' (a) because in many primitive societies it is fairly acceptable, (b) because in some advanced civilisations (ancient Greece, for example) it was even idealised, and (c) because it is quite widespread in animals. Dr. D. J. West, who reports this, goes on to quote Dr. F. A. Beach, an expert on animal sexuality, who because of animal homosexual behaviour says that to describe human homosexual behaviour as 'unnatural' is to 'depart from strict accuracy.'[23]

But these arguments express an extremely subjective view of what is 'natural' and 'normal.' We should not accept Norman Pittenger's statement that there are 'no external standards of normality or naturalness.'[24] Nor can we agree that animal behaviour sets standards for human behaviour! God has established a norm for sex and marriage by creation. This was already recognised in the Old Testament era. Thus, sexual relations with an animal were forbidden, because 'that is a perversion' (Leviticus 18.23), in other words a violation or confusion of nature, which indicates an 'embryonic sense of natural law.'[25] The same verdict is passed on Sodom by the second century B.C. *Testament of Naphtali:* 'As the sun and the stars do not change their order, so the tribe of Naphtali are to obey God rather than the disorderliness of idolatry. Recognising in all created things the Lord who made them, they are not to become as Sodom which changed the order of nature. . . .'[26]

The same concept was clearly in Paul's mind in Romans 1. When he wrote of women who had 'exchanged natural relations for unnatural ones,' and of men who had 'abandoned natural relations,' he meant by 'nature' (*phusis*) the natural order of things which God has established (as in 2.14, 27 and 11.24). What Paul was condemning, therefore, was not the perverted behaviour of heterosexual people who were acting against *their* nature, but any human behaviour which is against 'Nature,' that is, against God's created order. As C. K. Barrett puts it: 'In the obscene pleasures to which he (sc. Paul) refers is to be seen precisely that perversion of the created order which may be expected when men put the creation in place of the Creator.'[27]

(3) *The argument about quality of relationships*

The Gay Christian Movement borrows from Scripture the truth that love is the greatest thing in the world (which it is) and from the 'new morality' or 'situation ethics' of the 1960s the notion that love is an adequate criterion by which to judge every relationship (which it is not). Yet this view is gaining ground today.

The Friends' Report *Towards a Quaker View of Sex* (1963), for example, included the statements 'one should no more deplore "homosexuality" than lefthandedness'[28] and 'surely it is the nature and quality of a relationship that matters.'[29] Similarly in 1979, the Methodist Church's 'Division of Social Responsibility,' in its report *A Christian Understanding of Human Sexuality*, argued that 'homosexual activities' are 'not intrinsically wrong,' since 'the quality of any homosexual relationship is ... to be assessed by the same basic criteria which have been applied to heterosexual relationships. For homosexual men and women, permanent relationships characterised by love can be an appropriate and Christian way of expressing their sexuality.'[30]

The same year (1979) an Anglican working party issued the report *Homosexual Relationships: a contribution to discussion.* It was more cautious, judicious, and ambivalent than the Quaker and Methodist reports. Its authors did not feel able to repudiate centuries of Christian tradition, yet they 'did not think it possible to deny' that in some circumstances individuals may 'justifiably choose' a homosexual relationship in their search for companionship and sexual love 'similar' to those found in marriage.[31]

In his *Time for Consent*, Norman Pittenger lists six characteristics of a truly loving relationship. They are (1) commitment (the free self-giving of each to the other), (2) mutuality in giving and receiving (a sharing in which each finds his or her self in the other), (3) tenderness (no coercion or cruelty), (4) faithfulness (the intention of a lifelong relationship), (5) hopefulness (each serving the other's maturity), and (6) desire for union.[32]

If then a homosexual relationship, whether between two men or two women, is characterised by these qualities of love, surely (the argument runs) it must be affirmed as good and not rejected as evil? It rescues people from loneliness, selfishness, and promiscuity. It can be just as rich and responsible, as liberating and fulfilling, as a heterosexual marriage.

But the biblical Christian cannot accept the basic premise on which this case rests, namely that love is the only absolute, that besides it all moral law has been abolished, and that whatever seems to be compatible with love is *ipso facto* good, irrespective of all other considerations. This cannot be so. For love needs law to guide it. In emphasising love for God and neighbour as the two great commandments, Jesus and his apostles did not discard all other commandments. On the contrary, Jesus said 'if you love me you will keep my commandments,' and Paul wrote 'love is the fulfilling (not the abrogating) of the law.'[33]

So then the loving quality of a relationship is an essential, though by itself insufficient, criterion to authenticate it. For example, if love were the only test of authenticity, there would be nothing against polygamy, for a polygamist could certainly enjoy a relationship with several wives which reflects all Dr. Pittenger's six characteristics. Here, however, is a better illustration, drawn from my own pastoral experience. On several different occasions a married man has told me that he has fallen in love with another woman. When I have gently remonstrated with him, he has responded in words like these: 'Yes, I agree, I already have a wife and family. But this new relationship is the real thing. We were made for each other. Our love for each other has a quality and depth we have never known before. It *must* be right.' But no, I have had to say, it is not right. No man is justified in breaking his marriage covenant with his wife on the ground of the quality of his love for another woman. Quality of love is not the only yardstick by which to measure what is good or right.

Similarly, I do not deny the claim that homosexual relationships can be loving (although *a priori* I do not see how they can attain the same richness as the heterosexual mutuality God has ordained). But their love-quality is not sufficient to justify them. Indeed, I have to add that they are incompatible with true love because they are incompatible with God's law. Love is concerned for the highest welfare of the beloved. And our highest human welfare is found in obedience to God's law and purpose, not in revolt against them.

Some leaders of the Gay Christian Movement appear to be

following the logic of their own position, for they are saying that even monogamy could be abandoned in the interests of 'love.' Malcolm Macourt, for example, has written that the Gay Liberationist's vision is of 'a wide variety of life patterns,' each of which is 'held in equal esteem in society.' Among them he lists the following alternatives: monogamy and multiple partnerships; partnerships for life and partnerships for a period of mutual growth; same-sex partners and opposite sex partners; living in community and living in small family units.[34] There seem to be no limits to what some people seek to justify in the name of love.

(4) *The argument about acceptance and the gospel*

'Surely,' some people are saying, 'it is the duty of heterosexual Christians to accept homosexual Christians. Paul told us to accept—indeed welcome—one another. If God has welcomed somebody, who are we to pass judgment on him (Romans 14.1ff)?' Norman Pittenger goes further and declares that those who reject homosexual people 'have utterly failed to understand the Christian gospel.' We do not receive the grace of God because we are good and confess our sins, he continues; it is the other way round. 'It's always God's grace which comes *first*, . . . his forgiveness awakens our repentance.'[35] He even quotes the hymn 'Just as I am, without one plea,' and adds: 'the whole point of the Christian gospel is that God loves and accepts us just as we are.'[36]

This is a very confused statement of the gospel, however. God does indeed accept us 'just as we are,' and we do not have to make ourselves good first, indeed we cannot. But his 'acceptance' means that he fully and freely forgives all who repent and believe, not that he condones our continuance in sin. Again, it is true that we must accept one another, but only as fellow-penitents and fellow-pilgrims, not as fellow-sinners who are resolved to persist in our sinning. No acceptance, either by

God or by the church, is promised to us if we harden our hearts against God's Word and will. Only judgment.

Faith, Hope, and Love

If homosexual practice must be regarded, in the light of the whole biblical revelation, not as a variant within the wide range of accepted normality, but as a deviation from God's norm; and if we should therefore call homosexually oriented people to abstain from homosexual practices and partnerships, what advice and help can we give to encourage them to respond to this call? I would like to take Paul's triad of faith, hope, and love, and apply it to homosexually oriented people.

(1) *The Christian call to faith.*

Faith is the human response to divine revelation; it is believing God's Word.

First, *faith accepts God's standards.* The only alternative to heterosexual marriage is sexual abstinence. I think I know the implications of this. Nothing has helped me to understand the pain of homosexual celibacy more than Alex Davidson's moving book *The Returns of Love.* He writes of 'this incessant tension between law and lust,' 'this monster that lurks in the depths,' this 'burning torment.'[37]

The secular world says: 'Sex is essential to human fulfilment. To expect homosexual people to abstain from homosexual practice is to condemn them to frustration and to drive them to neurosis, despair and even suicide. It's outrageous to ask anybody to deny himself what to him is a normal and natural mode of sexual expression. It's "inhuman and inhumane."[38] Indeed, it's positively cruel.'

But no, the teaching of the Word of God is different. Sexual experience is not essential to human fulfilment. To be sure, it is a good gift of God. But it is not given to all, and it is not indispensable to humanness. People were saying in Paul's day that it was. Their slogan was 'Food for the stomach and the stomach for food; sex for the body and the body for sex' (1 Corinthians 6.13). But this is a lie of the devil. Jesus Christ was single, yet perfect in his humanity. Besides, God's commands are good and not grievous. The yoke of Christ brings rest not turmoil; conflict comes only to those who resist it.

So ultimately it is a crisis of faith: Whom shall we believe? God or the world? Shall we submit to the lordship of Jesus, or succumb to the pressures of prevailing culture? The true 'orientation' of Christians is not what we are by constitution (hormones), but what we are by choice (heart, mind, and will).

Secondly, *faith accepts God's grace*. Abstinence is not only good, if God calls us to celibacy; it is also possible. Many deny it, however. 'You know the imperious strength of our sex drive,' they say. 'To ask us to control ourselves is just not on.' It is 'so near to an impossibility,' writes Norman Pittenger, 'that it's hardly worth talking about.'[39]

Really? What then are we to make of Paul's statement following his warning to the Corinthians that male prostitutes and homosexual offenders will not inherit God's kingdom? 'And that is what some of you were,' he cries. 'But you were washed, you were sanctified, you were justified in the name of the Lord Jesus Christ and by the Spirit of our God' (1 Corinthians 6.11). And what shall we say to the millions of heterosexual people who are single? To be sure, all unmarried people experience the pain of struggle and loneliness. But how can we call ourselves Christians and declare that chastity is impossible? It is made harder by the sexual obsession of contemporary society. And we make it harder for ourselves if we listen to the world's plausible arguments, or lapse into self-pity, or feed our imagination with pornographic material and so inhabit a fantasy world in which Christ is not Lord, or ignore his command about plucking out our eyes and cutting off our hands and feet, that is, being ruthless with the avenues of temptation. But, whatever our 'thorn in the flesh' may be, Christ comes to us as he came to Paul and says: ' 'My grace is sufficient for you, for my power is made perfect in weakness" '(2 Corinthians 12.9). To deny this is to portray Christians as the helpless victims of the world, the flesh, and the devil, and to contradict the gospel of God's grace.

(2) *The Christian call to hope*

I have said nothing so far about the 'healing' for homosexual people, understood not now as self-mastery but as the reversal of their sexual bias. Our expectation of this possibility will depend largely on our understanding of the aetiology of the homosexual condition, and no final agreement on this has yet been reached. 'Research into the causes of homosexuality,' writes D. J. West, 'has left a lot of mysteries unsolved.'[40] In his view, however, 'children are not born with the sex instinct specifically directed to one sex or the other. Exclusive preference for the opposite sex is an acquired trait. . . .'[41]

Most agree that, lacking heterosexual outlets, and under cultural pressures, a large percentage of people would (or at least could) behave homosexually. Indeed, although there may be a genetic factor or component, the condition is more 'learned' than 'inherited.' Some attribute it to traumatic childhood experiences, such as the withdrawal of the mother's love, inhibiting sexual growth.[42] So, if it is learned, can it not be unlearned?

The possibility of change by the grace and power of God depends also on the strength of the person's resolve, which itself depends on other factors. Those whose sexuality is indeterminate may well change under strong influence and with strong motivation. But many researchers conclude that constitutional homosexuality is irreversible. 'No known method of treatment or punishment,' writes D. J. West, 'offers hope of making any substantial reduction in the vast army of adults practising homosexuality'; it would be 'more realistic to find room for them in society.' He pleads for 'tolerance,' though not for 'encouragement,' of homosexual behaviour.[43] Other psychologists go further and declare that homosexuality is no longer to be regarded as a pathological condition; it is therefore to be accepted not cured. In 1973 the trustees of the American Psychiatric Association removed homosexuality from the category of mental illness.

Are not these views, however, the despairing opinions of the secular mind? Christians know that the homosexual condition, being a deviation from God's norm, is not a sign of created order but of fallen disorder. How, then, can we acquiesce in it or declare it incurable? We cannot. The only question is *when* and *how* we are to expect the divine deliverance and restoration to take place. The fact is that, though Christian claims of homosexual 'healings' are made, either through regeneration or through a subsequent work of the Holy Spirit, it is not easy to substantiate them. Martin Hallett, who before his conversion was active in the gay scene, has subsequently founded the 'True Freedom Trust,' an interdenominational teaching and counselling ministry on homosexuality and related problems.[44] They have published a pamphlet entitled *Testimonies.* In it homosexual Christian men and women bear witness to what Christ has done for them. They have found a new identity in him, and a new sense of personal fulfilment as children of God. They have been delivered from guilt, shame, and fear by God's forgiving acceptance, and set free from thraldom to their former homosexual activity by the indwelling power of the Holy Spirit. But they have not been delivered from their homosexual orientation, and therefore some inner pain continues alongside their new joy and peace. Here are two examples: 'My prayers were not answered in the way I had hoped for, but the Lord greatly blessed me in giving me two Christian friends who lovingly accepted me for what I was.' 'After I was prayed over with the laying on of hands a spirit of perversion left me. I praise God for the deliverance I found that afternoon. . . . I can testify to over three years of freedom from homosexual activity. But I have not changed into a heterosexual in that time.'

Is there really, then, no hope of a substantial change of orientation? Dr. Elizabeth Moberly believes there is. She has been led by her research to the view that 'a homosexual orientation does not depend on genetic predisposition, hormonal imbalance, or abnormal learning processes, but on difficulties in the parent-child relationship, especially in the earlier years of life.' The 'underlying principle,' she continues, is 'that the homosexual—whether man or woman—has suffered from some deficit in the relationship with the parent *of the same sex;* and that there is a corresponding drive to make good this deficit through the medium of same-sex or "homosexual" relationships.'[45] The deficit and the drive go together. The reparative drive for same-sex love is not itself pathological, but 'quite the opposite—it is the attempt to resolve and heal the pathology.' 'The homosexual condition does not involve abnormal needs, but normal needs that have, abnormally, been left unmet in the ordinary process of growth.' Homosexuality 'is essentially a state of incomplete development' or of unmet needs.[46] So the proper solution is 'the meeting of same-sex needs without sexual activity,' for to eroticise growth deficits is to confuse emotional needs with physiological desires.[47]

How, then, can these needs be met? The needs are legitimate, but what are the legitimate means of meeting them? Dr. Moberly's answer is that 'substitute relationships for parental care are in God's redemptive plan, just as parental relationships are in his creative plan.'[48] What is needed is deep, loving, lasting, same-sex but nonsexual relationships, especially in the church. 'Love,' she concludes, 'both in prayer and in relationships, is the best therapy. . . . Love is the basic problem, the great need, and the only true solution. If we are willing to seek and to mediate the healing and redeeming love of Christ, then healing for the homosexual will become a great and glorious reality.'[49]

Even then, however, complete healing of body, mind, and spirit will not take place in this life. Some degree of deficit or disorder remains in each of us. But not for ever! The Christian's horizons are not bounded by this world. Jesus is coming again; our bodies are going to be redeemed; sin, pain, and death are going to be abolished; and both we and the universe are going to be transformed. Then we shall be finally liberated from everything which defiles or distorts our personality. This Christian assurance helps us to bear whatever our present pain may be, for pain there is, in the midst of peace. 'We know that the whole creation has been groaning as in the pains of childbirth right up to the present time. Not only so, but we ourselves, who have the firstfruits of the Spirit, groan inwardly as we wait eagerly for our adoption as sons, the redemption of our bodies' (Romans 8.22f). Thus our groans express the birthpangs of the new age. We are convinced that 'our present sufferings are not worth comparing with the glory that will be revealed in us' (Romans 8.18). This confident hope sustains us.

In the midst of his homosexuality Alex Davidson derives comfort from his Christian hope. 'Isn't it one of the most wretched things about this condition,' he writes, 'that when you look ahead, the same impossible road seems to continue indefinitely? You're driven to rebellion when you think of there being no point in it, and to despair when you think of there being no limit to it. That's why I find a comfort, when I feel desperate, or rebellious, or both, to remind myself of God's promise that one day it will be finished. . . .'[50]

(3) *The Christian call to love*

At present we are living 'in between times,' between the grace which we grasp by faith and the glory which we anticipate in hope. Between them lies love.

Yet love is just what the church has generally failed to show to homosexual people. Jim Cotter complains bitterly about being treated as 'objects of scorn and insult, of fear, prejudice and oppression.'[51] Norman Pittenger describes the 'vituperative' correspondence he has received, in which homosexuals are dismissed even by professing Christians as 'filthy creatures,' 'disgusting perverts,' 'damnable sinners,' and the like.[52] Pierre Berton, a social commentator, writes that 'a very good case can be made out that the homosexual is the modern equivalent of the leper.'[53] Rictor Norton is yet more shrill: 'The church's record regarding homosexuals is an atrocity from beginning to end: it is not for us to seek forgiveness, but for the church to make atonement.'[54]

The attitude of personal hostility towards homosexuals is nowadays termed 'homophobia.'[55] It is a mixture of irrational fear, hatred, and even revulsion. It overlooks the fact that the great majority of homosexual people are not responsible for their condition (though they are, of course, for their conduct). Since they are not deliberate perverts, they deserve our understanding and compassion (though many find this patronising), not our rejection. No wonder Richard Lovelace calls for 'a double repentance,' namely 'that gay Christians renounce the active life-style' and that 'straight Christains renounce homophobia.'[56] Dr. David Atkinson is right to add: 'We are not at liberty to urge the Christian homosexual to celibacy and to a spreading of his relationships, unless support for the former and opportunities for the latter are available in genuine love.'[57] I rather think that the very existence of the Gay Christian Movement, not to mention the so-called 'Evangelical Fellowship' within it, is a vote of censure on the church.

At the heart of the homosexual condition is a deep loneliness, the natural human hunger for mutual love, a search for identity, and a longing for completeness. If homosexual people cannot find these things in the local 'church family,' we have no business to go on using that expression. The alternative is not between the warm physical relationship of homosexual intercourse and the pain of isolation in the cold. There is a third alternative, namely a Christian environment of love, understanding, acceptance, and support. I do not think there is any need to encourage homosexual people to disclose their sexual orientation to everybody; this is neither necessary nor helpful. But they do need at least one confidante to whom they can unburden themselves, who will not despise or reject them, but will support them with friendship and prayer; probably some professional, private, and confidential pastoral counsel; possibly in addition the support of a professionally supervised therapy group; and many warm and affectionate friendships with people of both sexes. Same-sex friendships are to be encouraged, like those in the Bible between Ruth and Naomi, David and Jonathan, and Paul and Timothy. There is no hint that any of these was homosexual in the erotic sense, yet they were evidently affectionate and (at least in the case of David and Jonathan) even demonstrative.[58] Of course sensible safeguards will be important. But in African and Asian cultures it is common to see two men walking down the street hand in hand, without embarrassment. It is sad that our western culture inhibits the development of rich same-sex friendships by engendering the fear of being ridiculed or rejected as a 'queer.'

These relationships, both same-sex and opposite-sex, need to be developed within the family of God which, though universal, has its local manifestations. He intends each local church to be a warm, accepting and supportive community. By 'accepting' I do not mean 'acquiescing,' any more than in rejecting 'homophobia' I am rejecting a proper Christian disapproval of homosexual behaviour. No, true love is not incompatible with the maintenance of moral standards. There is, therefore, a place for church discipline in the case of members who refuse to repent and wilfully persist in homosexual relationships. But it must be exercised in a spirit of humility and gentleness (Galatians 6.1f); we must be careful not to discriminate between men and women, or between homosexual and heterosexual offences; and necessary discipline in the case of a public scandal is not to be confused with a witch-hunt.

Perplexing and painful as the homosexual Christian's dilemma is, Jesus Christ offers him or her (indeed, all of us) faith, hope, and love—the faith to accept his standards and his grace to maintain them, the hope to look beyond present suffering to future glory, and the love to care for and support one another. 'But the greatest of these is love' (1 Corinthians 13.13).

Conclusion

Chapter Nine

A Call for Christian Leadership

THERE IS A SERIOUS DEARTH OF LEADERS IN THE CONTEMPORARY world. Massive problems confront us, some of which we have looked at in this book. Globally, there are the terrifying build-up of nuclear arsenals, the widespread violations of human rights, the environmental and energy crises, and North-South economic inequality. Socially, there are the tragedy of long-term unemployment, the continuance of conflict in industrial relations, and the outbreaks of racial violence. Morally, Christians are disturbed by the forces undermining the stability of marriage and the family, the challenges to sexual mores and sexual roles, and the scandal of what is virtually abortion on demand. Spiritually, I might add, there is the spread of materialism and the corresponding loss of any sense of transcendent reality. Many people are warning us that the world is heading for disaster; few are offering us advice on how to avert it. Technical know-how abounds, but wisdom is in short supply. People feel confused, bewildered, alienated. To borrow the metaphors of Jesus, we seem to be like 'sheep without a shepherd,' while our leaders often appear to be 'blind leaders of the blind.'

There are many kinds and degrees of leadership. Leadership is not restricted to a small minority of world statesmen, or to the national top brass. In every society it takes a variety of forms. Clergy are leaders in the local church and community. Parents are leaders in their home and family. So are teachers in school and lecturers in college. Senior executives in business and industry, judges, doctors, politicians, social workers, and union officials all have leadership responsibilities in their respective spheres. So do the opinion-formers who work in the media—authors and playwrights, journalists, sound and vision broadcasters, artists and producers. And student leaders, especially since the 1960s, have been exercising influence beyond their years and their experience. There is a great need in all these and other situations for more clearsighted, courageous, and dedicated leaders.

Such leaders are both born and bred. As Bennie E. Goodwin, a black American educationist, has written: 'although potential leaders are born, effective leaders are made.'[1] In Shakespeare's famous lines, 'Be not afraid of greatness! Some are born great, some achieve greatness, and some have greatness thrust upon them.'[2] Books of management refer to 'B.N.L.s' ('born natural leaders'), men and women endowed with strong intellect, character, and personality. And we would want to add with Oswald Sanders that Christian leadership is 'a blending of natural and spiritual qualities,'[3] or of natural talents and spiritual gifts. Nevertheless, God's gifts have to be cultivated, and leadership potential developed.

What, then, are the marks of leadership in general, and of Christian leadership in particular? How can we give up sitting around, waiting for somebody else to take the initiative, and take one ourselves? What is needed to blaze a trail which others will follow?

Although different analyses of leadership have been made, I want to suggest that it has five essential ingredients.

Vision

'Where there is no vision, the people perish . . .' is a proverb from the King James Version of the Bible, which has passed into common usage. And although it is almost certainly a mistranslation of the Hebrew, it is nonetheless a true statement.[4] Indeed, it has been a characteristic of the post-Pentecost era that ' "your young men will see visions" ' and ' "your old men will dream dreams" ' (Acts 2.17). Monsignor Ronald Knox of Oxford concluded his critical though somewhat wistful book *Enthusiasm* with these words:

> *Men will not live without vision; that moral we do well to carry away with us from contemplating, in so many strange forms, the record of the visionaries. If we are content with the humdrum, the second-best, the hand-over-hand, it will not be forgiven us.*[5]

'Dreams' and 'visions,' dreamers and visionaries, sound somewhat unpractical, however, and remote from the harsh realities of life on earth. So more prosaic words tend to be used. Management experts tell us we must set both long-term and short-term goals. Politicians publish election manifestos. Military personnel lay down a campaign strategy. But whether you call it a 'goal,' a 'manifesto' or a 'strategy,' it is a *vision* that you are talking about.

So what is vision? It is an act of seeing, of course, an imaginative perception of things, combining insight and foresight. But more particularly, in the sense in which I am using the word, it is compounded of a deep dissatisfaction with what *is* and a clear grasp of what *could be*. It begins with indignation over the status quo, and it grows into the earnest quest for an alternative. Both are quite clear in the public ministry of Jesus. He was indignant over disease and death, and the hunger of the people, for he perceived these things as alien to the purpose of God. Hence his compassion for their victims. Indignation and compassion form a powerful combination. They are indispensable to vision, and therefore to leadership.

It will be remembered that Bobby Kennedy was assassinated in 1968 at the age of 42. In an appreciation of him which appeared ten years later, David S. Broder wrote that 'his distinguished quality was his capacity for what can only be called moral outrage. "That is unacceptable," he said of many conditions that most of us accepted as inevitable. . . . Poverty, illiteracy, malnutrition, prejudice, crookedness, conniving—all such accepted evils were a personal affront to him.'[6] Apathy is the acceptance of the unacceptable; leadership begins with a decisive refusal to do so. As George F. Will wrote in December 1981, after the declaration of martial law in Poland, 'what is outrageous is the absence of outrage.' There is a great need today for more righteous indignation, anger, outrage over those evils which are an offence to God. How can we tolerate what he finds intolerable?

But anger is sterile if it does not provoke us to positive action to remedy what has aroused our anger. 'One must oppose those things that one believes to be wrong,' writes Robert Greenleaf, 'but one cannot *lead* from a predominantly negative posture.'[7] Before Robert McNamara retired in 1981 as President of the World Bank after thirteen years, he addressed its annual meeting for the last time, and in his speech quoted George Bernard Shaw: 'you see things as they are and ask "why?" But I dream things that never were, and ask "why not?"'

History abounds in examples, both biblical and secular. Moses was appalled by the cruel oppression of his fellow-Israelites in Egypt, remembered God's covenant with Abraham, Isaac, and Jacob, and was sustained throughout his long life by the vision of the 'Promised Land.' Nehemiah heard in his Persian exile that the wall of the Holy City was in ruins, and its inhabitants in great distress. The news overwhelmed him, until

God put into his heart what he could and should do. ' "Come, let us rebuild the wall of Jerusalem," ' he said. And the people replied, ' "Let us start rebuilding" ' (Nehemiah 2.17, 18).

Moving on to the New Testament times, the early Christians were well aware of the might of Rome and the hostility of Jewry. But Jesus had told them to be his witnesses 'to the ends of the earth,' and the vision he gave them transformed them. Saul of Tarsus had been brought up to accept as inevitable and unbridgeable the chasm between Jews and Gentiles. But Jesus commissioned him to take the gospel to the Gentile world, and he was 'not disobedient to the heavenly vision.' Indeed the vision of a single, new, reconciled humanity so captured his heart and mind, that he laboured, suffered and died in its cause.[8]

In our own generation, presidents of the United States have had noble visions of a 'New Deal' and of a 'Great Society,' and the fact that their expectations did not altogether materialise is no criticism of their vision. Martin Luther King, Jr., incensed by the injustices of segregation, had a dream of dignity for blacks in a free, multiracial America; he both lived and died that his dream might come true.

There can be little doubt that the phenomenal success of Communists (within fifty years from the Russian Revolution of 1917 they had won over a third of the world) has been due to the vision of a better society which they have been able to inspire in their followers. This, at least, was the considered opinion of Douglas Hyde who in March 1948 resigned both from the British Communist Party (after twenty years' membership) and from being News Editor of the *Daily Worker*, and became a Roman Catholic. The subtitle he gave to his book *Dedication and Leadership* was 'Learning from the Communists,' and he wrote it to answer the question 'why are Communists so dedicated and successful as leaders, whilst others so often are not?' Here is how he put it: 'If you ask me what is the distinguishing mark of the Communist, what is it that Communists most outstandingly have in common, . . . I would say that beyond any shadow of doubt it is their idealism. . . .'[9] They dream of a new society in which (quoting from Liu Shao-chi) there will be 'no oppressed and exploited people, no darkness, ignorance, backwardness' and 'no such irrational things as mutual deception, mutual antagonism, mutual slaughter and war.'[10] Marx wrote in his *Theses on Feuerbach* (1888) 'the philosophers have only in various ways *interpreted* the world: the point, however, is to *change* it.'

That slogan, 'change the world,' comments Douglas Hyde, 'has proved to be one of the most dynamic of the past 120 years. . . . Marx concluded his *Communist Manifesto* with the words "You have a world to win." '[11] This vision fires the imagination and zeal of young idealistic Communists. Because of it 'the recruit is made to feel that there is a great battle going on all over the world,' and 'that this includes his own country, his own town, his own neighbourhood, the block of flats in which he lives, the factory or office where he works.'[12] 'One reason why the Communist is prepared to make his exceptional sacrifices,' Douglas Hyde argues, 'is that he believes he is taking part in a crusade.'[13]

But Jesus Christ is a far greater and more glorious leader than Karl Marx could ever be, and the Christian good news is a much more radical and liberating message than the Communist Manifesto. The world can be won for Christ by evangelism, and made more pleasing to Christ by social action. Why then does this prospect not set our hearts on fire? Where are the Christian people today who see the status quo, who do not like what they see (because there are things in it which are unacceptable to God), who therefore refuse to come to terms with it, who dream dreams of an alternative society which would be more acceptable to God, and who determine to do something about it? 'Nothing much happens without a dream. And for something great to happen, there must be a great dream. Behind every great achievement is a dreamer of great dreams.'[14]

We see with our mind's eye the three thousand million unevangelised peoples of the world, who have had no real opportunity to hear or respond to the gospel; the poor, the hungry, and the disadvantaged; people crushed by political, economic or racial oppression; the millions of babies aborted and incinerated; and the so-called 'balance' of nuclear terror. We see these things; do we not care? We see what is; do we not see what could be? Things could be different. The unevangelised could be reached with the good news of Jesus; the hungry could be fed, the oppressed liberated, the alienated brought home. We need a vision of the purpose and power of God.

David Bleakley calls such visionaries—'the people with a "hunch" alternative, those who believe that it *is* possible to build a better world'—'Pathfinders.' They are 'lovers of our planet, who feel a responsibility for God's creation and wish to give true meaning to the lives of all his people.' Indeed, he is confident, as I am, that such 'Pathfinders represent a growing ground-swell of change in our society and in societies elsewhere.'[15]

Industry

The world has always been scornful of dreamers. ' "Here comes that dreamer!" ' Joseph's older brothers said to one another. ' "Come now, let's kill him. . . . Then we'll see what comes of his dreams" ' (Genesis 37.19f). The dreams of the night tend to evaporate in the cold light of the morning.

So dreamers have to become in turn thinkers, planners, and workers, and that demands industry or hard labour. Men of vision need to become men of action. It was Thomas Carlyle, the nineteenth-century Scottish writer, who said of Frederick the Great that genius means first of all 'the transcendent capacity of taking trouble,' and it was Thomas Alva Edison, the inventor of electrical devices, who defined genius as '1 percent inspiration and 99 percent perspiration.' All great leaders, not least great artists, find this to be true. Behind their apparently effortless performance there lies the most rigorous and painstaking self-discipline. A good example is the world-renowned pianist, Paderewski. He spent hours in practice every day. It was not unknown for him to repeat a bar or phrase fifty times to perfect it. Queen Victoria once said to him, after she had heard him play, 'Mr. Paderewski, you are a genius.' 'That may be, Ma'am,' he replied, 'but before I was a genius, I was a drudge.'[16]

This addition of industry to vision is an evident hallmark of history's great leaders. It was not enough for Moses to dream of the land flowing with milk and honey; he had to organise the Israelite rabble into at least the semblance of a nation and lead them through the dangers and hardships of the desert before they could take possession of the Promised Land. Similarly, Nehemiah was inspired by his vision of the rebuilt Holy City, but first he had to gather materials to reconstruct the wall and weapons to defend it. Winston Churchill loathed the Nazi tyranny and dreamed of Europe's liberation. But he was under no illusions about the cost of the enterprise. On May 13, 1940, in his first speech to the House of Commons as Prime Minister, he warned members that he had 'nothing to offer but blood, toil, tears and sweat,' and 'many long months of struggle and suffering.'

Moreover the same combination of vision and industry is needed in our more ordinary individual lives. William Morris, who became Lord Nuffield the public benefactor, began his career repairing bicycles. What was the secret of his success? It was 'creative imagination wedded to indomitable industry.'[17] Thus dream and reality, passion and practicalities must go together. Without the dream the campaign loses its direction and its fire; but without hard work and practical projects the dream vanishes into thin air.

Perseverance

Thomas Sutcliffe Mort was an early nineteenth-century settler in Sydney, Australia, whose 'Mort Docks' are named after him.

He was determined to solve the problem of refrigeration, so that meat could be exported from Australia to Britain, and he gave himself three years in which to do it. But it took him twenty-six. He lived long enough to see the first shipment of refrigerated meat leave Sydney, but died before learning whether it had reached its destination safely. The house he built in Edgecliff is now Bishopscourt, the residence of the Anglican Archbishop of Sydney. Painted twenty times round the cornice of the study ceiling are the words 'To persevere is to succeed,' and engraved in stone outside the front door is the Mort family motto (a play on their Huguenot name) 'Fidèle á la Mort.'

Perseverance is certainly an indispensable quality of leadership. It is one thing to dream dreams and see visions. It is another to convert a dream into a plan of action. It is yet a third to persevere with it when opposition comes, for opposition is bound to arise. As soon as the campaign gets under way, the forces of reaction muster, entrenched privilege digs itself in more deeply, commercial interests feel threatened and raise the alarm, the cynical sneer at the folly of 'do-gooders,' and apathy becomes transmuted into hostility.

But a true work of God thrives on opposition. Its silver is refined and its steel hardened. Of course those without the vision, who are merely being carried along by the momentum of the campaign, will soon capitulate. So it is that the protesting youth of one decade become the conservative establishment of the next. Young rebels lapse into middle-class, middle-aged, middle-of-the-road mediocrity. Even revolutionaries, once the revolution is over, tend to lose their ideals. But not the real leader. He has the resilience to take setbacks in his stride, the tenacity to overcome fatigue and discouragement, and the wisdom (in a favourite phrase of John Mott's) to 'turn stumblingblocks into stepping-stones.'[18] The real leader adds to vision and industry the grace of perseverance.

In the Old Testament, Moses is again the outstanding example. On about a dozen distinct occasions the people 'murmured' against him, and he had the beginnings of a mutiny on his hands. When Pharaoh's army was threatening them, when the water ran out or was too bitter to drink, when there was no meat to eat, when the scouts brought back a bad report of the strength of Canaanite fortifications, when small minds became jealous of his position—these were some of the occasions on which the people complained of his leadership and challenged his authority. A lesser man would have given up and abandoned them to their own pettiness. But not Moses. He never forgot that these were *God's* people by *God's* covenant, who by *God's* promise would inherit the land.

In the New Testament the man who came to the end of his life with his ideals intact and his standards uncompromised was the apostle Paul. He too faced bitter and violent opposition. He had to endure severe physical afflictions, for on several occasions he was beaten, stoned, and imprisoned. He suffered mentally, too, for his footsteps were dogged by false prophets who contradicted his teaching and slandered his name. He also experienced great loneliness. Towards the end of his life he wrote 'everyone in the province of Asia has deserted me' and 'at my first defence . . . everyone deserted me' (2 Timothy 1.15; 4.16). Yet he never lost his vision of God's new, redeemed society, and he never gave up proclaiming it. In his underground dungeon, from which there was to be no escape but death, he could write: 'I have fought the good fight, I have finished the race, I have kept the faith' (2 Timothy 4.7). He persevered to the end.

In recent centuries perhaps nobody has exemplified perseverance more than William Wilberforce. Sir Reginald Coupland wrote of him that, in order to break the apathy of parliament, a would-be social reformer 'must possess, in the first place, the virtues of a fanatic without his vices. He must be palpably single-minded and unself-seeking. He must be strong enough to face opposition and ridicule, staunch enough to endure obstruction and delay.'[19] These qualities Wilberforce possessed in abundance.

In 1787 he first decided to put forward a motion in the House of Commons about the slave trade. This nefarious traffic had been going on for three centuries, and the West Indian slave-owners were determined to oppose abolition to the end. Besides, Wilberforce was not a very prepossessing man. He was little and ugly, with poor eyesight and an upturned nose. When Boswell heard him speak, he pronounced him 'a perfect shrimp,' but then had to concede that 'presently the shrimp swelled into a whale.'[20] In 1789 Wilberforce said of the slave trade in the House: 'So enormous, so dreadful, so irremediable did its wickedness appear that my own mind was completely made up for Abolition. . . . Let the consequences be what they would, I from this time determined that I would never rest until I had effected its Abolition.'[21] So abolition bills (which related to the trade) and foreign slave bills (which would prohibit the involvement of British ships in it) were debated in the Commons in 1789, 1791, 1792, 1794, 1796 (by which time Abolition had become 'the grand object of my parliamentary existence'), 1798, and 1799. Yet they all failed. The Foreign Slave Bill was not passed until 1806 and the Abolition of the Slave Trade Bill until 1807. This part of the campaign had taken eighteen years.

Next, soon after the conclusion of the Napoleonic wars, Wilberforce began to direct his energies to the abolition of slavery itself and the emancipation of the slaves. In 1823 the Anti-Slavery Society was formed. Twice that year and twice the following year Wilberforce pleaded the slaves' cause in the House of Commons. But in 1825 ill health compelled him to resign as a Member and to continue his campaign from outside. In 1831 he sent a message to the Anti-Slavery Society, in which he said: 'Our motto must continue to be *perseverance*. And ultimately I trust the Almighty will crown our efforts with success.'[22] He did. In July 1833 the Abolition of Slavery Bill was passed in both Houses of Parliament, even though it included the undertaking to pay £20,000,000 in compensation to the slave-owners. 'Thank God,' wrote Wilberforce, 'that I have lived to witness a day in which England is willing to give £20,000,000 sterling for the abolition of slavery.'[23] Three days later he died. He was buried in Westminster Abbey, in national recognition of his *forty-five years* of persevering struggle on behalf of African slaves.

Mind you, perseverance is not a synonym for pigheadedness. The true leader is not impervious to criticism. On the contrary, he listens to it and weighs it, and may modify his programme accordingly. But he does not waver in his basic conviction of what God has called him to do. Whatever the opposition aroused or the sacrifice entailed, he perseveres.

Service

A note of caution needs to be added at this point. 'Leadership' is a concept shared by the church and the world. We must not assume, however, that Christian and non-Christian understandings of it are identical. Nor should we adopt models of secular management without first subjecting them to critical Christian scrutiny, for Jesus introduced into the world an altogether new style of leadership. He expressed the difference between the old and the new in these terms:

> *'You know that those who are regarded as rulers of the Gentiles lord it over them, and their high officials exercise authority over them. Not so with you. Instead, whoever wants to become great among you must be your servant, and whoever wants to be first must be slave of all. For even the Son of Man did not come to be served, but to serve, and to give his life as a ransom for many.'*
>
> Mark 10.42–45

Among the followers of Jesus, therefore, leadership is not a synonym for lordship. Our calling is to be servants not bosses,

slaves not masters. True, a certain authority attaches to all leaders, and leadership would be impossible without it. The apostles were given authority by Jesus, and exercised it in both
teaching and disciplining the church. Even Christian pastors
today, although they are not apostles and do not possess apostolic authority, are to be 'respected' because of their position
'over' the congregation (1 Thessalonians 5.12f), and even
'obeyed' (Hebrews 13.17). Yet the emphasis of Jesus was not on
the authority of a ruler-leader but on the humility of a servant-
leader. The authority by which the Christian leader leads is not
power but love, not force but example, not coercion but rea-
soned persuasion. Leaders have power, but power is safe only
in the hands of those who humble themselves to serve.

What is the reason for Jesus' stress on the leader's service?
Partly, no doubt, because the chief occupational hazard of leadership is pride. The pharisaic model would not do in the new
community Jesus was building. The Pharisees loved deferential
titles like 'Father,' 'Teacher,' 'Rabbi,' but this was both an offence against God to whom these titles properly belong, and
disruptive of the Christian brotherhood (Matthew 23.1-12).

Jesus' main reason for emphasising the servant role of the
leader, however, was surely that the service of others is a tacit
recognition of their value. I have been troubled recently to observe that the 'service' model of leadership is being borrowed
by the world and commended for the wrong reasons. Robert K.
Greenleaf, for example, a specialist in the field of management
research and education, wrote in 1977 a long book called *Servant
Leadership*, to which he gave the intriguing subtitle 'a journey
into the nature of legitimate power and greatness.' He tells us
that the concept of 'the servant as leader' came to him from the
reading of Hermann Hesse's *Journey to the East*, in which Leo the
menial servant of a group of travellers turns out in the end to
have been their leader. The 'moral principle' which Greenleaf
draws from this is that 'the great leader is seen as the servant

first.' Or, expressed more fully: 'the only authority deserving one's allegiance is that which is freely and knowingly granted by the led to the leader in response to, and in proportion to, the clearly evident servant stature of the leader. Those who choose to follow this principle . . . will freely respond only to individuals who are chosen as leaders because they are proven and trusted as servants.'[24] I do not deny the truth of this, that leaders have first to win their spurs by service. But the danger of the principle as thus stated is that it regards service as being only a means to another end (namely qualifying one as a leader), and is therefore commended only because of its pragmatic usefulness. This is not what Jesus taught, however. To him service was an end in itself. T. W. Manson expressed the difference beautifully when he wrote: 'In the Kingdom of God service is not a stepping-stone to nobility: it *is* nobility, the only kind of nobility that is recognised.'[25]

Why then did Jesus equate greatness with service? Must not our answer relate to the intrinsic worth of human beings, which was the presupposition underlying his own ministry of self-giving love, and which is an essential element in the Christian mind? If human beings are Godlike beings, then they must be served not exploited, respected not manipulated. As Oswald Sanders has expressed it, 'true greatness, true leadership, is achieved not by reducing men to one's service but in giving oneself in selfless service to them.'[26] Herein also lies the peril of seeing leadership in terms of projects and programmes. Leadership will inevitably involve the development of these, but people take precedence over projects. And people must be neither 'manipulated' nor even 'managed.' Though the latter is less demeaning to human beings than the former, yet both words are derived from *manus*, a hand, and both express a 'handling' of people as if they were commodities rather than persons.

So Christian leaders serve, indeed serve not their own interests but rather the interests of others (Philippians 2.4). This

simple principle should deliver the leader from excessive individualism, extreme isolation and self-centred empire-building,
for those who serve others serve best in a team. Leadership
teams are more healthy than solo leadership, for several reasons. First, team members *supplement* one another, building on
one another's strengths and compensating for one another's
weaknesses. No leader has all the gifts, so no leader should
keep all the reins of leadership in his own hands. Secondly,
team members *encourage* one another, identifying each other's
gifts and motivating each other to develop and use them. As
Max Warren used to say, 'Christian leadership has nothing
whatever to do with self-assertion, but everything to do with
encouraging other people to assert themselves.'[27] Thirdly, team
members are *accountable* to one another. Shared work means
shared responsibility. We listen to one another and learn from
one another. Both the human family and the divine family (the
body of Christ) are contexts of solidarity in which any incipient
illusions of grandeur are rapidly dispelled. 'The way of a fool
seems right to him, but a wise man listens to advice' (Proverbs
12.15).

In all this Christian emphasis on service, the disciple is only
seeking to follow and reflect his teacher, for though he was lord
of all Jesus became the servant of all. Putting on the apron of
servitude, he got down on his knees to wash the apostles' feet.
Now he tells us to do as he did, to clothe ourselves with humility, and in love to serve one another.[28] No leadership is authentically Christlike which is not marked by the spirit of humble
and joyful service.

Discipline

Every vision has a tendency to fade. Every visionary is prone to
discouragement. Hard work begun with zest can easily degenerate into drudgery. Suffering and loneliness take their toll. The
leader feels unappreciated and gets tired. The Christian ideal of

humble service sounds fine in theory but seems impractical. So the leader may catch himself soliloquising: 'It is quicker to ride roughshod over other people; you get things done that way. And if the end is good, does it really matter what means we employ to attain it? Even a little prudent compromise can sometimes be justified, can't it?'

It is evident, then, that leaders are made of flesh and blood, not plaster or marble or stained glass. Indeed, as Peter Drucker has written, 'strong people always have strong weaknesses too.'[29] Even the great leaders of the biblical story had fatal flaws. They too were fallen and fallible and frail. Righteous Noah got drunk. Faithful Abraham was despicable enough to risk his wife's chastity for the sake of his own safety. Moses lost his temper. David broke all five commandments of the second table of the law, committing adultery, murder, theft, false witness, and covetousness, in that single episode of moral rebellion over Bathsheba. Jeremiah's lonely courage was marred by self-pity. John the Baptist, whom Jesus described as the greatest man who had ever lived, was overcome by doubt. And Peter's boastful impetuosity was doubtless a cloak for his deep personal insecurity. If those heroes of Scripture failed, what hope is there for us?

The final mark of a Christian leader is discipline, not only self-discipline in general (in the mastery of his passions, his time, and his energies), but in particular the discipline with which he waits on God. He knows his weakness. He knows the greatness of his task and the strength of the opposition. But he also knows the inexhaustible riches of God's grace.

Many biblical examples could be given. Moses sought God, and 'the Lord would speak to Moses face to face, as a man speaks with his friend.' David looked to God as his shepherd, his light and salvation, his rock, the stronghold of his life, and in times of deep distress 'found strength in the Lord his God.' The apostle Paul, burdened with a physical or psychological infirmity he called his 'thorn in the flesh,' heard Jesus say to him ' "My grace is sufficient for you" ' and learned that only when he was weak he was strong.

But our supreme exemplar is our Lord Jesus himself. It is often said that he was always available to people. This is not true. He was not. There were times when he sent the crowds away. He refused to allow the urgent to displace the important. Regularly he withdrew from the pressures and the glare of his public ministry, in order to seek his Father in solitude and replenish his reserves of strength. Then, when it came to the end, he and his apostles faced the final test together. How is it, I have often asked myself, that they forsook him and fled, while he went to the cross with such serenity? Is not the answer that he prayed while they slept?[30]

It is only God who 'gives strength to the weary and increases the power of the weak.' For 'even youths grow tired and weary, and young men stumble and fall; but those who hope in the Lord,' and wait patiently for him, 'will renew their strength. They will soar on wings like eagles; they will run and not grow weary, they will walk and not be faint' (Isaiah 40.29–31). Only those who discipline themselves to seek God's face, keep their vision bright. It is only those who live before Christ's cross whose inner fires are constantly rekindled and never go out. Those leaders who think they are strong in their own strength are the most pathetically weak of all people; only those who know and acknowledge their weakness can become strong with the strength of Christ.

I have tried to analyse the concept of Christian leadership. It appears to break down into five main ingredients—clear vision, hard work, dogged perseverance, humble service, and iron discipline.

In conclusion, it seems to me that we need to repent of two particularly horrid sins. The first is *pessimism*, which is dishonouring to God and incompatible with Christian faith. To be sure, we do not forget the fallenness, indeed the depravity, of human beings. We are well aware of the pervasiveness of evil. We are not so foolish as to imagine that society will ever become perfect before Christ comes and establishes the fulness of his rule. As the Lausanne Covenant rightly expressed it, 'we reject as a proud, self-confident dream the notion that man can ever build a utopia on earth.'[31] Nevertheless, we also believe in the power of God—in the power of God's gospel to change individuals and in the power of God's people (working like salt and light) to change society. We need then to renounce both naive optimism and cynical pessimism, and replace them with the sober but confident realism of the Bible.

The second sin of which we need to repent is *mediocrity*, and the acceptance of it. I find myself wanting to say, especially to young people: 'Don't be content with the mediocre! Don't settle for anything less than your full God-given potential! Be ambitious and adventurous for God! God has made you a unique person by your genetic endowment, upbringing, and education. He has himself created you and gifted you, and he does not want his work to be wasted. He means you to be fulfilled not frustrated. His purpose is that everything you have and are should be stretched in his service and in the service of others.'

This means that God has a leadership role of some degree and kind for each of us. We need, then, to seek his will with all our hearts, to cry to him to give us a vision of what he is calling us to do with our lives, and to pray for grace to be faithful (not necessarily successful) in obedience to the heavenly vision.

For then at the end of our life we shall be able to say with Paul, 'I have fought the good fight, I have finished the race, I have kept the faith,' and we shall hear Christ say to us those most coveted of all words, 'well done, good and faithful servant!'

NOTES

Chapter 1

1. James A. C. Brown, *The Social Psychology of Industry* (New York: Penguin, 1954), p. 186.
2. H. L. Mencken quoted by David Weir in *Men and Work in Modern Britain* (London: Fontana, 1973), p. 75.
3. Quoted from Dorothy Sayers' *Creed or Chaos?* by Ted W. Engstrom and Alec Mackenzie in *Managing Your Time* (Grand Rapids: Zondervan, 1967), pp. 21–3.
4. *Laborem Exercens*, Pope John Paul II's Encyclical on 'Human Work' (Catholic Truth Society, 1981), p. 4.
5. Ibid. p. 13.
6. Ibid. p. 12.
7. Ibid. p. 33.
8. E. F. Schumacher, *Good Work* (London: Abacus, 1980), p. 27.
9. Ibid. pp. 119, 120.
10. Ibid. p. 121.
11. Report in the *Guardian Weekly* on February 14, 1970.
12. From *Joy in Work* by Henri de Man (1929), quoted by Sherwood E. Wirt in *The Social Conscience of the Evangelical* (New York: Harper, 1968), p. 38.
13. *Good Work*, op. cit. pp. 3, 4.
14. Op. cit. p. 122.
15. The story is told by Basil Willey in *Religion Today* (A & C Black, 1969), p. 74.
16. From one of thirteen interviews in *Just the Job* by David Field and Elspeth Stephenson (Leicester: IVP, 1978), pp. 93, 94.
17. Quoted in *William Temple* by F. A. Iremonger (Oxford University Press, 1948), p. 440.
18. *The Manpower Implications of Micro-Electronic Technology*, a report by Jonathan Sleigh, Brian Boatwright, Peter Irwin, and Roger Stanyon (H.M.S.O., 1979), pp. 9 and 6.
19. Sir Fred Catherwood's essay is entitled 'The New Technology: The Human Debate,' and is published in *The Year 2000 AD*, ed. John Stott (Marshalls, 1983), pp. 126–145.
20. David Bleakley, *In Place of Work: The Sufficient Society*, 'A Study of

Technology from the Point of View of People' (London: SCM, 1981), p. 89.

21. David Bleakley, *Work: The Shadow and the Substance*, 'A Reappraisal of Life and Labour' (London: SCM, 1983), p. 42.

22. *In Place of Work*, op. cit. p. 6.

23. E.g., *In Place of Work*, op. cit. pp. 2 and 51 and *Work*, op. cit. pp. 20–33.

24. *Work*, op. cit. p. 56. See also *In Place of Work*, op. cit. p. 3.

25. Church Action with the Unemployed, Campaign Office, P.O. Box 576, Aston, Birmingham, England B6 5QL.

26. *Work or What? A Christian Examination of the Employment Crisis* (London: CIO, 1977), pp. 28, 29.

27. David Bleakley's *Work*, p. 61.

28. Marshall McLuhan, *Understanding Media* (1964, Abacus 1973), p. 381.

Chapter 2

1. John V. Taylor, *Enough is Enough* (SCM, 1975), p. 102.

2. Mark 10.43; Philippians 2.4 and 5–8.

3. See Proverbs 14.31; 17.5; 22.2.

4. A. J. M. Sykes's report was published in the journal *Sociology*, vol. iii (1969), pp. 21–34.

5. Ibid. p. 206.

6. Ibid. pp. 211, 112.

7. From a news report in *Christianity Today* in 1979, a tape-recorded conference address, and especially R. C. Sproul's *Stronger Than Steel*, 'The Wayne Alderson Story' (San Francisco: Harper & Row, 1980).

8. From *The Social Foundations of Wage Policy* (London: Allan & Unwin, 1955; 1962 ed.), p. 146.

9. Richard Hyman and Ian Brough, *Social Values and Industrial Relations:* 'a study of fairness and inequality' (Oxford: Blackwell, 1975).

10. Ibid. p. 11.

11. E. F. Schumacher, *Good Work* (London, 1979, Abacus, 1980), p. 79.

12. William Temple, *Christianity and the Social Order* (New York: Penguin, 1942), p. 87.

13. Ibid. p. 61.

14. Erving Goffman, *Asylums*, 'Essays on the Social Situation of Mental Patients and other Inmates' (New York: Anchor Books, Doubleday, 1961).

15. Ibid. p. xiii.

16. Ibid. p. 6.

17. Ibid. p. 7.

18. Ibid. p. 9.

19. Ibid. p. 43.

20. See my *I Believe in Preaching* (Sevenoaks: Hodder & Stoughton, 1981), pp. 174–178.

21. From Charles Colson's lecture entitled 'The Rehabilitation of Prisoners,' published in *Crime and the Responsible Community* (Sevenoaks: Hodder and Stoughton, 1980), p. 156.

22. The Nuremberg Code (1947); reproduced in *Dictionary of Medical Ethics*, edited by A. S. Duncan, G. R. Dunstan, and R. B. Welbourn (DLT, 1981), pp. 130–132.

23. Declaration of Helsinki (1964; revised 1975); reproduced in *Dictionary of Medical Ethics*, op. cit., pp. 132–135.

24. Aleksandr Solzhenitsyn, *Cancer Ward* (1968, Penguin 1971).

25. Ibid. p. 240.

26. Ibid. pp. 85, 86.

27. Ibid. p. 320.

28. *Christianity and the Social Order*, p. 96.

29. Ibid. p. 96.

30. Quoted by David Bleakley in *In Place of Work: The Sufficient Society* (SCM, 1981), pp. 16, 17.

31. *Christianity and the Social Order*, p. 87.

32. Ibid. p. 99.

33. *The Donovan Report* (1968) was produced by the fifth Royal Commission on Trade Unions and Employers' Associations, which was set up by the Labour Government and sat between 1965 and 1968.

34. P. J. Armstrong, J. F. B. Goodman and J. D. Hyman, *Ideology and Shop-Floor Industrial Relations* (Beckenham: Croom Helm, 1981).

35. The principle of 'codetermination,' first developed in the 1930s was put into practice in West Germany after World War II. In essence it advocated (1) a 'works council,' which represented the workers, (2) a 'supervisory board' (two-thirds of whose members being owners and one-third workers' representatives), which appointed (3) the executive board, which ran the company. West Germany's postwar economic progress and good record of labour relations are thought by many to be at least partly due to this arrangement. See H. F. R. Catherwood, *A Better Way*, The Case for a Christian Social Order (IVP, 1975), p. 121.

36. Bishop Robin Woods of Worcester, letter to *The Times* (16 Feb. 1977).

37. See *Employee Share Schemes*, published in 1979 by the Wider Share Ownership Council, Juxon House, St. Paul's Churchyard, London EC4M 8EH. The booklet also explains the profit-sharing provisions of the 1978 Finance Act. Other businesses which early adopted dividend limitation and profit sharing were I.C.I., Courtaulds and Rowntrees in U.K., and Sears Roebuck of Chicago in U.S.A.

38. Thomas J. Peters and Robert H. Waterman, *In Search of Excellence*, lessons from America's best-run companies (New York: Harper & Row, 1982).

39. Richard Tanner Pascale and Anthony G. Athos in *The Art of Japanese Management* (New York: Simon & Schuster 1981; Penguin 1982), p. 50.

40. George Goyder, *The Responsible Company* (Oxford: Basil Blackwell 1961), p. ix.

41. Ibid. pp. 109–111.

42. Ibid. pp. 118, 126.

43. The Christian Association of Business Executives, 114 Mount Street, London, WIY 6AH.

Chapter 3

1. Martin Luther King, Jr.'s 'I have a dream' speech is recorded in Coretta Scott King's *My Life with Martin Luther King, Jr.* (London: Hodder & Stoughton, 1969), p. 249.

2. From an address by Roy Jenkins, Home Secretary, in May 1966 to a meeting of Voluntary Liaison Committees.

3. David Brion Davies, *The Problem of Slavery in Western Cultures* (Ithaca: Cornell University Press, 1966), p. 31.

4. Edward Long, *The History of Jamaica* (Lowndes, London, 1774), pp. 351–356.

5. J. H. Guenebault, *The Natural History of the Negro Race* (English translation published by Dowling, Charleston, South Carolina, 1837), pp. 1–19. See also the references to this book in *A Tribute for the Negro* by Wilson Armistead (Manchester, 1848), e.g. p. 36.

6. Stanley M. Elkins, *Slavery*, A Problem in American Institutional and Intellectual Life (1959; 2nd ed. University of Chicago Press, 1968), p. 82.

7. Ibid. p. 84.

8. Ibid. p. 113.

9. Ibid., especially Chapter III 'Slavery and Personality.'

10. Wilson Armistead, op. cit. p. 5.

11. M. F. Ashley Montagu, *Man's Most Dangerous Myth: the Fallacy of Race* (1942. 5th ed. revised and enlarged, Oxford University Press, 1974), p. 101.

12. Ibid. p. 67.

13. Ibid. p. 416.

14. Ibid. p. 3.

15. Columbus Salley and Ronald Behm, *What Color is your God?*, 'Black Consciousness and the Christian Faith,' first published 1970 under the title *Your God is Too White* (Downers Grove: IVP, revised ed. 1981).

16. Ashley Montagu, op. cit. p. 420.

17. Adolf Hitler, *Mein Kampf* (1925, translated by James Murphy. Hutchinson, 1940), p. 150.

18. Ibid. p. 284.

19. Richard Gutteridge, *Open Thy Mouth for the Dumb*, 'The German Evangelical Church and the Jews 1879–1950' (Oxford: Basil Blackwell, 1976), p. 69.

20. Ibid. p. 48.

21. Quoted by Ashley Montagu, op. cit. p. 50.

22. Quoted in *The Church Struggle in South Africa* by John W. de Gruchy (Grand Rapids: Eerdmans, 1979), pp. 30, 31.

23. *Human Relations and the South African Scene in the Light of Scripture*, a 1974 report of the Dutch Reformed Church (Dutch Reformed Publishers, 1976), pp. 14, 32, 71.

24. *Mein Kampf*, p. 248.

25. Professor Dr. A. B. Dupreez, *Inside the South African Crucible* (H.A.U.M., Kaapstad-Pretoria, 1959), p. 63.

26. M. F. Ashley Montagu, op. cit. p. 10.

27. Ibid. pp. 190–193.

28. Ibid. p. 202.

29. Ibid. pp. 204–234.

30. Margery Perham, *The Colonial Reckoning*, the 1961 Reith Lectures (London: Collins, 1961), p. 39.

31. Jeremy Murray-Brown, *Kenyatta* (London: Allan & Unwin, 1972), p. 306.

32. Mzee Jomo Kenyatta, *Suffering without Bitterness* (East African Publishing House, 1968), p. 166. For similar African reactions to French colonial rule, see *Black Skin, White Masks* by Frantz Fanon (1952).

33. Paul Scott, *The Jewel in the Crown* (1966, Granada, 1973), p. 260.

34. Arnold Toynbee, *A Study of History* (Vol. I, p. 213) quoted by Archbishop Cyril Garbett in *World Problems of Today* (Sevenoaks: Hodder and Stoughton, 1955), p. 135.

35. See *Sheep and Goats*, 'British Nationality Law and its Effects,' and *Families Divided*, 'Immigration Control and Family Life' by Anne Owers (CIO, 1984).

36. Martin Walker, *The National Front* (London: Collins, 1977), p. 34.

37. Ibid. pp. 78–84.

38. Ibid. p. 185.

39. David J. Smith, *Racial Disadvantage in Britain* (New York: Penguin, 1977), p. 17.

40. Ibid. Part 2, 'Employment', pp. 109, 110. Similarly, David Sheppard, Bishop of Liverpool, writes: 'Rates of unemployment for black people are generally more than double those for other workers of the same age group' (*Bias to the Poor*, 1953, p. 69).

41. Ibid. Part 3, 'Housing' pp. 210–213, 222 and 288.

42. Lord Scarman, *The Scarman Report*, the Brixton Disorders April 10–12, 1981 (New York: Penguin, 1981), pp. 77, 78.

43. Ibid. p. 209.

44. Ibid. p. 196.

45. H. J. Eysenck versus Leon Kamin, *Intelligence: The Battle for the Mind* (Pan Books & Macmillan, 1981), p. 74.

46. *The Autobiography of Malcolm X* (Bramcote: Grove Press, 1964), pp. 175, 275.

47. Ibid. pp. 179, 272.

48. Ashley Montagu, op. cit. p. 74.

49. Ibid. p. 307.

50. Quoted by Martin Walker, op. cit. p. 47.

51. *The Lausanne Covenant*, para. 10, 'Evangelism and Culture.'

52. J.C.G. Klotze, *Principle and Practice in Race Relations According to Scripture* (SCA Publications, Stellenbosch, 1962), p. 55.

53. O. R. Johnston, *Nationhood: towards a Christian Perspective* (Latimer Studies No. 7, 1980), p. 14.

54. *The Pasadena Report* (Lausanne Occasional Paper No. 1, 1977), p. 6.

Chapter 4

1. From an article by Malcolm Muggeridge which first appeared in *The Observer* on June 26, 1966 and was subsequently published in *Jesus Rediscovered* (London: Collins Fontana, 1969), p. 57.

2. *Poverty and the Churches*, Newsletter No. 112 of the Church of England General Synod's Board for Social Responsibility, January 1983, p. 3. See also *Church Action on Poverty*, the Christian Action Journal, Winter 1982.

3. *Puebla*, 'Evangelization at present and in the future of Latin America,' Conclusions of the Third General Conference of Latin American bishops (St. Paul Publications, 1980), p. 107, para. 494.

4. *World Development Report* (World Bank, Washington, D.C., 1978), p. iii.

5. Compare Acts 17.16f with e.g. Mark 8.1–3.

6. Bishop David Sheppard's Richard Dimbleby Lecture, 'The Poverty that Imprisons the Spirit,' was published in *The Listener* (April 19, 1984 edition).

7. See, for example, *The Poor of Yahweh* by Albert Gélin (1467; English translation by the Liturgical Press, Minnesota, 1953); *Good News to the Poor* by Julio de Santa Ana (WCC 1977) and *Towards a Church of the Poor* ed. Julio de Santa Ana (Maryknoll: Orbis, 1979); *Rich Man, Poor Man and the Bible* by Conrad Boerma (1975, SCM, 1979); *Christians and the Poor* by Athol Gill (Zadok Centre Series, Canberra, No. 9, undated); *Christian Witness to the Urban Poor* (Lausanne Occasional Paper No. 22, 1980), a group report from the Consultation on World Evangelisation at Pattaya, Thailand, which incorporates as an Appendix Jim Punton's analysis of the nine Hebrew words for the poor; *Your Kingdom Come*, the report of the World Conference on Mission and Evangelism, held in Melbourne 1980; *Evangelism and the Poor* by Vinay Samuel and Chris Sugden (Partnership in Mission Asia, Bangalore, revised ed. 1983); and *The Wealth of Christians* by Redmond Mullin (Exeter: Paternoster, 1983).

8. Proverbs 6.6–11 cf. 24.30–34. Similarly, 'lazy hands make a man poor, but diligent hands bring wealth' (Proverbs 10.4) cf. 19.15; 20.13; 28.19.

9. Proverbs 23.20f. cf. 21.17.

10. For national blessings and curses, see for example Leviticus 26; Deuteronomy 8 and 28; Isaiah 1.19f and 5.8ff.

11. Raymond Fung's speech 'Good News to the Poor' is published in *Your Kingdom Come* (WCC, 1980), pp. 83–92.

12. Deuteronomy 15.7ff; Leviticus 25.35ff; Deuteronomy 14.29; Leviticus 26.12.

13. Exodus 22.25; Leviticus 25.36f; Deuteronomy 24.10f; Exodus 22.26f; Deuteronomy 24.12.

14. Leviticus 19.13; Deuteronomy 24.14f; Leviticus 19.9f; 23.22; Deuteronomy 16.9ff; 24.19f; 14.28f; 26.12f; Exodus 23.10f; Leviticus 25.1ff.

15. Psalms 111.1–9; Proverbs 21.13 cf. Proverbs 14.20f; 19.7; 31.20; Job 31.16ff; Ezekiel 16.49.

16. Proverbs 17.5; 19.17.

17. Luke 12.33; 14.12ff; Matthew 25.35–40.

18. Psalms 109.31; 140.12

19. Exodus 23.6, 8; Leviticus 19.15; Deuteronomy 24.17; 27.19; 15.15.

20. Psalms 82.1–3; Proverbs 31.8, 9 cf. Job 29.11ff; Proverbs 22.22f; 29.7, 14.

21. Isaiah 1.17; Zechariah 7.8f; 1 Kings 21; Amos 2.6f; 4.1f; 5.11f; 8.4ff; 5.24; Jeremiah 22.13ff. Other examples of the prophetic stress on justice are Isaiah 3.13ff; 5.7ff; 10.1f; Jeremiah 5.28f; Ezekiel 18.10ff; James 5.1ff.

22. Isaiah 11.1–5.

23. Zephaniah 2.3; 3.12; Isaiah 66.2 cf. 49.13.

24. See, for example, Psalms 22, 25, 37, 40, 69, 74, 149.

25. Psalms 25.16; 37.5, 7; 40.1; 22.26; 37.11; 149.4.

26. Psalms 34.1–6; 15–18.

27. Psalms 86.1–4; 14–17.

28. Luke 4.18f; Matthew 11.5; Luke 7.22; Matthew 5.3; Luke 6.20.

29. David Sheppard, *Bias to the Poor* (Sevenoaks: Hodder 1983), p. 16.

30. Ibid. p. 225.

31. *Puebla*, op. clt. p. 178 para. 1134.

32. Ibid. p. 179 paras. 1141, 1142.

33. Ibid. p. 180, para. 1154.

34. *Your Kingdom Come*, p. 171.

35. This was Professor Kosuke Koyama's expression at Melbourne (*Your Kingdom Come*, p. 161).

36. Robert Holman, *Poverty: Explanations of Social Deprivation* (Oxford: Martin Robertson, 1978).

37. Luke 2.21ff; Leviticus 12.6ff; Luke 9.57f; Mark 4.1; 11.1ff; 14.12ff; 15.42ff; John 12.6; Luke 8.1ff.

38. Martin Hengel, *Property and Riches in the Early Church*, 'Aspects of a Social History of the Early Church' (1973; English translation SCM and Fortress, 1974), pp. 26, 27.

39. Luke 14.33; Mark 1.16ff; 2.13f; 10.21, 28.

40. Matthew 6.19ff; Luke 12.33f; Matthew 6.33; Luke 12.15; Matthew 6.24.

41. Matthew 27.57; Luke 19.8f.

42. Acts 2.44f; 4.32ff.

43. Martin Hengel, op. cit. pp. 32, 33.

44. Quoted by Bishop Otto Dibelius in his autobiography, *In the Service of the Lord* (New York: Holt, Rinehart & Winston, 1964), p. 31.

45. Luke 12.15 (RSV); Colossians 3.5 cf. Ephesians 5.5.

46. John V. Taylor, *Enough Is Enough* (London: SCM, 1975), pp. 81, 82.

47. See *The Lausanne Covenant–An Exposition and Commentary* by John Stott (Lausanne Occasional Papers, No. 3) pp. 21, 24, 25.

48. *An Evangelical Commitment to Simple Lifestyle* Exposition and Commentary by Alan Nichols (Lausanne Occasional Papers, No. 20, 1980). The papers

prepared for the 'International Conference on Simple Lifestyle' have been published in *Lifestyle in the Eighties*, ed. Ronald J. Sider (Exeter: Paternoster, 1982). See pp. 16 and 35, 36.

Chapter 5

1. Plato, *Timaeus*, Loeb Classical Library, trans. R. G. Bury (London: Heineman, 1929), p. 249, para. 91a.

2. Aristotle, *The Generation of Animals*, II. iii. Loeb Classical Library, trans. A. L. Peck (London: Heineman, 1943), p. 175.

3. Josephus, *Against Apion* or *On The Antiquity of the Jews*, Book II, para. 201. Loeb Classical Library, trans. H. St. J. Thackeray (London: Heineman, 1926), p. 373.

4. William Barclay, *Ephesians*, Daily Study Bible (Edinburgh: St. Andrew Press) pp. 199ff.

5. Tertullian, *On The Apparel of Women*, Book 1, Chapter 1, The Ante-Nicene Fathers, Vol. IV (Grand Rapids: Eerdmans, reprinted 1982), p. 14.

6. Germaine Greer, *The Female Eunuch* (London: Paladin 1971), p. 12.

7. Ibid. pp. 18, 22.

8. Ibid. pp. 59, 60.

9. Janet Radcliffe Richards, *The Sceptical Feminist*, 'a philosophical enquiry' (1980, Penguin 1982), p. 11.

10. Ibid. pp. 13, 14, 16.

11. *An Inclusive Language Lectionary: Readings for Year A* (Cooperative Publication Association, 1983). The quotations are from the Preface and the Introduction.

12. Deuteronomy 32.18; cf. Isaiah 42.14; 49.15; 66.13; Psalms 131.1ff; Luke 15.8ff; Matthew 23.37.

13. *Gandhi: An Autobiography* (1949; Jonathan Cape 1966), p. 155.

14. *The Koran*, translated by N. J. Dawood (New York: Penguin, 1956), pp. 360f.

15. Raymond de Coccola, *Ayorama* (1955; Paper Jacks, Ontario 1973), p. 212.

16. Luke 1.28, 42.

17. Luke 8.1ff; Mark 15.41; John 8.1ff; Luke 7.36ff.

18. Luke 10.38ff; John 20.10ff. John Wenham argues cogently in *Easter Enigma* (Exeter: Paternoster, 1984) that 'Mary of Bethany' was in fact Mary Magdalene (pp. 22–33).

19. John Howard Yoder, *The Politics of Jesus* (Grand Rapids: Eerdmans, 1972), p. 177 footnote 23.

20. Betty Friedan, *The Feminine Mystique* (New York: Pelican, 1963), p. 68.

21. Leslie F. Church, ed. *Matthew Henry's Commentary* (1708, Marshall Morgan & Scott, 1960), p. 7.

22. *The Sceptical Feminist*, p. 65.

23. George F. Gilder, *Sexual Suicide* (1973; Bantam, 1975), p. v.

24. Ibid. p. 46.

25. Ibid. p. 246.

26. Ibid. p. 63.

27. Paul K. Jewett, *Man as Male and Female* (Grand Rapids: Eerdmans, 1975), p. 86.

28. Ibid. p. 86.

29. Ibid. p. 112.

30. Ibid. p. 134.

31. Ibid. p. 138.

32. See *Discovering An Evangelical Heritage* by Donald W. Dayton (New York: Harper & Row, 1976). In his chapter entitled 'The Evangelical Roots of Feminism' (pp. 85–98), Dr. Dayton traces the roots of the American feminist movement to the revivals of Charles G. Finney, whose Oberlin College 'became the first coeducational college in the world' (p. 88).

33. James B. Hurley, *Man and Woman in Biblical Perspective*, 'a study in role relationships and authority' (Leicester; IVP, 1981), pp. 206–214.

34. James B. Hurley gives us a thorough treatment of 'veils.' He points out that the Old Testament contains no law about wearing a veil, and that the Hebrew and Graeco-Roman custom was for women to be normally unveiled. In both cultures too it was usual for women to put their hair up; loosed or hanging hair was a sign either of mourning or of separation from the community (e.g. because of leprosy, Nazirite vows or being suspected of adultery). Dr. Hurley argues, therefore, that the 'covering' and 'uncovering' Paul mentions refers to the putting up and letting down of the hair. The NIV margin also adopts this interpretation. (Ibid. pp. 45–47, 66–68, 162–171, 178–179 and 254–71).

35. The 'origin' argument is apparently derived from S. Bedale's article 'The Meaning of *Kephalē* in the Pauline Epistles' (*Journal of Theological Studies*, 5, 1954), which has been mistakenly thought to deny the element of 'authority.' See James B. Hurley op. cit. p. 164 (footnote).

36. Stephen B. Clark opts for this word in his magisterial survey *Man and Woman in Christ*, an examination of the roles of men and women in the light of Scripture and the social sciences (Ann Arbor: Servant Books, 1980), pp. 23–45. Despite his distinctions between 'coercive,' 'mercenary,' and 'voluntary' subordination, I remain uncomfortable with the word.

37. Margaret Mead, *Male and Female* (1949, Penguin 1962), e.g. pp. 41, 71, 86 and 192ff. Consider also the very ancient Chinese teaching about the equilibrium between Yin (the feminine or passive principle) and Yang (the masculine or active). Stephen B. Clark summarises the findings of psychology and anthropology on the differences between the sexes (op. cit. pp. 371–465).

38. *The Sceptical Feminist*, p. 192.

39. Ibid. p. 175.

40. *Male and Female*, p. 88.

41. Letha Scanzoni and Nancy Hardesty, *All We're Meant To Be*, a biblical approach to women's liberation (Waco: Word, 1974), pp. 12 and 206.

42. 1 Corinthians 14.34; 1 Timothy 2.12.
43. 2 Kings 22.11ff; 2 Chronicles 34.19ff; Exodus 15.20; Judges 4 and 5.
44. John 20.10ff; Matthew 28.8ff.
45. Acts 21.9; 1 Corinthians 11.5 cf. Joel 2.28; Acts 2.17; Acts 18.26.
46. Philippians 4.2ff; Romans 16.1ff.
47. Acts 2.17ff; 1 Corinthians 12.4ff.
48. In an interesting article entitled 'Pandemonium and Silence at Corinth' in *The Reformed Journal* Vol. 28 No. 6 (June 1978), Richard and Catherine Clark Kroeger point out that ancient Corinth was a well known centre of the worship of Bacchus (Dionysus), which included frenzied shouting, especially by women. They therefore suggest that Paul was urging self-control in worship, and that the *lalein* he was forbidding (an onomatopoeic word) was either the mindless ritual shouting of 'alala' or the babbling of gossip.
49. In *The Reformed Journal* Vol. 30 No. 10 (October 1980), Richard and Catherine Clark Kroeger refer in general to the emphasis in the Pastoral Epistles on the need to 'silence' heretics (e.g. Titus 1.10) and in particular to later Gnostic systems which 'based their *gnosis* on a special revelation given to a woman,' notably Eve. She was the *first* to eat of the tree of knowledge (*gnōsis*) and had also (some taught) enjoyed a prior existence. She thus had two qualifications to instruct Adam. If such a heresy was already current (which is speculative), Paul's insistence that Adam was created first and Eve deceived (not enlightened) first would certainly take on extra significance.
50. e.g. Acts 14.23; 20.17; Philippians 1.1: Titus 1.5.
51. e.g. Matthew 18.17; 1 Corinthians 5.4f: Hebrews 13.17.
52. Matthew 23.1ff and Mark 10.42ff.
53. 1 Peter 5.1ff.
54. 1 Thessalonians 5.12: Hebrews 13.17.

Chapter 6

1. Matthew 19.11f; 1 Corinthians 7.7.
2. Mark 12.25.
3. Hebrews 13.4; 1 Timothy 4.1ff.
4. See O. Raymond Johnston's 1978 London Lectures in Contemporary Christianity, published under the title *Who Needs the Family?* (Sevenoaks: Hodder & Stoughton, 1979).
5. Jack Dominian, *Marriage, Faith and Love* (London: Darton, Longman & Todd, 1981) pp. 49–88. See also his earlier book *Christian Marriage* (London: Darton, Longman & Todd, 1965).
6. See Judson J. Swihart and Steven L. Brigham, *Helping Children of Divorce* (Downers Grove: InterVarsity Press, 1982).
7. Statistics taken from *Social Trends* No. 13, ed. Deo Ramprakash (HMSO, 1983), pp. 29–31; an article by John Witherow in *The Times* on November 21, 1983; and *Spotlight 2*, a pamphlet issued by the Office of Population Censuses and Surveys (HMSO, 1980).
8. George and Nena O'Neill, *Open Marriage: a new lifestyle for couples* (New

York: Evans, 1972). This book is referred to and quoted by George F. Gilder in *Sexual Suicide* (1973, Bantam 1975) pp. 47ff.

9. John Williams, *For Every Cause?* 'a biblical study of divorce' (Exeter: Paternoster, 1981), p. 12.

10. Jack Dominian, *Marital Breakdown* (New York: Penguin, 1968), p. 42.

11. John Murray, *Divorce* (Committee on Christian Education, Orthodox Presbyterian Church, 1953), p. 1.

12. Deuteronomy 22.20ff cf. Leviticus 20.10.

13. The details may be found in the tract *Gittin* in the Babylonian Talmud. See also Ecclesiasticus 25.26.

14. William L. Lane, *The Gospel of Mark*, New International Commentary Series (Grand Rapids: Eerdmans and Marshall Morgan & Scott, 1974), p. 353.

15. James B. Hurley, *Man and Woman in Biblical Perspective* (IVP, 1981), pp. 22–28.

16. *The Biblical View of Marriage and Divorce*, three articles published in *Third Way* in October and November 1977 (Vol. 1, numbers 20–22).

17. It is true that in Mark 10.3ff Jesus is recorded as having used the verb 'command,' but there he seems to have been referring either to the Mosaic legislation in general or in particular to the issuing of the divorce certificate.

18. C. E. B. Cranfield in *The Gospel according to Mark*, Cambridge Greek Testament Commentary (Cambridge University Press, 1959), pp. 319, 320.

19. Matthew 19.9; Mark 10.11; Luke 16.18.

20. Matthew 5.32; Luke 16.18.

21. John Murray, op. cit. p. 21.

22. James B. Hurley, op. cit. p. 103 cf. also p. 111. John Murray's conclusions are very similar (op. cit. pp. 27, 28).

23. John Murray, op. cit. p. 65.

24. In *The Teaching of the New Testament on Divorce* (London: Williams & Norgate, 1921), R. H. Charles argued that, since in 1 Corinthians 7.39 the opposite of 'bound' is 'free to marry,' therefore in v. 9 'the right of remarriage is here conceded to the believing husband or wife who is deserted by an unbelieving partner' (p. 58).

25. David Atkinson, *To Have and To Hold*, 'the Marriage Covenant and the Discipline of Divorce' (London: Collins, 1979), p. 28.

26. Ibid. p. 70.

27. Ibid. p. 71.

28. Ibid. pp. 75, 76.

29. Ibid. p. 91.

30. Ibid. p. 151.

31. Ibid. p. 152.

32. Ibid. p. 154.

33. *Marital Breakdown*, p. 61.

34. See Lynn R. Buzzard and Laurence Eck, *Tell It To The Church: Reconciling Out Of Court* (Elgin: David C. Cook, 1982). The Christian Legal Society's address is P.O. Box 2069, Oak Park, Illinois 60303, USA. See also *Reconciliation and Conciliation in the Context of Divorce* (the Order of Christian Unity, 1982)

and *Marriage Breakdown and Conciliation* (Board for Social Responsibility, Newsletter No. 111, December 1982).

35. Oliver O'Donovan, *Marriage and Permanence*, Grove Booklet on Ethics No. 26 (Bramcote: Grove Books 1978), p. 20.

36. Ibid. p. 21.

Chapter 7

1. Acts 17.25, 28; Psalms 104.29; Job. 1.21.

2. Desmond Doig, *Mother Teresa: Her People and her Work* (London: Collins, 1976), p. 162.

3. Francis A. Schaeffer and C. Everett Koop, *Whatever Happened to the Human Race?* (Old Tappan: Revell, 1979; revised British edition by Marshall Morgan & Scott, 1980). See particularly Chapter 1 'The Abortion of the Human Race' (pp. 2–27) and Chapter 4 'The Basis for Human Dignity' (pp. 68–99).

4. The Japanese abortion statistics are given by C. Everett Koop in his *The Right to Live; The Right to Die* (Wheaton: Tyndale House, and Coverdale House UK, 1976), p. 46.

5. Report of the Committee on the Working of the Abortion Act 1967, Vol. I (HMSO Cmnd. 5579, April 1974), p. 11.

6. The Registrar General's Statistical Review of England and Wales for the years 1968–73: Supplement on 'Abortion' (HMSO).

7. A full description and discussion of the *Roe v. Wade* case may be found in *Death Before Birth* by Harold O. J. Brown (Nashville: Thomas Nelson, 1977), pp. 73–96.

8. These figures are taken from (1) *Statistical Abstract of the United States: 1982–83* (U.S. Bureau of the Census, 1982), p. 68, and (2) 'Intercessors for America Newsletter,' Vol. 10, No. 2 (Feb. 1983).

9. Quoted from Daniel Callahan's *Abortion: Law, Choice and Morality*, p. 298 by Lewis B. Smedes in *Mere Morality* (Grand Rapids: Eerdmans, 1983), p. 267 footnote 21.

10. John Powell, S. J., *Abortion: the Silent Holocaust* (Allen: Argus Communications, 1981), e.g. pp. 20–39.

11. For ancient perspectives and practices, see *Abortion and the Early Church, Christian, Jewish and Pagan attitudes in the Graeco-Roman world*, by Michael J. Gorman (Downers Grove: InterVarsity Press, 1982).

12. Quoted from *Abortion Law Reformed* (1971) by R. F. R. Gardner in *Abortion: The Personal Dilemma* (Exeter: Paternoster, 1972), p. 62.

13. *Abortion: The Personal Dilemma*, p. 126.

14. See, for example, James 1.18; 1 Peter 1.23–25; and 1 John 3.9.

15. Quoted by John T. Noonan in *The Morality of Abortion* (Cambridge: Harvard University Press, 1970), p. 45.

16. Quoted by C. Everett Koop in *The Right to Live; the Right to Die* (op. cit.), pp. 43, 44.

17. John M. Frame discusses this passage fully, including the meaning of the Hebrew words used, in his chapter in *Thou Shalt Not Kill*, the Christian Case against Abortion, ed. Richard L. Ganz (New York: Arlington House, 1978), pp. 50–57.

18. First published by Faber in 1965.

19. For Oliver O'Donovan's position see his *The Christian and the Unborn Child* (Grove Booklets on Ethics, No. 1, 1973) and his 1983 London Lectures in Contemporary Christianity *Begotten Not Made?*, 'human procreation and medical technique' (Oxford University Press, 1984).

20. See also Donald MacKay's 1977 London Lectures in Contemporary Christianity, *Human Science and Human Dignity* (Sevenoaks: Hodder & Stoughton, 1979), especially pp. 64, 65 and 98–102.

21. Tertullian's *Apology*, chapter ix. Michael J. Gorman gives a popular but thorough account of the unanimous prolife, antiabortion stance of the first five centuries of Christianity in his *Abortion and the Early Church* (Downers Grove: InterVarsity Press, 1982). His references to Tertullian are on pp. 54–58.

22. Paul Ramsey, *Fabricated Man*, the ethics of genetic control (New Haven: Yale University Press, 1970), p. 11.

23. Lewis B. Smedes, *Mere Morality* (Grand Rapids: Eerdmans, 1983), p. 129.

24. From Professor G. R. Dunstan's contribution to the article on 'Abortion' in the *Dictionary of Medical Ethics*, ed. by A. S. Duncan, G. R. Dunstan, and R. B. Welbourn (London: Darton, Longman and Todd, revised and enlarged edition, 1981).

25. The expression used by Mr. Justice McNaughten in the Rex v. Bourne case of 1938.

26. Glanville Williams, *The Sanctity of Life and the Criminal Law* (London: Faber, 1958), p. 212.

27. Op. cit. p. 31.

28. Quoted from his book *Humanly Possible* by C. Everett Koop at the beginning of his *The Right to Live; The Right to Die* (q.v.).

29. Quoted by Norman St. John Stevas in *The Right to Life* (Sevenoaks: Hodder & Stoughton, 1963), p. 20.

30. Op. cit. pp. 225, 226.

31. The addresses of these organisations are as follows: Birthright, 686 N. Broad St., Woodbury, NJ 08096, or 21 Donegal Drive, Toronto 17, Canada; LIFE, 7 The Parade, Leamington Spa, Warwickshire, England; SPUC, 7 Tufton St., London, SW1, England.

32. Quoted by Rex F. R. Gardner in *Abortion: The Personal Dilemma*, p. 276. See also *The Story of Birthright: the Alternative to Abortion* by Louise Summerhill (Libertyville: Prow Books, 1973).

33. *Abortion: an Ethical Dilemma*, a report of the Board for Social Responsibility (CIO, 1965), p. 57.

34. Op. cit. pp. 248–262.

Chapter 8

1. See A. C. Kinsey's *Sexual Behaviour in the Human Male* (1948) and *Sexual Behaviour in the Human Female* (1953). His research methods and findings have been criticised, however; the former for being selective and the latter in consequence for showing a misleadingly high percentage of abnormality.

2. Donald J. West, *Homosexuality* (1955; 2nd ed. Pelican 1960; 3rd ed. Duckworth, 1968), p. 12.

3. From an article entitled 'God, Sex and You' in *Eternity* magazine, August 1972.

4. J. N. D. Anderson, *Morality, Law and Grace* (Leicester: Tyndale Press 1972), p. 73.

5. Malcolm Macourt ed., *Towards a Theology of Gay Liberation* (SCM Press 1977), p. 3. The quotation comes from Mr. Macourt's own Introduction to the book.

6. Derrick Sherwin Bailey, *Homosexuality and the Western Christian Tradition* (Harlow: Longmans, Green 1955), p. 4.

7. Isaiah 1.10ff; Jeremiah 23.14; Ezekiel 16.49ff. Cf. the references to pride in Ecclesiasticus 16.8 and to inhospitableness in Wisdom 19.8.

8. Matthew 10.15; 11.24; Luke 10.12.

9. Sherwin Bailey gives references in the *Book of Jubilees* and the *Testaments of the Twelve Patriarchs* (op. cit. pp. 11–20). There is an even fuller evaluation of the writings of the Intertestamental period in Peter Coleman's *Christian Attitudes to Homosexuality* (SPCK, 1980), pp. 58–85.

10. Sherwin Bailey, op. cit. p. 27.

11. So James D. Martin in *Towards a Theology of Gay Liberation*, ed. Malcolm Macourt (London: SCM, 1977), p. 53.

12. Sherwin Bailey, op. cit. p. 30.

13. Peter Coleman, op. cit. p. 49.

14. See, for example, 1 Kings 14.22ff; 15.12; 22.46 and 2 Kings 23.7.

15. Sherwin Bailey, op. cit. p. 39.

16. Peter Coleman, op. cit. pp. 95, 96.

17. Peter Coleman, op. cit. p. 277.

18. Peter Coleman, op. cit. p. 101.

19. Rictor Norton in *Towards a Theology of Gay Liberation*, q.v., p. 58.

20. Letha Scanzoni and Virginia R. Mollenkott, *Is The Homosexual My Neighbour?* (New York: Harper & Row, and SCM, 1978), p. 111.

21. Sherwin Bailey, op. cit. p. 1.

22. Norman Pittenger, *Time for Consent* (3rd ed. SCM, 1976), pp. 7, 73.

23. Donald J. West, op. cit. pp. 17–32.

24. Norman Pittenger, op. cit. p. 7.

25. So Peter Coleman, op. cit. p. 50.

26. Chapter 3.3–5, quoted by Peter Coleman, op. cit. p. 71.

27. C. K. Barrett, *Commentary on the Epistle to the Romans* (London: A. & C. Black, 1962), p. 39.

28. p. 21.

29. p. 36.

30. Chapter 9.

31. Chapter 5.

32. Norman Pittenger, op. cit. pp. 31–33.

33. John 14.15; Romans 13:8–10.

34. Malcolm Macourt, op. cit. p. 25.

35. Norman Pittenger, op. cit. p. 2.

36. Ibid. p. 94.

37. Alex Davidson, *The Returns of Love* (Leicester: IVP, 1970) pp. 12, 16, 49.

38. Norman Pittenger in *Towards a Theology of Gay Liberation*, q.v., p. 87.

39. *Time for Consent*, q.v.; p. 7.

40. Donald J. West, op. cit. p. 261.

41. Ibid. p. 15.

42. Professor R. J. Berry provides a useful summary of current opinion on aetiology in his contribution to the 1982 London Lectures *Free To Be Different* (Basingstoke: Marshalls, 1984), pp. 108–116.

43. D. J. West, op. cit. pp. 266, 273.

44. The address of the True Freedom Trust is P.O. Box 3, Upton, Wirral, Merseyside L49 6NY, England.

45. Elizabeth R. Moberly, *Homosexuality: A New Christian Ethic* (James Clarke, 1983), p. 2.

46. Ibid. p. 28.

47. Ibid. pp. 18–20.

48. Ibid. pp. 35, 36.

49. Ibid. p. 52.

50. Alex Davidson, op. cit. p. 51.

51. *Towards a Theology of Gay Liberation*, q.v. p. 63.

52. *Time For Consent*, q.v. p. 2.

53. Quoted from *The Comfortable Pew* (1965) by Letha Scanzoni and Virginia Mollenkott.

54. *Towards a Theology of Gay Liberation*, q.v., p. 45.

55. The word seems to have been used first by George Weinberg in *Society and the Healthy Homosexual* (New York: Doubleday, 1973).

56. Richard F. Lovelace, *Homosexuality and the Church* (Old Tappan: Revell, 1978, 1984) p. 129 and cf. p. 125.

57. David J. Atkinson, *Homosexuals in the Christian Fellowship* (Oxford: Latimer House, 1979), p. 118. Dr. Roger Moss concentrates on pastoral questions in his *Christians and Homosexuality* (Paternoster, 1977).

58. E.g. 1 Samuel 20.41 and 2 Samuel 1.26.

Chapter 9

1. Bennie E. Goodwin II, *The Effective Leader: a Basic Guide to Christian Leadership* (Downers Grove: InterVarsity Press, 1981), p. 8.

2. William Shakespeare, *Twelfth Night*, Act II, iv. 158.

3. J. Oswald Sanders, *Spiritual Leadership* (Basingstoke: Marshall, Morgan & Scott, 1967, Lakeland ed. 1981), 20.

4. Proverbs 29.18. The NIV rendering is 'Where there is no revelation, the people cast off restraint.'

5. Ronald A. Knox, *Enthusiasm*, a chapter in the history of religion (Oxford University Press, 1950), p. 591.

6. From the *Washington Post*, republished in *The Guardian Weekly* in June 1978.

7. Robert K. Greenleaf, *Servant Leadership*, 'a journey into the nature of legitimate power and greatness' (Paulist, 1977), p. 236.

8. For Paul's vision see, e.g. Acts 26.16–20, Ephesians 2.11–3.13.

9. Douglas Hyde, *Dedication and Leadership*, 'Learning from the Communists' (University of Notre Dame Press, 1966), pp. 15, 16.

10. Ibid. p. 121.

11. Ibid. pp. 30, 31.

12. Ibid. p. 52.

13. Ibid. p. 59.

14. Robert K. Greenleaf, op. cit. p. 16.

15. David Bleakley, *Work: The Shadow and the Substance*, 'a reappraisal of life and labour' (London: SCM), 1983), p. 85.

16. Quoted by William Barclay in his *A Spiritual Autobiography* or *Testament of Faith* (Mowbray and Eerdmans, 1975), p. 112.

17. From a review by Canon R. W. Howard of *Wheels To Fortune*: 'the life and times of Lord Nuffield' by James Leasor (1955).

18. Basil Matthews, *John R. Mott, World Citizen* (London: SCM, 1934), p. 357.

19. Reginald Coupland, *Wilberforce* (London: Collins 1923; second edition 1945), p. 77.

20. John C. Pollock, *Wilberforce* (Tring: Lion, 1977), p. 27. Sir Reginald Coupland recounts the same incident in different words, op. cit. p. 9.

21. Ibid. p. 56.

22. Ibid. p. 304.

23. Ibid. p. 308.

24. Robert K. Greenleaf, op. cit. pp. 7–10.

25. T. W. Manson, *The Church's Ministry* (Sevenoaks: Hodder & Stoughton, 1948) p. 27.

26. J. Oswald Sanders, op. cit. p. 13.

27. M. A. C. Warren, *Crowded Canvas* (Sevenoaks: Hodder & Stoughton, 1974) p. 44.

28. John 13.12–17; 1 Peter 5.5; Galatians 5.13.

29. Peter F. Drucker, *The Effective Executive* (New York: Harper & Row, 1966), p. 72.

30. For Moses, see Exodus 33.11 and Deuteronomy 34.10; for David, Psalms 23.1, 27.1, and 1 Samuel 30.6; for Paul, 2 Corinthians 12.7–10; and for Jesus, Mark 4.36, 6.45f, 14.32–42 and 50.

31. Paragraph 15.

INDEX